TABLE TALK
WITH TOVEY

Also by John Tovey

ENTERTAINING WITH TOVEY
How to star in your own kitchen

TABLE TALK
WITH TOVEY

A COOK'S TOUR
OF HIS
CULINARY EDUCATION

JOHN TOVEY

Photographs by Mick Duff
Drawings by
Lorna Turpin

Macdonald & Co
London & Sydney

Copyright © John Tovey, 1981

First published in Great Britain in 1981 by
Macdonald & Co. (Publishers) Ltd.
London & Sydney
Holywell House
Worship Street
London EC2A 2EN

ISBN 0 354 04722 1

Front cover photograph by Mick Duff shows a selection of terrines
and the view of Windermere from Miller Howe

Commissioned photographs by Mick Duff, copyright © Macdonald,
London 1981

Photographs by Mick Duff of Steamed Sponge Puddings, Wheatmeal
Guinness Cake, Suprêmes of Chicken, Goujons of Turkey and Terrines
reproduced by courtesy of *The Caterer and Hotelkeeper*

Photograph of pavlovas by David Jordan, reproduced by permission of *Woman's
Own*
Drawings by Lorna Turpin, copyright © Macdonald, London, 1981

Design: Anne Davison

Filmset in 'Monophoto' Century Schoolbook by
Servis Filmsetting Limited, Manchester

Printed and bound in Great Britain
Purnell & Sons Ltd, Paulton near Bristol

CONTENTS

Contents continued

LIST OF ILLUSTRATIONS

Colour plates

Between pages 64 and 65
Leah's Cottage Pie; Orange and Syrup Sponge Pudding; how to make a basic gravy; apple starter or salad, Sausage and Apple Bake and Toffee Apples; Wheatmeal Guinness Cake; Suprêmes of Chicken; a picnic spread, with Casserole of Chicken, Liquorice Allsort Sandwiches and Apricot Chutney; various ways of using avocadoes.

Between pages 128 and 129
Sautéed Duck Livers; making a terrine; Savoury Duck Slice; Goujons of Turkey with Sweet and Sour Sauce; Canapés and Portuguese Savoury; American Wheatmeal Chocolate Rum Slice; a tuna fish salad; Pavlova; a Sunday Morning Bloody Mary; Vegetable Terrine, Prawn and Smoked Salmon Terrine and Marinated Breast of Chicken in Cheese Terrine; Lamb Tournedos with Blackcurrant Croutons.

MEASUREMENTS

The recipes in this book were originated in pounds and ounces, and the metric equivalents are based on the approximations most commonly used:
1 oz = 25 g, 1 fl oz = 25 ml.

Conversion Tables (Britain, Australia etc.)

Weight		Capacity	
Imperial	*Metric*	*Imperial*	*Metric*
1 oz	25 g	1 fl oz	25 ml
2 oz	50 g	2 fl oz	50 ml
3 oz	75 g	4 fl oz	100 ml
4 oz ($\frac{1}{4}$ lb)	100–125 g	5 fl oz ($\frac{1}{4}$ pt)	150 ml
5 oz	150 g	6 fl oz	175 ml
6 oz	175 g	7 fl oz	200 ml
7 oz	200 g	8 fl oz	225 ml
8 oz ($\frac{1}{2}$ lb)	225 g	10 fl oz ($\frac{1}{2}$ pt)	300 ml
9 oz	250 g	15 fl oz ($\frac{3}{4}$ pt)	400 ml
10 oz	275 g	20 fl oz (1 pt)	500–600 ml
11 oz	300 g	$1\frac{1}{4}$ pt	700 ml
12 oz ($\frac{3}{4}$ lb)	350 g	$1\frac{1}{2}$ pt	900 ml
13 oz	375 g	$1\frac{3}{4}$ pt	1 litre
14 oz	400 g	2 pt	1.1 litre
15 oz	425 g	$2\frac{1}{4}$ pt	1.3 litre
16 oz (1 lb)	450 g	$2\frac{1}{2}$ pt	1.4 litre
$1\frac{1}{2}$ lb	700 g	$2\frac{3}{4}$ pt	1.6 litre
2 lb	900 g	3 pt	1.7 litre
$2\frac{1}{2}$ lb	1.1 kg		
$2\frac{3}{4}$ lb	1.3 kg		
3 lb	1.4 kg		

Conversion Tables (America)

If you are using standard American cup and spoon measures when cooking from recipes in this book, the following measuring equivalents will be useful for reference. They have been very slightly adjusted for ease of calculation.

Liquid

1 Imperial pint = 20 fl oz = $2\frac{1}{2}$ cups
$\frac{1}{2}$ Imperial pint = 10 fl oz = $1\frac{1}{4}$ cups
$\frac{1}{4}$ Imperial pint = 5 fl oz = $\frac{5}{8}$ cup

1 Imperial gill = 5 fl oz = $\frac{5}{8}$ cup

1 standard UK tablespoon = $1\frac{1}{4}$ standard American tablespoons
1 standard UK teaspoon = $1\frac{1}{4}$ standard American teaspoons

Dry

Imperial/Metric		American
1 lb (450 g)	almonds, slivered	4 cups
	whole	3 cups
1 lb	breadcrumbs, fresh	16 cups
1 lb	butter or margarine	2 cups
1 lb	cheese, fresh grated	4 cups
1 lb	cherries, glacé	$2\frac{1}{4}$ cups
1 lb	coconut, shredded	4 cups
1 lb	cooking fat	2 cups
1 lb	dried fruit (average)	3 cups
1 lb	flour, all-purpose	4 cups
1 lb	honey	$1\frac{1}{3}$ cups
1 lb	meat, ground	2 cups
1 lb	mushrooms, sliced	5 cups
1 lb	rice, cooked	6 cups
	uncooked	2 cups
1 lb	sugar, confectioners'	$3\frac{1}{2}$ cups
	demerara	$2\frac{1}{4}$ cups
	granulated	2 cups
1 lb	syrup	$1\frac{1}{4}$ cups
1 lb	walnuts, halved	4 cups

1 oz flour = 30 g = 2 level tablespoons
1 oz sugar = 30 g = 1 level tablespoon

Terms

biscuit crumbs	...graham cracker crumbs	icing sugar	.........confectioners' sugar
cornflour	...........cornstarch	minced meat	......ground meat
double cream	......heavy cream	rich shortcrust	...rich pie pastry
flour	.................all-purpose flour	shortcrust	.........pie pastry
grill	.................broil	single cream	......light cream

INTRODUCTION

I am constantly being asked when giving interviews (that sounds rather grand, but it's true) how I became so involved with food, wine and cooking. I always used to say 'It just happened' but once, under pressure, I found myself obliged to analyse my life. I suddenly realized that each individual stage of my life had contributed to what I am now – a talented amateur cook, with a flair for the occasion and the theatrical.

Literally at my grandmother Leah's knee, I learned to appreciate the taste of food, and more important, the *feel* of food, and helping in the school kitchen to extend my pocket money taught me more. When I was out in Africa, where I worked first, it was a case of 'sink or swim' when it came to living, eating and entertaining; I could have lived indifferently and expensively, but a little interest from me soon changed this. My years in the theatre business taught me what life was all about in many, many ways and in retrospect, they were my happiest and most formative days: frugal fare was never dull, and although money was practically non-existent, we laughed and lived to the full. Hotels – which have played such a major role in my life – came mostly as a necessity, as I wanted to earn as much as I could, spending as little as possible on living, whilst learning a new trade. I worked for other people for seven mostly happy years, but the turning point came when I threw in my hat and bought Miller Howe.

That was a traumatic day, the 1st July 1971, and even now, each evening when the hotel is open, the adrenalin flows at 8 to 8.30 and the tension builds up. Will the 'performance' be good tonight, or will we have a disaster, major or minor? Each and every performance is a challenge, as is every new venue when I travel round the world, with my staff, promoting British food and cooking for British Airways. We are *never* complacent, but only grateful for being allowed to do what we enjoy so much.

John Tovey, March 1981

ONE

NURSERY

SCHOOL

NURSERY SCHOOL

I was born prematurely in the North Lonsdale Hospital, Barrow-in-Furness, in 1933 (thus I feel quite justified in reading both Taurus and Gemini horoscopes – but neither ever tells me anything new!). I spent most of my childhood in Barrow, apart from the years my parents and I lived in Nottinghamshire where I went to grammar school, but holidays were always spent in Barrow, I would hasten back to Barrow on my leaves from the Colonial Service, and I have now returned indisputably to my roots, having settled once more in the area, in Windermere.

The magnet in Barrow was my maternal grandmother, Leah Hewetson, whom I called Nanna or Nan. She was the major influence in my childhood, and I realize now how much I owe to her, seeing many of her qualities and characteristics in myself. The sheer joy with which she entertained – nothing gave her greater pleasure than pulling out the legs and flaps of the living-room table to seat her own brood and friends for a Sunday high tea – is very definitely echoed in what I now do, both professionally and personally (although entertaining at my own house, Brantlea, is a rare treat these days, due to my hectic schedule).

As far as food and cooking were concerned, the foundations of my future tastes were laid then. Those were the days when, of necessity, most food had to be made, grown, concocted from what there was – I grew up scrubbing earth from the allotment off potatoes, and watching the bread dough rising: most children nowadays think bread and potatoes start their lives in plastic bags! – and it never ceases to amaze me how hard people like my Nan worked.

Money was always in short supply; husbands frequented the pubs more often than they should – presumably to drown their sorrows – leaving the women to fend for the family and keep the home together. I never saw a cleaner house than Leah's, even nowadays when there is so much labour-saving gadgetry: the black-leaded grate gleamed; the brass shone; the carpets were watered and brushed by hand daily; mats were hung over the line and beaten with those wonderful Indian cane beaters; the furniture was rubbed down daily with waxed cloths (none of those pressurised silicone polishes). She would wash heaps of laundry in the wash-house boiler, and festoon the house, yard and even back-street with dripping washing (with panic ensuing when the coalman or dustman was due); she would starch and iron with those heavy steel irons heated on the fire; and make-over for me clothes she got from some of the better-off ladies she cleaned for in the afternoons.

She was always up at the crack of dawn, making breakfast, shooing me and my grandfather John off to work and school, preparing the mid-morning 'bait' for John and some of his mates (an extra small source of income). How she found time to cook and keep us going, I do not know, but do so she did. Breakfasts, afternoon teas, high teas, suppers, all tasty, nourishing and filling, and prepared on the black-leaded range with two ovens and a trivet for the kettle – hot soups, plain roast meats, eggs in all their guises, fresh vegetables, steamed puds, and lots of home-made breads, cakes and sponges. None of this 'oat' cuisine, as she called it!

Her days never had enough hours in which to cope with all the work. It seems so silly that nowadays, with all our mod. cons., we have to resort to a multitude of pills to get us to sleep. Poor old Leah used literally to fall asleep each night from sheer exhaustion. But it was obviously a fairly healthy life, as she lived well into her seventies. I miss her still.

Starters

Wild Spring Nettle Broth

serves 4

2 pints (1·1 litre) good lamb stock (see method)

4 oz (100–125 g) each of carrots, parsnips, turnips, leeks and onions

2 oz (50 g) butter

4 tablespoons pearl barley

at least 4 young wild nettle plants

Wild nettles usually appear towards the end of March, particularly around patches of bracken, but even at this early stage gloves are definitely needed when you pick the plants! Allow 1 stem of young leaves per person, and do beware, as they are rather bitter in taste if you over-cook them. Serving this soup is by no means a gimmick, as it was traditional in our family and we believed it helped clean the system of the ills of winter!

First of all, make the stock from 2 lb (900 g) lamb bones, using the onion skins, tops of the leeks, washed skin off the carrots, parsnips and turnips, and the stalks from the young wild nettles. Brown the bones in a very hot oven and then transfer them to a saucepan with all the other ingredients. Completely cover with water and simmer slowly (topping up from time to time with further supplies of water) for at least 2 hours. Pass through a clean strainer and this is the base for your broth.

Finely and very evenly dice the vegetables. Gently fry them off in the butter and then leave to strain on kitchen paper.

Simmer the pearl barley for 25 minutes in the strained stock and then add the part-cooked vegetables, and cook for a further 10 to 15 minutes. Five minutes prior to serving sprinkle the finely chopped leaves of the nettles on top and stir well.

Peasant Soup

serves 6 generous portions

2 medium tomatoes

1 medium onion

3 medium courgettes

8 oz (225 g) frozen French beans (or fresh if in season)

5 tablespoons olive oil

2 pints (1·1 litre) chicken stock

1 medium potato

3 cloves garlic

1 teaspoon salt

4 large sprigs parsley

4 sprigs fresh basil

½ 15 oz (425 g) can red kidney beans

Skin and seed the tomatoes and chop roughly. Chop the onion finely, and wipe and slice the courgettes thinly. Cut the French beans into easily edible lengths (defrosted if they're frozen).

Heat 3 tablespoons of the olive oil in a large saucepan and gently cook off the prepared vegetables until light gold. Add the chicken stock and bring to the boil. Add the potato, chopped into small cubes, and cook slowly for 15 minutes.

Meanwhile, in a pestle and mortar, pound the garlic to a paste with the salt and add the chopped parsley and basil and the other 2 tablespoons olive oil. Drain the red kidney beans and lightly wash them under slow-running cold water to remove the taste of the brine. Add the garlic and oil mixture to the soup and whisk around fairly vigorously and then add the red kidney beans. Simmer for a few minutes. Test for temperature and seasoning. Serve with chunks of brown bread (pages 35–6).

per person

2 oz (50 g) shrimps, defrosted

1½ oz (40 g) salted butter, melted

freshly ground black pepper

1 teaspoon gin

generous pinch of freshly ground nutmeg

Potted Shrimps

Flookburgh shrimps (although rather earthy) are sold commercially nowadays, frozen. They are ideal for this dish, served as a starter in 3 inch (7·5 cm) ramekins.

Defrost the shrimps thoroughly (see page 127 for more details). With some of the melted butter paint the walls and base of the ramekin and then sprinkle generously with freshly ground black pepper. Place the shrimps into the ramekin, mix together the melted butter, gin and nutmeg, and pour over the shrimps.

When cool, put into the fridge to set. When ready to serve, turn out and allow to come round to room temperature (but not a hothouse temperature, otherwise the butter will melt!). Serve with thin slices of lavishly buttered brown bread (pages 35–6), slices of cucumber and skinned tomato, and I sometimes garnish with a teaspoon of horseradish cream.

EGGS

'An egg every day
Keeps the bugs at bay',
(cheekily re-sung under my breath)
'An egg every day
Keeps the buggers away.'

During the Second World War we were fortunate in being able to get an ample supply of black-market eggs and, as a kid, I think I learned to enjoy them all the more because of the intrigue of picking them up from the 'woman' at Haverthwaite. It involved a quite lengthy weekly bus ride on the old Florence motor coach which ran hourly from Barrow to Grange-over-Sands. In those days, Grange supposedly had class, brimming over with well-heeled retired folk from the industrial towns and cities of the north. Even their Florence buses were different from the Ribble ones, with a bit of style about them and a smell of real leather.

As soon as I got home with the bag containing several dozen eggs, my Nan always separated them into browns and whites, and insisted that the brown ones were the best for boiling, poaching or scrambling. For years I believed this, always tending to seek out brown eggs, although the colour of the shell has nothing at all to do with the goodness of the inside. However, a brown boiled egg *does* look so attractive at breakfast!

Nowadays it is much more of a job finding truly fresh farm eggs, for although the notices may well state, 'Fresh Farm Eggs for Sale Today', the eggs roll out of the bottoms of balding chickens cooped up in batteries, fed on pellets and water. I want the true flavour of the free-range, fresh farm egg when the hen has been nosing around picking up worms here, insects there, bits of grit all over, and even the odd bit of muck. Mother Nature automatically rejects what is bad, and produces those marvellous deep-coloured yolks.

The average egg weighs 2 oz (50 g) out of the shell, the yolk and the albumen or white each weighing 1 oz (25 g). Eggs should not be stored at extremes of temperature and why, oh why, do makers of fridges invariably put the little compartment for eggs so close to the freezing compartment? And why do they make them for 8 or 16 eggs? Who buys 8 eggs? Eggs should almost always be used when at room temperature, but I break this rule when frying, or making any kind of meringue. When poaching, boiling, frying or scrambling eggs, never rush the cooking process as eggs respond so well to slow cooking. The only exception is making omelettes, and I write about these on pages 75–6.

When beating egg whites, never, never use a plastic or polystyrene bowl but always stainless steel, tinned metal or – of course – hammered copper. Always begin on a slow speed so that you can break up the mass of clinging white and thus start getting the volume you are looking for. For each 4 egg whites, add a pinch of salt and a pinch of cream of tartar which act as stabilizers, preventing the egg whites from breaking up once you have achieved the desired consistency. Increase the speed to high very gradually and, if you're making meringues, never start to beat in the tablespoons of sieved castor sugar until you have initially got lovely shining peaks of beaten egg white.

Many people say to me that they have difficulty in getting their egg whites stiff and I can only say that somewhere along the line there was grease or oil on their equipment. It is absolutely essential that the mixing bowl and the beater are scrupulously clean. Also there should not be the slightest trace of egg yolk in the whites. If a little egg yolk does drop into the bowl when you are separating the egg, use a piece of the egg shell as a scoop to get it out.

Boiled Eggs

I often hear people complaining that they can't boil eggs successfully, and then seem comforted when I admit that I often have the same problem. Many books are so dictatorial about this 'simple' method, and dismiss it with a sentence like, 'Put eggs into cold water, bring to boil, simmer for 3 minutes for soft, 4 minutes for medium hard and 8 minutes for hard-boiled.' Period.

The first thing you have to bear in mind is the source of your eggs. Are they actually free-range or battery and how old are they? Size, too, plays a part, but I am afraid all that bureaucratic nonsense about grading eggs by numbers is anathema to me. What was wrong with small, medium or large, which any idiot could understand?

When boiling eggs I always take a needle and poke it sharply into the egg. This prevents that sordid mess of white floating all round the saucepan, and having to sort out a cracked egg at serving time. I then put my fresh, farm, free-range eggs in a pan of cold water, bring them to the boil and simmer for just over 3 minutes to get them soft and runny in the middle, and just cooked to a gentle, solid white mass beneath the shell. Each minute's subsequent cooking gives me the other desired effects I might want. For a good hard-boiled egg, put the egg into cold water, and cook for 8 to 10 minutes after the water comes to the boil.

But at breakfast so many people cook their eggs before they sit down to start their meal, popping them into egg-cups with hand-made cosies on top. And then, after going through their grapefruit and cereal, they're disappointed by the boiled egg. Standing as it has, well wrapped in its cosy, it ends up a well and truly well-coddled egg. No, I always get up from the table and boil the eggs when I need them, and in the time it takes for the cold water to boil, I can make the toast and re-charge the coffee-maker.

Baked Eggs

Baked eggs are eggs baked in the oven in a container which you can serve at the table. These containers are placed in a bath of water or bain marie (usually a roasting tray). I use ramekins, and now you can have your pick of these: good old-fashioned French white, with fluted sides; brown earthenware by your favourite potter; gold-leaf or bramble-decorated ones by a posh firm (I always buy seconds of these at the sales, and they really are a good bargain).

Some people like plain baked eggs, with runny yolks and cooked whites but, for me, it is all the savoury additions you can concoct inexpensively that make this supper dish so interesting. You can add most pâtés; tomatoes and bacon left over from breakfast mixed together (a bit of black pudding too!); finely chopped kidneys; potatoes, onions and red peppers finely chopped and fried together; spinach puréed with lots of butter and freshly ground nutmeg; diced apple and bacon with grated cheese and coarsely chopped herbs; left-over bits of cooked chicken; finely chopped duck brought together with well-fried breadcrumbs and skinned, seeded and chopped tomatoes. Put any of these into buttered, salted and peppered ramekins and then warm them through in the oven at 350°F (180°C), Gas 4, for about 10 minutes. Then add the eggs and bake for 8 to 10 minutes.

Baked Egg in Fried Cob

per dinner cob

at least 1½ oz (40 g) butter, melted

1 teaspoon cheese and herb pâté (page 173)
or **1 teaspoon cheese, grated**

1 egg

salt, freshly ground black pepper

at least 1 tablespoon fresh tomato sauce (page 175)
or **1 tablespoon cheese, finely grated**

sprig of parsley or watercress

This is an ideal recipe for using up any stale dinner cobs or rolls you may have left over from a party – but it's so good, it's well worth going out and buying some especially. The crispy, crunchy, buttery cob baked in the oven is a marvellous container for the softly cooked egg yolk. One roll is sufficient per person at the beginning of a meal, but you'll need 2 or 3 each as a main, one-only supper course.

With a sharp serrated bread knife shape your dinner cob into a cube. Make sure you keep the top sliced round bit, which you will use at the end as a 'lid' for the box you are going to present. Then, using a small, sharp, pointed knife, cut out a deep square from the cob (a relatively easy task if the dinner cob is stale, but slightly more difficult if it is fresh). Now you have shaped a box from the cob, in which you will bake off the egg.

Coat the cob with 1 oz (25 g) of the melted butter (it will absorb the full amount easily) and simply put on a baking tray in a pre-heated oven at 350°F (180°C), Gas 4, and bake for 30 minutes. Your little cube will be crispy golden. Remove from the oven and paint with the remaining butter. On the base of the cube place the teaspoon of cheese and herb pâté – or if you haven't any just put a teaspoon of finely grated cheese in – and break a small egg into the hole of the cube. Return to the oven (which is set at the same heat as before), and the egg will be cooked in 12 to 15 minutes. When I first tested this recipe I thought the egg would be cooked in about 4 minutes, but after testing and re-testing, 12 to 15 minutes was the time needed in my gas oven!

Serve topped with the fresh tomato sauce or some finely grated cheese (and a few chopped fresh herbs if you like). Garnish with the parsley or watercress.

Egg Flip Sauce

makes 1½ pints (900 ml)

4 eggs

1 14 oz (400 g) tin condensed milk

½ pint (300 ml) sherry

¼ pint (150 ml) cooking brandy

freshly grated nutmeg

War-time Christmases were never complete without a drop of Egg Flip. This I sipped, daringly and with trepidation, never quite knowing whether it was because the eggs used were black-market, the condensed milk 'obtained', or because it was so devilishly sinful to actually consume booze before lunch (although my Nan always had a noggin around 11 o'clock – knowing now just how hard she slogged, I think her body and soul *needed* something to give her a boost). This recipe is much better than the modern expensive commercial advocaat and, quite apart from being a good pick-you-up after the 'flu, I use it quite often as a sauce.

Beat the eggs lightly into the condensed milk, then beat in the sherry and the brandy. Grate a touch of fresh nutmeg over the liquid, chill, and serve as a drink. To use as a sauce, pour it over ripe melon balls mixed with apple slices and pipped grapes as a starter to a dinner. Or you can use it with a fruit salad as a sweet, or combined with finely diced preserved ginger on kiwi fruit, grapes, apple slices and with sprigs of mint. I can also remember having it with cold left-over Christmas pudding.

Main Courses

serves 10

1 onion

1 large carrot

handful of parsley stalks

8–10 lb (3½–4½ kg) leg of lamb

sea salt, freshly ground black pepper

4 oz (100–125 g) butter

redcurrant jelly

Roast Leg of Spring Lamb

Lamb is, without doubt, my very favourite meat. Roasted, baked in hay, or casseroled with exotic spices and accompaniments, it is the meat I would most like to encounter on my eventual desert island. Apparently we consume approximately 560 million pounds of home-produced lamb each year, which means we eat annually about nine and a half million sheep. Just fancy – 130 million chops and 19 million legs of English lamb!

English lambs vary from those fed on the rich salty marshland grasses of Kent to the sheep bred on the Lakeland fells but, providing the animal is well hung, it is relatively easy to cook by many different methods, and is always a joy to serve and eat. When buying English lamb, for goodness sake do not look for a bright red colour and clean white fat, but go for the very dark meat that is slightly dry on the edge with straw-coloured fat.

Roughly chop up the onion and the carrot, and place them on the bottom of a roasting tin with a generous handful of fresh parsley stalks. Simply wipe the leg with a dry kitchen cloth, and coat it generously with the salt, pepper and butter. Place it in a pre-heated oven set at 425°F (220°C), Gas 7, and roast it for 1¼ hours if you prefer the meat medium-cooked, with just a mere trace of blood. About every 20 minutes baste the joint and keep on easing it off the base of the roasting tray with a large spoon.

Fresh mint is often unavailable, so to add a little sweetness to the dish I usually put a couple of tablespoons of redcurrant jelly into the roasting tray when making the gravy.

Basic Gravy

This gravy – for roast meats, chops, a multitude of uses – is what I would call a basic gravy, but it's far removed from the gravy-browning school. It perhaps *is* a bit lengthy, but it's well worth the trouble.

Brown raw or cooked bones in a roasting tray in a hot oven with diced onion, carrot and celery, and a little butter. This will take about 1 hour and it doesn't matter at all if the vegetables become quite dark and horrible. Pour in 1 pint (550 ml) water and bring to the boil on top of the stove. Simmer, skimming occasionally, for about 45 minutes. Strain. This then is the basic stock for your basic gravy.

In about 2 oz (50 g) butter, brown 1 chopped medium onion, 1 chopped stick of celery and 1 finely chopped carrot. Add 2 tablespoons chopped parsley, plus the stalks, a chopped sprig of rosemary or a teaspoon of another herb (depending on the basis of your stock, and what the gravy is to accompany). Cook until brown, stir in a tablespoon tomato paste, a teaspoon Meaux or other mustard, and a tablespoon of sieved plain flour. Brown the flour, and stir continually, as you slowly add the reserved pint (550 ml) of strained stock. Bring gently to the boil, simmer for 15 minutes, then strain. Re-heat if necessary and spoon over the meat.

serves 6–8

**shoulder of pork, boned
and rolled (about 4 lb or 1·8
kg)**

**bunch of fresh sage leaves
(or 2 tablespoons, dried)**

1 tablespoon dripping

$\frac{1}{2}$ tablespoon sea salt

Roast Shoulder of Pork with Sage and Apple

One of the things I like best in the world is pork crackling, and it was one of the joys of my childhood. Now, whenever we serve roast pork at the hotel, I'm invariably asked how we get such delicious crackling. I'm not sure how Leah did it, but we achieve it simply by roasting well-hung meat. The longer pork is hung, the drier the skin becomes, and the more the actual joint shrinks. It stands to reason that dry skin will give crisp crackling, whereas wet skin will produce a chewy unspeakable horror. We do nothing at all to a joint of pork before it goes in the oven apart from thoroughly drying it with a tea towel, and then greasing and salting the skin. I have known people to use a hair-drier on the skin and swear that it works: but I just prefer to roast rather well-hung joints, at least 12 days old.

A whole shoulder will serve 8 easily, but you could use just half the joint – either the hand and spring, or the blade, which is easy to carve if the butcher bones, rolls and ties it for you. Carving crackling can be difficult, so ask him to score the skin straight across at intervals as thick as the slices you will carve, or do this yourself before roasting.

Prepare the skin for crackling with the dripping and salt. Sprinkle on the sage. Roast, uncovered, at 450°F (230°C), Gas 8, for 1 hour. Reduce the heat to 400°F (200°C), Gas 6, and cook for another hour. Serve with apple sauce and fresh vegetables.

**1 lb (450 g) Granny Smith
apples**

$\frac{1}{4}$ teaspoon cinnamon

**1 tablespoon soft brown
sugar**

$\frac{1}{2}$ oz (15 g) butter

**1 tablespoon Calvados
(optional)**

Apple Sauce
Peel, core and slice the apples, and put in a lightly buttered ovenproof dish, mixed with the cinnamon and soft brown sugar. Dot with the butter. Cover, and put into the oven at the lower temperature with the pork for about 35 minutes, stirring occasionally. When the apple has softened, transfer to the top of the stove (in a pan if necessary). At this stage you could add a tablespoon of Calvados; first light it with a match, and then pour over the apples.

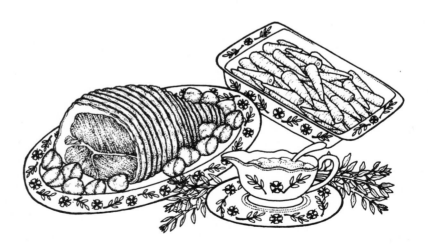

Leah's Cottage Pie

serves 4

2 tablespoons olive oil

2 oz (50 g) butter

1 medium onion, about 6 oz (175 g), finely chopped

2 cloves garlic, crushed with 1 teaspoon salt

1 lb (450 g) minced beef

1 tablespoon Bovril

$\frac{1}{8}$ pint (75 ml) beer

6 oz (175 g) leeks, cleaned and finely sliced

$\frac{1}{4}$ pint (150 ml) milk

6 oz (175 g) carrots

4 sticks celery

salt, freshly ground black pepper

1$\frac{1}{4}$ lb (575 g) potatoes

2 tablespoons parsley, chopped

1 egg yolk

Gently heat the oil in a frying pan and then add 1 oz (25 g) of the butter. When it's melted, fry the finely chopped onions with the 2 crushed cloves of garlic and salt. Cook until golden and then add the minced beef. Cook, stirring, for 15 minutes, and then mix in the Bovril and the beer.

Meanwhile, simmer the leeks for 10 minutes in the milk. Dice the cleaned carrots very small, and chop the celery into thin slices.

On the base of a 2 pint (1·1 litre) casserole dish, place half the cooked strained leeks. Spread over them half of the partly cooked beef, with half the chopped carrots and celery sprinkled over that. Season between the layers. Build up the layers again in the same order as before, finishing off with the carrots and celery, remembering to season.

Peel the potatoes, boil them until soft and tender, and then mash with the parsley, egg yolk, the remaining butter and more seasoning. Spoon on top of the cottage pie base, and with the back of a fork make a pattern across the top. At this stage the dish can be frozen.

To cook, put the dish in the oven for 40 minutes at 350°F (180°C), Gas 4, with further knobs of butter or grated Cheddar cheese on top of the potato. A tablespoon of onion marmalade (page 83) goes down well with this, and there is absolutely nothing wrong either with a good dollop of HP sauce!

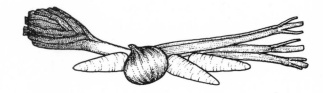

Savoury Mince and Macaroni

serves 4–6

2 medium onions, finely chopped

4 oz (100–125 g) mutton fat, cooking oil, or half butter, half oil

1$\frac{1}{2}$ lb (700 g) raw lamb, minced

2 tablespoons tomato purée

4 oz (100–125 g) cooked, drained, macaroni pieces, about 1 inch (2·5 cm) in length

sea salt, freshly ground black pepper

This was a wash-day favourite in my Nan's household as, apart from being economical (on some empty purse weeks, there was more macaroni than mince), it had a touch of excitement because it was Italian! Any Italian worth his salt would, I'm sure, raise his brows and hands to heaven – but it *is* nice in this updated version.

Fry off the chopped onions in the fat until nice and golden and then add the lamb mince. Cook over a low heat for 30 minutes, stirring from time to time. Mix in the tomato purée, cook for a few more minutes, and then fold in the cooked and drained macaroni pieces. I personally like to cook this dish for a little bit longer at this stage, in order to slightly brown the macaroni, and let it really take up the lamb flavour.

If feeling the pinch, use 1 lb (450 g) lamb mince with 8 oz (225 g) macaroni, and if you like garlic (as I do), add as much or as little as you want when frying off the onions. Just before serving, sprinkle the dish generously with sea salt and freshly ground black pepper.

Vegetables and Salads

POTATOES

So, so many people these days, when eating out, refuse potatoes as they are 'fattening', and then go on to consume another half bottle of wine and a quarter pint of double cream with the pudding, and liqueurs to follow. I think they miss so much, as one potato isn't going to make all that much difference.

Potatoes seem to have gone through a full circle in availability, for although first found by the Spaniards around 1560 in Ecuador, they did not come to the British Isles until 1584 when Sir Walter Raleigh planted them on his country estate in County Cork, Ireland. During the eighteenth and nineteenth centuries numerous delicious varieties and strains were developed, and potatoes were served on every table, but of late, like apples, the number of varieties has been greatly reduced, and the Potato Marketing Board has done more harm than good in my opinion. Nowadays one has little control over the type of potato one can freely purchase, and some of the 'new' potatoes that appear on the market around Christmas are perfectly horrible.

Few people realize that most potatoes contain more than two-thirds water, and have nearly 3 times less carbohydrate than the equivalent amount of fresh bread. So if you are diet-conscious, take a potato at a dinner party rather than the second hot dinner roll you were thinking of smothering with butter!

Baked Potatoes

I have always liked baked potatoes, as they were the winter fillers for supper, the spring dish for school holiday lunches, the summer savoury for picnics and, in autumn, always the bonfire treat. I used to love them the way Leah baked them. They were never, as I recall, served with a meal but as a light lunch dish before a high tea when somebody special would be coming (Auntie Janie who once lived in America and who, according to my Nan, hadn't been a very nice lady, or Maisie who 'had been' a nun but was now living out of the order – or perhaps she meant out of order – with Miss Jackson), or as an early evening dish when we had been out for the day. Accompanied by fresh chives and parsley grown in the backyard window boxes, we would eat them sitting in front of the fire listening to Max Miller in *Saturday Night Music Hall* on the radio. (My Nan was always convulsed by Max Miller and I laughed equally, but only at her face and infectious giggling. When he used to say 'Ay, you must have a mucky mind', she used suddenly to become respectable, but only temporarily!)

It is extremely difficult to give exact cooking times for potatoes as I don't know how large yours are going to be. Pick out the largest potatoes, one for each person, and put them in a sink of cold water. With a clean nailbrush (not one stinking of smelly soap or carbolic) simply brush them vigorously until free from grime and looking reasonably clean. Dry them well with a tea towel. Line the base of the tray you are going to use with sea salt to a depth of about $\frac{3}{4}$ inch (18 mm), and place the dried potatoes in this base, leaving ample room around each potato for the heat to cook them. Set the oven at 400°F (200°C), Gas 6, and the potatoes usually take at least $1\frac{1}{2}$ hours to bake, but you have to press one first to see if it's done to your liking. When nearly finished (if ready too soon, simply transfer the dish to a warming drawer to arrest the cooking, and then you can finish them off when you want), sprinkle generously with sea salt and freshly ground black pepper. When serving them, make a criss-cross incision on the top with a small knife, and simply get hold of each end of the potato and push gently up towards the middle. This then opens the potato out ready to receive whatever flavouring you are going to serve with it – cheese and herb pâté, sour cream, mayonnaise, curried hollandaise, tomato sauce, baked beans, bacon fat and bacon bits, chopped walnuts and watercress, herbed French dressing, mushroom pâté, or any of the savoury butters mentioned on page 50. Experiment!

Another way of baking potatoes is in the ashes of your hearth underneath a lovely open coal or log fire. It's economical, *provided* you have the luxury of that old-fashioned kind of grate which collects the ashes.

All you do is scrub your potato/es clean and then dry well on kitchen paper. Get pieces of tinfoil large enough to completely enclose the potato/es and paint liberally with butter and season with salt and pepper. Completely wrap the potatoes in the foil, and then put them in the ashes underneath your lit fire. Turn over at the end of the first hour and the potatoes should be ready at the end of the second.

Mashed Potato

This is a feast if served with baked sausage and onions or similar simple fare, but you have to be fairly generous with the cream (or yoghurt) and butter.

I tend to slightly over-cook the potatoes in salted water and then drain and return to the saucepan over a high heat for a few seconds to dry out as much as possible before mashing (and there is nothing more effective for this than an old-fashioned potato masher). Mash the potatoes fairly roughly and then add to each pound (450 g) of boiled potatoes at least $\frac{1}{4}$ pint (150 ml) cream, top of the milk or yoghurt, and a really generous knob of butter. Mash away some more (if you are really particular, force the potatoes through a strong nylon sieve) until you have no lumps whatsoever. Leave to re-heat in a low oven.

A form of potato I used to love in my youth was Riced Potatoes, and although I still have the original pyramid-shaped ricer I don't use it any more as so many of the cooked potatoes nowadays just do not seem to hold their lovely wormy shape when passed through it.

Boiled Potatoes, Old

When boiling peeled potatoes do try to see you have them all more or less the same size. It is no use putting 2 very large potatoes and 4 small ones into your cold water, as when you want to eat them the small ones will, naturally, be over-cooked and the large ones still hard in the middle. Put the peeled potatoes into cold salted water and cover. Bring to the boil and then turn down the heat and simmer for at least 15 minutes. All you do is remove the lid and test the potatoes with a sharp, pointed knife. When cooked to your liking, drain well, return to the saucepan with a knob of butter and put back on the heat to dry out, just for a few minutes.

Boiled Potatoes, New

Never, ever peel new potatoes, simply scrub with a nail brush kept for that purpose. I bring my salted water up to the boil (with stalks of fresh mint too) and then throw in the prepared new potatoes and simmer them for about 10 to 15 minutes. Once again cooking times are difficult to define as I don't know how large your new potatoes are or how fast or slow your stove simmers.

Boiled New Potatoes with Chicken Bits

Boil the new potatoes as above, but for 5 minutes only, and have to hand a very strong well-reduced chicken stock along with any bits of meat scraped from the bones of the cooked roast chicken. After the potatoes have simmered for the 5 minutes, drain them well and put into another saucepan with about $\frac{1}{2}$ inch (12 mm) depth of the reduced chicken stock (making sure no potatoes sit on top of each other), and finish the cooking off in the stock. Serve with the stock, scattering the chicken bits liberally over the dish and garnishing with either fresh parsley or watercress. One pound (450 g) new potatoes will serve 2 to 4 as a supper dish, and it's a feast fit for a king!

Potatoes with Cream and Cheese

serves 6–8

2 cloves garlic

1 oz (25 g) butter

about 1½ lbs (700 g) potatoes, peeled

½ pint (300 ml) cold milk

salt, freshly ground black pepper

generous pinch freshly grated nutmeg

½ pint (300 ml) double cream

2 oz (50 g) Cheddar cheese, finely grated

You will need a baking dish big enough to take just over 2 pints (1·1 litre) liquid volume. Peel the garlic, gently bruise it, and rub your dish all over quite briskly with the cloves to get a good garlicky flavour. Butter the dish. Slice the peeled potatoes very thinly using either a mandoline or a steel knife. Do *not* soak the potatoes in water, as this allows the starch to come out of them.

In a large saucepan bring the milk to the boil with the pepper, salt, and nutmeg, add the sliced potatoes, and simmer slowly for 10 minutes. Drain the potatoes, discarding the milk, and bring the double cream slowly to the boil with the potatoes, and cook slowly for another 10 minutes. At this stage check the seasoning for your own personal taste, and then spoon the potatoes and cream into the prepared baking dish. Sprinkle on the finely grated cheese and, if serving immediately, put under the grill until the top browns and bubbles. However at this stage the potatoes can be kept for a day or two, and then re-heated, and put under the grill when required.

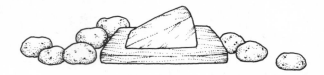

Watercress Salad

Watercress seems very much in vogue these days for iron-full diets, but I can remember so well the watercress man coming down the back street selling the wares that he had picked about an hour before from the streams in the woods. I used to love the watercress simply served with sliced tomatoes in a warmed-up, well-buttered breakfast bun, but I suppose nowadays those on diets would have to miss out on the bun.

Watercress salads are such a change from the good old lettuce, and many starters can use watercress as a base instead of lettuce – terrines, pâtés and vegetable salads – but only use the freshest ends of each stem and keep them in the fridge until as late as possible. Fresh cherries scattered liberally on watercress look quite stunning, and toasted pine kernels provide a clever contrast in colour and texture. You could even sprinkle hot bacon bits over the watercress and use the bacon fat as dressing, but I prefer a very light dressing made up of equal parts of white wine and a good oil, sweetened to taste with icing sugar and then sharpened with as much or as little white wine vinegar as you care to use. Don't make the dressing in a liquidizer, but simply add the ingredients to a mixing bowl and beat gently with a wire whisk, and keep on dipping in your finger and tasting until you get what you want.

Pineapple Cheese Salad

I vividly recall the days of rationing in the last war when tinned goods were bought with coupons. The more scarce and luxurious the item the more of the coupons were needed to aid your purchase. It was then, with great joy (and much anticipation), that my Nan would occasionally fork out both cash and coupons for a small tin of pineapple chunks. For days this would sit with pride of place in the store-cupboard, and my mouth would water just *thinking* about this pineapple and cheese salad. It was the main course for a high tea.

Lots of lettuce leaves were spread on the plate, with spring onions, radish slices, watercress sprigs, parsley, grated carrots, and perhaps some apple slices artfully scattered around. Then each plate got 4 pineapple chunks, and the whole thing was coated with very, very finely grated, tasty Lancashire cheese. Nowadays I use fairly thick slices of fresh pineapple with the merest touch of French dressing, and lots of the white Lancashire cheese, but *then*, always topped off with large crumbs of my favourite cheese – the blue Cheshire. This fairly strong, soapy tasting cheese is the perfect accompaniment to the sweet tangy pineapple.

APPLES

The Granny Smith is my favourite apple, and it is said to have got its name from Elsie Smith, a Covent Garden flower girl. She was always surrounded by children, for whom she used to beg fruit from the various stallholders, and who used to call her 'Granny' Smith. When one of the wealthy fruit merchants who purchased his daily buttonhole from Elsie developed a new strain of apple, he called it 'Granny Smith', as he knew the name at least would be popular. Elsie Smith later emigrated to Australia, taking with her some of 'her' apple trees, and there they grew and flourished.

Apples are marvellous fruit. When I am on one of my spasmodic diets I use them frequently as a good nibble and filler-up. An apple has traces of vitamins A, B and C and is a good source of roughage but, more important still, an apple is said to have up to 3 times the filling power of the various expensive 'slimming' products. An apple with a thin slice of cheese and a small amount of yoghurt will make a good breakfast for diet-conscious people, and one eaten by itself 10 minutes before a meal will stop you eating so much.

I find apples go well in or with almonds, batters, cake mixings, caramel, cloves, curry, chutney, cinnamon, chicken, dates, duck, ginger, lemon rind, marmalade, nutmeg, pork, piecrust, rice, sausages, sandwiches, stuffings, salads and soups. So there! When purchasing the weekly shopping convenience snack products, think again and put a couple of pounds of Granny Smiths in the shopping bag. Your purse will be the richer and your health the better for it.

Apple Starters or Salads

Practically any left-overs go well with diced raw apple – in particular various cheeses, chutney, sour cream, gherkins, olives, dates, banana, celery or tomato – all served on a bed of dressed lettuce or watercress. A peeled, cored and halved apple, stuffed with cheese and herb pâté and coated with a tarragon cream was apparently one of the most successful dishes in my last book, and is certainly the most popular starter at Miller Howe or when on tour overseas. An apple stuffed with peanut butter with finely grated Cheddar cheese as a coating is very filling and satisfying. Apples go well too with avocados (making an expensive fruit go further), and with walnuts and a few prawns added, this makes a very exciting starter or salad. Finely grated young root vegetables served on a bed of thinly sliced, peeled and cored apples coated with a dressing of curried natural yoghurt is unusual. Or you can grate apples and carrots and set them with peas in individual lime jelly moulds – a delicious starter to a spring or summer menu.

1 lb (450 g) Granny Smith apples

$\frac{1}{4}$ pint (150 ml) white wine

sprig of fresh mint

$\frac{1}{2}$ pint (300 ml) home-made mayonnaise (page 177)

Apple Sauce Mayonnaise

This is excellent with cold pork, and also goes well with grilled plaice or sole. Simmer the peeled, cored and sliced apples in the wine with the mint and, when fallen, liquidize and combine, after passing through a sieve, with the mayonnaise. A teaspoon of grated horseradish adds a delicious spiciness.

Apple Stuffing

Apples make excellent stuffings as they preserve the moisture, tend to reduce the richness, and increase the quantity of your meat or whatever at little expense. They may be used to stuff a bird or laid on top of or between portions of pork.

Fry a few chopped onions (or spring onions) in dripping or butter, then add the peeled, sliced apples, and fry gently. At this stage, you can also add a little sausagemeat and seasoning of choice – herbs, finely chopped red peppers, walnuts, wine, grated cheese, or mushrooms. You want to achieve a slightly fluffy, mushy texture, and if it dries out add a little apple juice or cider. When sufficiently cooked you can gently fold in a few breadcrumbs.

When you stuff your loin of pork, breast of chicken, or shoulder of lamb, don't press the stuffing down hard as you want to leave room for it to expand slightly when the joint is being cooked, and to be light at the end.

Honey Apples

Heat until bubbling a cup of runny honey with $\frac{1}{2}$ cup of wine vinegar and when ready drop in thinly sliced rings of apple. Skim them out when they are more or less transparent and serve as a marvellous garnish for roast pork or ham.

serves 4

4 level tablespoons plain flour

2 eggs

$\frac{1}{2}$ pint (300 ml) milk

pinch salt

pinch nutmeg

4 oz (100–125 g) butter

2 medium onions, about 6 oz (175 g), finely chopped

6 large sausages

3 Granny Smith apples

3 tablespoons demerara sugar

Sausage and Apple Bake

Even in wartime, sausages were scarce, and were usually just highly-seasoned breadcrumbs and wheat stuck into india-rubber skins, but they went further and tasted better when cooked with apples in a batter.

For the batter, mix the plain flour slowly with the eggs, milk, salt and nutmeg until smooth (this can be done in a liquidizer).

Melt the butter and cook the finely chopped onions until golden. Roughly cut the sausages into pieces, add them to the pan, and brown them quickly and fiercely. Peel, core and roughly dice the apples and add them, along with the demerara sugar, to the sausages and onions, and cook gently for a minute. Spread this mixture on the base of an 8 inch (20 cm) casserole dish, pour on the batter and bake in a pre-heated oven for $\frac{3}{4}$ hour at 375°F (190°C), Gas 5.

I well remember this dish served with mashy, mushy marrowfat peas cooked with the stalks of fresh mint. Go on, get down to basics for a change and try it – it was marvellous then, and still is!

coats 6 large Granny Smith apples

1 lb (450 g) granulated sugar

4 tablespoons golden syrup

¼ pint (150 ml) cold water

Toffee Apples

When did you or your family last have a toffee apple? Each year on Guy Fawkes night we make them at Miller Howe and I still get as excited as ever. They are well worth the trouble, and good for you into the bargain. There used to be a stall in Barrow market that sold only toffee apples and I was often tempted to spend part of my meagre pocket money on one, but a certain winning smile I could conjure up would melt my Nan's heart and get her to bring out the apple saucepans. I would clumsily chop a stick or two of firewood into sensibly sized pieces for the toffee apple sticks, and we would be in business.

First of all prepare the apples. Stick wooden skewers right into the core of each, and wipe the apples perfectly dry. Have ready a well-buttered tray on which to place the coated apples.

Place all the ingredients in a thick bottomed saucepan, and stir over a low heat until the sugar has dissolved. When the mixture is clear, increase the heat and continue cooking until the mixture begins to caramelise. (If you have the luxury of a sugar thermometer, this is when it shows a temperature of 310°F or 155°C.) Remove the saucepan from the heat immediately, and tip it up so that the toffee is all at the bottom of one side of the saucepan.

Dip the apples, holding them securely by the skewer, into the toffee, and turn until fully coated. Lift up, and allow the excess toffee to drain back into the saucepan, and then place the apples on the buttered tray to set. When they are quite cold, wrap each apple in lightly buttered good greaseproof paper.

Desserts, Cakes and Biscuits

STEAMED SPONGE PUDDINGS

These sweets are much-maligned (rather like mothers-in-law in music-hall jokes), and most people dismiss them, remembering the horrors of school dinners (actually mine at Henry Mellish Grammar School for Boys were interesting, as I used to earn pocket money by helping in the kitchen each lunch-time, which made both my pocket and my body heavier!). I can vividly recall having them throughout my childhood when they were often served with aplomb by my grandmother on even the hottest day, accompanied by jugs of cream from the top of the milk or, on high days and holidays, by a carton of double cream. They might have come to the table hot but we used to wait for them to cool a little before attacking them, and then we could go straight on to the seconds which had been left on the side-table in the wash-house. One slice is no more fattening than a wedge of sponge-cake, and in the summer, served at lunch, it will bring on that lovely half hour's doze, or will make you good and warm for that brisk walk in the cold crisp air in winter.

A steamer is necessary for steamed puds, but don't rush out to buy one until you have decided that you like steamed puds, and there is a place for them in your repertoire (I bet my bottom dollar you do eventually invest in one). You won't need one of those new-fangled pressure steamers but just an old-fashioned colander which can also be used for straining boiled vegetables or for steaming vegetables and fish etc – in other words a round saucepan with holes on the base which will fit on top of a pan three-quarters filled with boiling water. If you haven't one, be a Boy Scout or Girl Guide and adapt what you have to make one. Simply find a deep metal sieve that will fit over the top lip of a saucepan and which will hold your pudding basin, covered by a saucepan lid or, if that isn't big enough, coated completely in tinfoil.

3 tablespoons golden syrup

rind and juice of 2 oranges

2 tablespoons fine breadcrumbs (or liquidized cornflakes)

4 oz (100–125 g) butter

4 oz (100–125 g) castor sugar

2 eggs, lightly beaten

4 oz (100–125 g) self-raising flour, sieved

grated rind and juice of 1 lemon

1 tablespoon butter, melted

Orange and Syrup Sponge Pudding

These days so many people are hung up on 'dieting' and being slim that I think our forefathers would have thought us a real rum lot. I can cast cholesterol and calories to the winds, as without a doubt this is one of my favourite sweets all year round. This sponge can also be made with treacle instead of syrup, which gives it a more pungent taste.

Gently warm the golden syrup through in a small saucepan, with the rind and juice of the oranges, in order to make a runny sauce. Pour onto the bread or cornflake crumbs in a small bowl. Meanwhile, in a separate bowl, cream the butter and sugar together until white and fluffy. Little by little beat in the eggs and then fold in the sieved self-raising flour. Lastly, add the rind and juice of the lemon.

Warm a small pudding basin (a 2 pint or 1·1 litre one is large enough), and start bringing your double steamer to the boil. Liberally coat your warmed pudding basin with the melted butter, put in the warm syrup sauce and breadcrumb mixture, and top with the creamy butter, egg and flour mixture. Cover with a double layer of foil or greaseproof paper (or use the paper removed from the butter). Place the pudding basin in the top of your double steamer, with the water boiling, and immediately put on the lid. Boil merrily away for about $1\frac{1}{4}$ hours, but for goodness sake do keep looking in the bottom saucepan to check it has not burned dry!

In summer serve this on the hottest of days accompanied by a dollop of home-made icecream (page 166), and in the winter serve it with custard sauce (page 32). On a very special occasion, make the following sauce for your sponge pudding.

1 pint (550 ml) double cream

2 tablespoons cube or preserving sugar

juice and rind of 2 oranges

Orange Cream Sauce

Put the cream and cube or preserving sugar into a large clean saucepan. (A large saucepan is important as the cream can very suddenly and unexpectedly boil over.) Put the pan over a low heat and simmer for about 45 minutes, keeping your eye closely on the mixture or else you will have a devil of a job cleaning the stove. The cream should reduce by half, and at this point it will have taken on a lovely golden buttery colour and the smell is absolutely sensuous. Add to this thickened cream the juice and finely grated rind of the oranges, and hey presto, a sauce for the gods!

$\frac{1}{4}$ pint (150 ml) apple purée (page 168)

2 Granny Smith apples, peeled, cored and thinly sliced

1 tablespoon butter

4 oz (100–125 g) butter

4 oz (100–125 g) castor sugar

2 eggs, lightly beaten

4 oz (100–125 g) self-raising flour, sieved

Steamed Apple Sponge

Make the apple purée (you can freeze the remaining $\frac{1}{2}$ pint (300 ml) from the recipe). Using the tablespoon of butter, grease all round the inside of the pudding bowl (a 2 pint or 1·1 litre one will be about right). On the base and around the sides arrange about half the thin circles of apples. In a mixing bowl cream the sugar and butter, and little by little add the lightly beaten eggs to this creamy base. Then beat in the apple purée and gently fold in the sieved flour.

Set your double steamer on to boil. Coat the base of the prepared pudding bowl with a dollop of the sponge mixture and then cover this with some of the remaining apple circles, and repeat this process until your sponge and apples are finished. Cover with a double layer of greaseproof paper or foil securely tied on the outside of the bowl and put in the boiling steamer and cook for $1\frac{1}{4}$ hours (don't let the water boil dry). Serve with custard sauce.

4 oz (100–125 g) butter

4 oz (100–125 g) castor sugar

2 eggs, lightly beaten

4 oz (100–125 g) self-raising flour, sieved

4 pieces preserved ginger, finely chopped

3 oz (75 g) currants

juice and rind of 1 orange

1 tablespoon butter

Spotty Ginger Dick

The basic sponge mixture for all these steamed puddings is the same, as is the cooking method. Fold into the basic sponge mixture the finely chopped ginger, currants and rind and juice of the orange. Grease the bowl with the tablespoon of butter and cook the sponge as before for $1\frac{1}{4}$ hours.

4 oz (100–125 g) butter

4 oz (100–125 g) castor sugar

2 eggs, lightly beaten

4 oz (100–125 g) self-raising flour, sieved

1 pear

$\frac{1}{2}$ pint (300 ml) stock syrup (page 178)

1 tablespoon butter

Steamed Pear Sponge

Once again make up the basic sponge, but steam the pudding with the pear in the middle. Choose a pear that will fit your pudding bowl comfortably (the same size bowl, about 2 pint or 1·1 litre should be about right). Peel and core the pear and poach it gently for about 10 minutes in the stock syrup.

Put all the sponge mixture in the butter-greased bowl. Push a spill or wooden skewer through the base of the pear, and push the pear, stalk or narrow end down, into the centre of the batter in the bowl. The spill, the same length as the width of the bowl or slightly larger, balancing across the bowl, ensures that the pear remains exactly in the middle of the bowl, with a little bit sticking up, throughout cooking. Cook as before for $1\frac{1}{4}$ hours.

Remove the spill before serving (of course), and I usually pour some warmed butterscotch sauce over this sponge (page 33).

Steamed Coffee Pudding

To the basic sponge pudding mixture of butter, sugar, eggs and flour, add simply 2 tablespoons Camp Coffee. Don't forget to butter the bowl well, and steam in the same way as all the others.

4 oz (100–125 g) butter

4 oz (100–125 g) castor sugar

2 eggs, lightly beaten

2 oz (50 g) self-raising flour, sieved

2 oz (50 g) drinking chocolate

1 tablespoon butter (for greasing bowl)

Steamed Chocolate Pudding

Make the basic sponge mixture, substituting half the flour with drinking chocolate powder. Walnuts add a marvellous nutty texture, and these can be folded in before baking – about 3 oz (75 g), finely chopped. Steam this pudding for $1\frac{3}{4}$ hours, not $1\frac{1}{4}$ hours.

*   *   *

serves 8

about 6–8 $\frac{1}{4}$ inch (6 mm) slices of good stale bread

1 oz (25 g) butter

$\frac{1}{2}$ pint (300 ml) single cream

3 eggs

1 egg yolk

2 tablespoons castor sugar

fresh seasonal fruit

for the crumble topping

3 oz (75 g) self-raising flour

1 dessertspoon cornflour

2 oz (50 g) soft brown sugar

1 oz (25 g) butter

teaspoon ground cinnamon

pinch ground nutmeg

1 tablespoon demerara sugar

Crumbles

Everybody, but everybody, has his or her own recipe for crumbles, just as for trifles. In my early days crumbles were often served at my Nan's, and nowadays, whenever I have a surplus of practically any fruit, I follow her recipe. I know only too well it's not traditional, but *she* called them crumbles, and I have followed suit. It's really like a cross between a traditional crumble and a bread and butter pudding.

Gooseberries, apples, pears, cherries, plums, rhubarb – all summer fruits can be used and will be eagerly consumed. It's difficult to be precise about the amount of fruit to use as each fruit behaves differently when cooked, but we made a wonderful apple crumble when testing, with $1\frac{3}{4}$ lb (800–825 g) Granny Smith apples.

Remove the crusts from the bread. Grease a $2\frac{1}{2}$ pint (1·4 litre) dish with the butter. Line the base and the sides of your dish (my Nan used an oval Pyrex one) with the slices of bread, and then mix together the cream and eggs. Beat the extra egg yolk with the castor sugar, and mix into the cream and egg 'custard'. Pour this over the base of the bread – encourage it up the sides as well – and leave for an hour or so for the bread to absorb most of the custard.

Peel and slice the fruit if necessary, and place it on top of the soggy bread (push the bread sides down a bit if the fruit doesn't come up far enough). Pre-heat the oven to 350°F (180°C), Gas 4.

Bring all the crumble ingredients together slowly and lightly as if you were making pastry, and scatter over the uncooked fruit. Bake in the pre-heated oven for 1 hour until the custard is set. Serve at once with soured cream (if available) or lightly whipped fresh cream. (The apple crumble was amazingly sleep-inducing served with the egg flip sauce on page 18).

$\frac{1}{2}$ pint (300 ml) single cream

1 vanilla pod

3 egg yolks

1 generous tablespoon castor sugar

1 level teaspoon cornflour

Custard Sauce

I'm sure many people are perfectly happy with packet custard sauce, but there really is absolutely nothing like the proper stuff and it's so easy to make. However I must admit I do cheat a bit as I put in a little cornflour as a guarantee that it will not split, assuring me of a lovely, slightly thick, rich custard.

Heat the cream with the vanilla pod in a saucepan, gently. Do not let it boil. Mix together the other ingredients to a smooth paste in a mixing bowl that is large enough to hold the hot cream. Place a fine plastic sieve over the mixing bowl and quickly pour in the cream (minus the pod) and then stir it all vigorously until smooth. Return to the saucepan and, stirring all the time, cook until the custard thickens. This takes an incredibly short time. However, don't go boiling the custard, as you must remember those egg yolks!

3 oz (75 g) butter

$4\frac{1}{2}$ oz (130 g) soft brown sugar

3 oz (75 g) granulated sugar

1 1 lb (450 g) tin golden syrup

$\frac{1}{4}$ pint (150 ml) double cream

few drops vanilla essence

Butterscotch Sauce

My Nan used painstakingly to make butterscotch sweets for high days and holidays and I, more than once, got a burnt tongue by greedily endeavouring to eat a piece as it was cooking. It was Delia Smith who told me about this butterscotch sauce, and I now invariably have a jam jar of it in the fridge at home and use it regularly at Miller Howe. As it stores so well (several weeks in the fridge) and has so many uses – spooned over poached peaches, pears or apples; on top of a generous blob of icecream; with apple pie or better still, banana, walnut and date pie; combined with whipped cream, broken meringue, and chunky bits of over-ripe bananas; even used to restore a bit of nearly over-the-top sponge gâteau – I usually make a large mixing when I cook it. This quantity will make enough to fill about 2 1 lb (450 g) jars.

Put the butter into a fairly large, very thick bottomed saucepan, along with the sugars and the syrup. To get every drop of the syrup out of the tin, leave it in a warm kitchen for a few hours prior to use, or put the opened tin into a saucepan, half fill up its sides with hot water and simmer away for about 20 minutes (a damned sight easier than trying to scrape every bit out of the tin, with your hands, spoons and work surface becoming increasingly sticky!).

Put the saucepan containing the butter, sugars and syrup over a gentle heat and, when formed into a liquid, stir slowly and continue to cook for about another 10 minutes. Remove from heat and, after a few minutes, begin to stir in the double cream a little at a time, along with a few drops of vanilla essence. It is important to continue stirring at this time for about another 3 to 5 minutes to ensure the sauce is smooth. Leave it then to use more or less right away or put into clean screw-top jam jars.

BAKING

Baking days were at least 3 times a week in my Nan's house and there weren't then the modern wonders of refrigeration, freezers, mixers or food chemistry (I can clearly remember her suspicion, for instance, just before the war, of the new-fangled self-raising flour – she used to sieve and re-sieve plain flour to which she had added baking powder in order to get a 'rise'). No quick-to-hand Kenwood mixer or, better still, a Kenwood Chef to speed up the work time, but only a rather tattered cream enamel bowl (with the odd black spot in parts where the enamel had worn through) and her hand. I never saw her beat batters or cream butter and sugar with anything other than her hand, and she used to say she could 'feel' how the mixing was going on. In a similar way *I* 'know', using an electric hand beater, when the butter and sugar have reached the creamy stage as suddenly the 'feel' is different.

For me there is nothing more basic than baking and, for that matter, nothing more satisfying. Rubbing fat into flour, beating sugar into soft butter, folding in ground almonds – I find it all quite sensuous! You may well say there is a lot of 'faffing' about to baking. Getting out the scales, weights, tins, bowls, jars, ingredients, pans, greaseproof paper for lining the tins, melting butter, all that endless washing-up afterwards. I agree, *but* if you make up your mind to have one real blitz, either once a week or fortnight (depending on your storage facilities), it is all worth the effort.

A good bake-day can produce endless items, especially if you double up on the recipes as I do. But most baked products can be frozen (some to their advantage), and many can be stored in polythene bags in airtight tins or containers for up to 10 days and are none the worse for it. There are very few baked goods that *need* to be eaten straightaway. And also do remember that old North-country saying, 'What you sow you reap', and so give, give, give. See the look on friends' faces when you present them with something you have actually baked for them! Time is the most expensive item in most of our lives these days – even surrounded by time-saving, new-fangled gadgetry – and however old-hat it may sound, next time you go visiting, take something home-baked with you and see how satisfied you feel afterwards.

But good baking *does* require good materials and care. You must weigh out all your ingredients accurately, and follow the recipe exactly (if you don't you can't then blame the cookery writer for a poor result!).

The first essential is a good weighing machine, and I find the old-fashioned balancing scale absolutely vital. The new-fangled spring-balancing, plastic machines look so attractive in their multi-colour ranges, but they just can't compete with the older scales, and indeed are often 'out' just enough to ruin a recipe. (I'm also anti-metrication: fuddy-duddy that I am, I still convert new pence back to shillings and pence, and all my recipes are evolved in pounds and ounces).

Greaseproof paper, too, plays an important part in a baking kitchen, but it varies so much in quality. I think the high-quality 'silicone-treated' paper is the best buy even though it appears expensive – it can often be used over and over again, particularly if you have used it as a lining when cooking meringues or biscuits – while the flimsy lavatory paper type of greaseproof that may initially appeal to your purse will have you cursing when the cooked goodies will not detach themselves from it!

If you followed my advice in *Entertaining with Tovey*, you will have bought yourself an oven thermometer, and will be putting it to good use. *Do* remember each time you go to grab it out of the oven to use an oven cloth, and never put it down immediately on to a cold surface. I give full marks to those glass-doored ovens with electric lights – even though they don't sport a thermometer on the door – but why, oh why, are the replacement bulbs so difficult to find and so difficult to fit back in! But if you have to open the oven (about two-thirds through recommended cooking time) do it *gently*, and close it even more gently as a sudden gust of wind can do damage to your baking. If you see that one side is cooking more than another, or the bottom shelf more than the top, change the items round, from side to side, back to front, top to bottom.

Butter is the only ingredient I will mention as it is vital, in my opinion, for baking. Nothing at all quite compares with the rich, nutty flavour it gives. OK, if you have a cholesterol problem, use margarine, but don't inflict me with your problems as, without a doubt, butter is best for baking.

But it is the too hurried storing of cooked items that often spoils baking. Nothing, repeat nothing, should be stored away in foil, polythene bags or airtight tins until it is perfectly *cold*. The commercial open-wire cooling trays are a great help – and don't, whatever you do, put lovely piping hot cooked cakes to cool near a draughty window (just think what happened to the Queen of Hearts). Just use your basic common sense, of which you have plenty!

However, I'm getting away from the basic point of persuading you to return to the old-fashioned style of baking at least once a week. Believe you me, if you have a Kenwood Chef or Mixer, your life will be easier, *but* even without these, you can cope admirably with most of the following recipes (and those elsewhere in the book) and your store-cupboard, biscuit tins and the freezer will always have something in to satisfy the hungry demands of unexpected visitors or a famished family turning up with friends at the last moment. For a warm welcoming host or hostess collects acquaintances and people to be fed like a flame attracts moths, but that is what life and cooking is all about: giving, caring and sharing.

Rich Easy Brown Bread

2 lb (900 g) wheatmeal flour

8 oz (225 g) soft butter

2 generous teaspoons sea salt

1 oz (25 g) fresh yeast

1 oz (25 g) castor sugar

1 pint (550–600 ml) warm milk

The night before, lightly rub the butter into the wheatmeal flour and salt, and leave. (A *large* bowl should be used, as after adding the yeast mixture you have to allow for the bread mixture rising.)

When you want to make the bread, cream the yeast with the sugar with a wooden spoon in a pudding bowl and then add the warm milk – at about blood heat temperature (if too hot, you will kill the yeast). Then quickly stir the milk mixture into the bowl of mixed wheatmeal flour and butter, cover with a damp cloth and leave in a warm draught-free place for 2 hours. It will double in size. Turn this light springy mixture out onto a floured surface and roughly knock back and shape into 2 round loaves. Leave once again to rise for 15 to 20 minutes (only a minimal rise this time) and then bake off in a pre-heated oven at 400°F (200°C), Gas 6, for 30 to 40 minutes.

The beauty of this bread is that it requires no kneading and little care, and will last for about 8 days.

Walnut and Date Loaf

makes 2 1 lb (450 g) loaves

8 oz (225 g) dates

7 fl. oz (200 ml) boiling water

1½ lb (700 g) plain flour

1 teaspoon salt

6 oz (175 g) butter

1 lb (450 g) castor sugar

1 teaspoon bicarbonate of soda

2 eggs, lightly beaten

6 oz (175 g) walnuts, chopped

Stone the dates, chop roughly, and cover with the boiling water. Leave until they are quite cool. Sieve the flour and salt into a Kenwood bowl, add the butter and castor sugar, and mix on a low speed until the mixture has a breadcrumb texture. Drain the water from the dates and dissolve the bicarbonate of soda in it. Mix in the 2 lightly beaten eggs and then combine with the dry ingredients along with the chopped walnuts and the dates.

Mix to a paste and turn out into 2 well-greased and floured bread tins and bake in a pre-heated oven at 325°F (160°C), Gas 3, for approximately 1½ hours, but test with a sharp pointed knife after 1 hour.

Auntie Millie's Dropscones

makes 18–20 scones

8 oz (225 g) self-raising flour

½ teaspoon salt

4 oz (100–125 g) castor sugar

1½ oz (40 g) soft butter

2 eggs

10 tablespoons milk

12 drops fresh lemon juice

Mix all the dry ingredients together and then gently rub in 1 oz (25 g) of the soft butter. Beat the eggs, milk and lemon juice together, make a well in the flour, and add the liquid, stirring the flour in slowly until you have a smooth paste mixture.

Heat your griddle pan, paint liberally with the remaining butter, and place 3 separate dessertspoons of the mixture on the griddle at a time. You will see when the base is cooked and, using a palette knife, flick them over to cook on the other side. Have to hand a clean tea towel folded in half on a plate, and as you make the dropscones, put them in between the halves to keep them warm.

Rock Cakes

makes about 20–24 cakes

5 oz (150 g) butter

10 oz (275 g) self-raising flour

4 oz (100–125 g) demerara sugar

2 oz (50 g) each of dates, walnuts, cherries, finely chopped, separately

2 eggs, lightly beaten

I just do not know how this name originated, but believe you me, these cakes are not like rocks, but a good standby to have in any store-cupboard cookie tin'.

The whole mixing can be done with the K beater of a Kenwood. Place all the ingredients into the bowl and mix on a slow speed until they are all combined.

If you haven't a mixer, simply rub the butter into the flour, fold in the sugar, dates, walnuts and cherries, and then combine with the lightly beaten eggs.

Have to hand a baking tray lined with greaseproof paper, and at wide intervals drop blobs of the mixture onto it. Bake for about 20 minutes in a pre-heated oven set at 375°F (190°C), Gas 5. When cold, store in an airtight container.

Victorian Sponge

8 oz (225 g) soft butter

8 oz (225 g) castor sugar

4 eggs (weighing 8 oz or 225 g out of the shell!)

8 oz (225 g) self-raising flour, sieved

grated rind of 2 oranges and juice of 1

juice of 1 lemon

This is the best recipe I know, with everything weighing 8 oz or 225 g. Weigh out *very* accurately and go through each basic step of the recipe with care and patience. Your end product will reflect this love.

Cream the butter and sugar together until nice and fluffy and then beat until white (about 10 minutes). Add the beaten eggs little by little. *Never* add more egg until that which you have already put in has been taken up by the butter and sugar mixture. When all the egg is in, scatter on the grated rind of the oranges, fold in the sieved flour, and finally incorporate the juice of the 1 orange and the lemon.

Put the batter into 4 7–8 inch (17·5–20 cm) sponge tins (about 1½ inch or 3·5 cm deep). Bake in a pre-heated oven at 325°F (160°C), Gas 3, for about 20 to 30 minutes. They are ready when the centres feel springy and no imprint of your finger remains. Take out and cool.

I use the juice from the second orange to flavour the icing. Mix 1 lb (450 g) icing sugar with the juice, and add boiling water until you get the desired texture. Topped with this flavoured icing and filled with lemon curd (page 180) and lightly whipped cream, the calories are prolific but the taste and texture truly prodigious.

You can also make individual sponge cakes with this recipe. These quantities should fill about 24 paper cake cases, and I serve these with the top taken off, and the middle filled with jam and cream and the 'lid' popped back on.

makes approximately 30 biscuits

6 oz (175 g) self-raising flour

1 level teaspoon bicarbonate of soda

1 level teaspoon ground ginger

2 oz (50 g) soft butter

4 oz (100–125 g) castor sugar

1½ oz (40 g) golden syrup

1 egg, lightly beaten

Ginger Snaps

Sieve the flour, bicarbonate of soda and ground ginger together and mix well. Beat together the butter, castor sugar, golden syrup and lightly beaten egg, and then fold in the flour mixture. The dough should not be too soft.

Turn out on a floured board and roll into the shape of a snake ¾ inch (18 mm) thick. Cut off pieces, at ½ inch (12 mm) intervals, and roll these into balls. Place the balls well apart on a baking tray lined with good greaseproof paper (they will spread, obviously). Bake in batches of 12. They take about 15 minutes at 350°F (180°C), Gas 4, to cook but do watch then from time to time as, I warn you, they burn easily. Leave to cool on the baking trays.

ENTERTAINING OCCASION
Picnics

Some say you need sun for picnics. I say you only need a little flair and imagination and even the dullest days can be transformed!

In my childhood, when summers were really summers, picnics played an important part in my life. Being sent to the shops in the morning for things forgotten didn't seem such a chore, as it was all part of the great anticipated feast. No tasks were too menial or boring, provided we would be packed and off, in time to catch the 1 o'clock bus from the Cemetery over to North Scale on Walney Island. Each single corner of the 13-cornered lane was ticked off as we walked from the bus terminus to the Irish Sea and I didn't resent the mile-and-a-half trek. But once on the beach, I didn't want to go far as the sooner we all got settled, the sooner the picnic and eating got into full swing. When the spot was mutually agreed, there were hundreds of things to do: a wall-surround made from pebbles to protect us from wind and sand; castles to be built; crabs and winkles sought out; pools explored; flat stones skimmed over the sea; boats sailed and kites flown; shells to collect and sand worms to be disturbed.

But none of these appealed to me. Little Fatso Tovey just wanted to get on with the eating of

the picnic. 'Nanna, don't you think the tomato sandwiches are ever so soft now?' 'Shall I go and get some Marsh's Sass?' 'Is it time to get the hot water for the tea?' No posh thermos flasks in those days, merely a large blue teapot with tealeaves inside, which was filled up with hot water from the Pavilion for tuppence. People actually made a living at that, and by selling tuppenny ice lollies during the lovely endless warm summers.

Which weren't in fact so endless. I can remember going on one picnic with my Nan on the miniature open-air train to Eskdale. The sun shone as we set out at 8 in the morning, but very soon the sky became cloudy, the heavens opened, and down lashed the rain. But Nanna smiled, insisting that it wouldn't last, and we and a few others braved the elements, huddled together in the open wooden coaches. We were soon soaked to the skin, although the picnic bags were safe and dry under the seat. Leah said, 'Well, lad, we won't get wet whilst passing under the bridges' (some consolation as there were only 3 on that stretch of line), but we ate, wonderfully, in the waiting-room at Eskdale Station!

Another time, in the late 40s, Marjorie and Norman (my aunt and uncle) called for us around 3 on a Sunday in their highly polished second-hand car. Right proud we were as we got in, knowing full well that the neighbours were watching from behind their net curtains. First of all, the luggage needed for Nan's picnic – travel rugs, newspapers, library books, towels etc, plus the food – was put in the boot. Heads held high, we got in too, but our smugness was deflated when the ruddy car moved 3 yards, spluttered and stopped. Madly did Norman get out and start looking under the bonnet, but after what seemed ages, out we had to get, unpack the picnic luggage, and go back into the house. With style and aplomb, however, we had tea in the back-yard, passing some of the tasty delicacies over the wall to Mrs Morgan in order to create the impression that all had gone as planned!

On the way to our picnic site, my Nan would have tempted us with titbits – home-made treacle toffee or mints, a Nuttall's Mintoe or stick of chewy pink spearmint, apples or oranges, or lovely bought Cadbury's chocolate biscuits (*so* much better then). But when we had arrived and the goodies started to emerge from the various baskets and boxes, my excitement reached its peak. There were soft tomato sandwiches, salad rolls, and well-buttered, home-made teacakes to go with the generous slices of cold meat carved there and then to prevent them drying up on the journey. Followed by trifles, jellies, swiss rolls, currant slices, apple pie, puff pastry dreams filled with cream and home-made jam, eccles cakes and sausage rolls with chunks of Lancashire cheese. And, of course, lots and lots of sandwiches.

SANDWICHES

I love sandwiches and eat them for a light lunch, and we *never* had a picnic in my childhood without a vast selection. Many people will be cautious about taking their fill of these as their rigorous diets forbid bread. Well, all I can say is all the more for the sensible ones as, on a picnic, tasty, soggy, fresh, buttery, salty sandwiches are super!

Use good brown bread (the bread on pages 35–6 is eminently suitable), and be generous with your butter. Spread it when it's nice and soft

and don't take it right up to the edges of each slice as, if you're like me, you will cut off the crusts and later make them into breadcrumbs (or put them in a separate plastic bag and feed to the ducks, birds, fish etc somewhere in the countryside). To make your butter spread further and the sandwiches taste better (provided the fillings don't clash), beat in a little of the following – lemon juice, salt, horseradish, tomato sauce, fresh herbs, garlic, cream cheese, crushed garlic, or mustard.

Always make thick chunky sandwiches, using a lot of filling. Use any cold meat, with lots of salady ingredients, and tasty garnishes, or cheese, or any of the fillings mentioned in the liquorice allsort sandwiches.

Sandwiches can be made the night before and still taste wonderful if you follow my instructions. Lay out a large sheet of tinfoil and onto this place slightly damp outside leaves of lettuce, damp tops of celery, or outer leaves of cabbage or spinach. Place the sandwiches on top, and arrange them compactly. The damp leaves ensure they are always moist – soggy ones don't turn me off, only rather dried-out hard ones! Garnish the sandwiches with as much attention and affection as you do your Christmas parcels. Generous sprigs of parsley, cucumber slices, strips of raw vegetables all combine to make exciting eating. Top your finished array with more lettuce/cabbage/spinach/celery leaves, and parcel them up with the foil into brick-shape parcels. Leave them on a tray in the fridge covered with a slightly damp tea towel, and they should taste wonderful the next day.

Orange and Banana Sandwiches

Oranges and bananas were very much 'black-market' items during my young picnic days but when we managed to get them, they went much further when made into sandwiches. I can clearly recall getting my first real banana on my blue ration book in about 1946. I kept it for days, showing it to all and sundry, and thinking about all the ways in which I could eat it. But I protracted the ecstacy too much as when I came to eat it the yellow skin had gone really brown and each end dark and soggy. The flavour was good, though, and I still enjoy a banana sandwich – good nursery food which may sound revolting, but *isn't*!

Just mash slightly over-ripe bananas to a pulp, fold in a tablespoon of condensed milk, and

spread on your buttery bread. Grate on the
merest touch of nutmeg, and put the top piece
of bread on. Delicious.

Orange and watercress is a tasty combination
– in salads too. Remove the skin from the
orange and then slice the flesh crossways into
fairly thick slices. Place these onto the
buttered bread base and coat liberally with
fresh watercress. Grind on black pepper and
sea salt, before topping off with the other slice
of bread.

Liquorice Allsort Sandwiches

Bought sliced bread is best for these, I must
admit. Use white, brown and pumpernickel, if
you can find it, as they will add to the colours
of your finished product. Spread each slice
generously with softened butter and lay the
slices out in front of you. You want to build a
multi-coloured skyscraper, and one way of
doing this is as follows.

On a base of buttered white bread lay a filling
of tuna fish purée (page 161). Top this with a
slice of buttered pumpernickel bread, and then
spread on a filling of mashed hard-boiled eggs
with a little anchovy. Put a slice of buttered
brown bread on top, with a filling of cheese
and herb pâté (page 173). Top this off finally
with a further slice of white bread, butter side
down. When you have your finished triple-
decker sandwich in front of you, press firmly
down to make the square fairly compact, and
then with a sharp bread knife, remove the
crusts on all the 4 sides, and cut into squares
of the size you want.

A second set of sandwiches would be filled
with mashed tinned salmon or sardines, pea
purée and cream cheese. A third set could
have peanut butter, chutney and tomato and
onion served on a bed of lettuce.

These sandwiches look tempting, and are most
appetizing, but all the fillings must be strongly
flavoured. To make the bread content go
further (and therefore not so fattening) I have
been known to take a wooden rolling pin to
each separate slice before buttering, and force
it to a wafer-thinness. These sandwiches can
also be made the night before, but are better
made the morning of your picnic. If you make
them earlier and store in the fridge (in their
leaf and foil parcels) do remember to take
them out in plenty of time to allow them to
lose any fridgy taste or texture they may have
acquired.

BRANTLEA PICNICS

Nowadays, when I have a proper picnic – rarer and rarer, I must admit, primarily because of the lovely summer house at the top of my garden, from which the views are enviable – I tend to make an MGM production number out of it all. I take blankets, cushions, flysprays, picnic hampers, portable radio, newspapers, books, thermos flasks, cooler boxes filled with ice and bottles of white wine, best glasses wrapped in tissue paper, bottle openers and plates and dishes. Quite a safari!

The food is almost always the same, and it all tastes *so* good in the open air. For a starter I take the chilled apple chive soup (page 120) in thermos flasks, or a selection of cold quiches. For the main course, I cook the casserole of chicken (following), and serve it with its jellied vegetables, hard-boiled eggs, and fresh salads of all kinds packed in plastic bags. As a pudding I would take individual trifles or mousses, plate pies, or banana, yoghurt rum slice (page 142).

Everything, but everything, can be prepared the day before.
 HAPPY PICNICKING!

Casserole of Chicken with Vegetables in Wine

serves 8

$\frac{1}{2}$ pint (300 ml) good strong clear chicken stock

1 pint (600 ml) dry white wine

$\frac{1}{4}$ pint (150 ml) dry sherry

$\frac{3}{4}$ lb (350 g) assorted root vegetables, finely diced

$\frac{1}{4}$ lb (125 g) onions, finely diced

fresh herbs of choice

2 chickens, about $1\frac{1}{2}$ lb (700 g) each

2 small pig's trotters

salt, freshly ground black pepper

Place the stock, wine, sherry and vegetables into a casserole dish big enough to hold everything, along with the chopped fresh herbs, and then place the 2 chickens, breast down, in the casserole and add the pig's trotters. Season and bring to the boil, then cover and cook for $1\frac{1}{2}$ hours in a pre-heated oven at 350°F (180°C), Gas 4. At the end of the cooking time, turn the oven off and leave the casserole until quite cool. Take the casserole out, leave to go quite cold, and then chill in the fridge. The juices set to a lovely soft jelly full of partly-cooked vegetables, surrounding the very tender juicy chickens. You may need to skim some fat off the top of the jelly, though.

On a picnic, as long as I don't have too far to go, I take the casserole dish itself in a cardboard box, and portion the birds out at the picnic site, with the chopped, jellied vegetables as an additional salad.

TWO
INFANT SCHOOL

INFANT SCHOOL

At the age of 16, in 1949, having forged my father's signature on the application form, I set sail in a troop ship for Rhodesia (now Zimbabwe) as a Junior Cadet Officer in the Colonial Service. Even the weeks on board ship opened my eyes to food as there appeared to be no sign of shortages once we sailed out of Southampton and rationing-bound Britain.

It took $3\frac{1}{2}$ days to travel from Cape Town, where we docked, to Salisbury where I worked for two years. It was here that I picked up my secretarial skills, by going 5 nights a week to Salisbury Technical College to learn shorthand and typing (quite an effort as I lived in the Mount Hampden Government Hostel, 10 miles out of Salisbury on a dusty strip road). We ate well in the hostel, but when I transferred to the Government mess at Msasa, I discovered real gourmet cooking at the hands of Ann Taylor – a neurotic but superb caterer who loved nothing more than for us bachelors to entertain friends in the evening so that she could pull out all the stops. Every meal was an enlightenment, but it was dinner at 7 for 7.30 that was my daily highlight: tables polished to perfection, glasses shining, cutlery glimmering, flowers everywhere, waiters in beautiful stiffly-starched white uniforms with red fez hats.

But not for long such inexpensive luxury as I was once again transferred, to Nyasaland (now Malawi) to become Private Secretary to Geoff Spicer, General Manager of the Native Labour Organization. He and his wife Eileen lived in great colonial style at Chipande (their beautiful telegraphic address simply SPICER CHIPANDE NJULI), and we enjoyed a wonderful relationship over the following years. It was in their house that I began to learn about style – the right way to present food, the right way to accompany foods, how to combine this guest with that guest – all the little touches that make entertaining such fun and so stimulating.

It was indubitably during those years in Nyasaland that I learned most about food, a complete education to one such as I who had grown up with lack of money and rationing. And the *quality* differed as well as the tastes: the fish from Lake Nyasa were fresh and delicious, as were the chickens Eileen Spicer produced on the farm; the vegetables – ordinary or exotic – grew in abundance, and I learned a multitude of ways in which to serve avocadoes for instance (as you shall see!); the meat, if not one hundred per cent, was wonderfully edible, spiced up in Eastern and African ways, and many of those tastes, new as they were then, have strongly influenced my present-day cooking.

In 1958, after an illness, I was once again transferred, this time to the Gold Coast (now Ghana), where I was secretary to the Court of Inquiry for the Timber and Gold Concessions of the Ashanti. This stint only lasted about a year as I had already fallen in love with the theatre, with *a* theatre. I returned to the UK in 1959, and threw myself wholeheartedly into my new life.

Starters

serves 6–8 portions

2 tablespoons raisins

1 tablespoon cooking brandy

1 cucumber

$\frac{1}{2}$ pint (300 ml) single cream

$\frac{1}{2}$ pint (300 ml) natural yoghurt

2 cloves fresh garlic, crushed

1 tablespoon tarragon vinegar

1 tablespoon fresh mint, finely chopped

1 tablespoon cocktail gherkins, finely chopped

2 hard-boiled eggs, finely chopped

Cold Cucumber Soup

The day before you wish to serve the soup, leave the raisins soaking in the brandy for at least 12 hours.

Wash and dry the cucumber and then grate it coarsely. Stir together all the other ingredients and then mix with the grated cucumber and leave to chill overnight.

Serve in chilled soup bowls and garnish if you can with lovely sprigs of fresh dill (or tops of fresh fennel).

AVOCADOES

I first came to know and like avocadoes when I worked in Africa, and soon discovered how versatile they could be in cooking. Having them literally growing by the dozens in the garden also helped me to use my brains to see how I could serve them differently, day after day, and also helped my then very slender budget. I have literally seen them grow to about $2\frac{1}{2}$ lb (1·1 kg) in weight (resembling a small rugby ball rather than a pear), and even at this size full of that slightly buttery flavour. I think, though, that it is the texture people like most, and the fact that being rather bland, avocadoes can easily be combined with and complemented by other foodstuffs.

Of course we all know Avocado Vinaigrette – half an avocado with its hole (left by removing the stone) filled with a French dressing – and Avocado with Prawns appears on many *à la carte* menus. I gave an easy Avocado Mousse recipe in the last book. Fried, fanned-out quarter wedges of avocado are delicious with most grilled fish dishes or grilled calves' liver. It's a very versatile fruit.

The skin of the avocado is very tough and can vary from a dark greenish brown when ripening, to a rich purple when over the hill. You should use a stainless steel knife to first cut your pear in half from stem to base and then break in two. One half will inevitably then hold the whole large stone which you remove by jiggling it back and forth to loosen it. It should come out with ease provided the pear is ripe and ready for eating. If you find you have been sold a 'pup' by the greengrocer and your pear is quite hard, simply wrap it (in its skin, of course) in some old newspaper and leave in an airing cupboard or close to your central heating boiler. Test daily, and it should only need 3 or 4 days to become nice and ripe. (Use the stone to grow avocado plants. Stick a couple of cocktail sticks or matches into the stone and suspend it in a jam jar of cold water. Leave the jar in a warm place, and the stone should soon start to grow roots and shoots.)

Make certain you remove the dark brown skin from the hole left by the removal of the stone and, using a large silver or stainless steel tablespoon, ease the spoon down one side of the flesh and skin and remove the whole half of the pear leaving the skin behind. Discard the skins, unless you're planning to re-fill them.

Chilled Avocado, Orange and Mint Soup

A delightful soup for a summer's evening that can be done in the flash of the eye. I give you vague quantities as a guide, but it's a recipe that you will find fits exactly to your taste if you keep dabbing your finger in, and actually tasting it!

You can use either a good clear chicken stock, single cream, or natural yoghurt (less fattening than cream and easier on the pocket). Use avocadoes that are just right for eating or slightly over the hill. Use either frozen concentrated orange juice or fresh, and put in the finely grated rind too, if you like.

For each avocado you use, the soup will take $\frac{1}{2}$ pint (300 ml) liquid easily, and this will easily absorb a $\frac{1}{4}$ pint (150 ml) fresh orange juice with the rind or let-down concentrated juice. Use mint whimsically or lavishly depending on your taste, but what you *do* need is a liquidizer. Simply use some of the liquid as a base in the liquidizer, add the lightly chopped avocado, and just play around.

Serve the soup chilled in ice-cold bowls (2 avocadoes and about $1\frac{1}{2}$ pints or 900 ml will serve 4 to 6), garnished with a dollop of cream and a sprig of fresh mint. To add a bit of colour, you can sprinkle on some very finely diced red pepper, or you could use chopped walnuts.

Avocado Pear with Fresh Pear

When avocadoes are expensive, this is a good recipe to help your pocket and delight your palate. You will need a quarter of fresh skinned avocado (see above) and fresh pear per person (therefore one of each will serve 4 people). Choose pears which are of similar size. Divide each pear (avocado and fresh) into quarters, lengthwise, then simply slice *each* quarter – again lengthwise – into 4 sections. Then put together a 'half' pear per person, alternating avocado sections with fresh. Serve with a light French dressing.

Avocado Pear with Horseradish Yoghurt

per person

½ **avocado pear**

½ **oz (15 g) carrot, finely grated**

1 **teaspoon horseradish cream**

2 **tablespoons natural yoghurt**

Fill the centre of the skinned half pear lightly with the grated carrot, and place the pear on the serving plate, round side up. Whip the horseradish cream and natural yoghurt together, and coat the pear. Garnish with chopped parsley.

Avocado Pear with Preserved Ginger

Everybody serves avocado pear with vinaigrette dressing, but for a change, finely chop up one piece of preserved ginger for each half section of avocado, and place this in the hole. Pour over a teaspoon of the preserved ginger juice. Quick and different.

Healthfood Avocado

serves 6

2 **ripe avocadoes, skinned and chopped**

2 **tablespoons cream cheese**

2 **tablespoons double cream**

1 **egg yolk**

juice and rind of 1 fresh lime

2 **teaspoons runny honey**

3 **egg whites**

6 **tablespoons natural yoghurt**

12 **teaspoons toasted sunflower seeds**

Place the chopped avocado flesh in a Magimix or blender with the cream cheese, cream, egg yolk, juice and rind of the lime, and runny honey, and whizz around until very smooth. If you are doubtful about the mixture, pass it through a fine plastic sieve. Beat up the egg whites in a metal or glass bowl until stiff and fold gently into the avocado purée.

Portion into 6 glasses and just as you are about to serve, top off each glass with a tablespoon of natural yoghurt and sprinkle onto each 2 teaspoons of the toasted sunflower seeds. Serve with the rich, easy brown bread on pages 35–6.

Avocado and Smoked Salmon

Make parisian balls of your avocado (using what is left inside the skin for a soup or mousse or even liquidized as a sauce), and wrap each ball in a strip of smoked salmon. To keep the smoked salmon in place and for easy serving, pierce with a wooden cocktail stick.

Avocado Cocktail

Avocado balls can also be arranged in the saucer type of champagne glass, and mixed with finely chopped apple, red pepper, and celery. At the last minute add a French dressing if you like, or you can top it off with the purée of avocado (left after making the parisian balls) and a twirl of whipped double cream to which you have added some horseradish cream.

Stuffed Avocado and Bacon

per person

½ **avocado pear**

1 **oz (25 g) cheese and herb pâté (page 173)**

1 **slice middle bacon, smoked**

Remove the skin from the avocado. Pipe the cheese and herb pâté into the middle of each half avocado, and then generously wrap it all up with the bacon. Make sure the cheese and herb pâté filling is completely covered, then place the avocadoes, filling down, on a baking tray. Simply cook through in a pre-heated oven at 350°F (180°C), Gas 4, for about 10 minutes. Finish off under the grill.

Avocado Pear Stuffed with Tuna, Smoked Salmon and Water Chestnuts

per person

1 avocado pear

1 oz (25 g) smoked salmon

2 oz (50 g) tuna (canned, in oil)

3 water chestnuts (canned)

2 oz (50 g) lemon mayonnaise (page 177)

I was 'landed' with unexpected visitors one day in the winter and the only thing I had in fresh were some avocadoes and a few offcuts of smoked salmon. The rest came from tins or cans (see pages 157–62) for hints on store-cupboard cookery). It makes a substantial and interesting starter, the crispy waterchestnuts providing such a lovely change of texture.

Roughly chop the smoked salmon, flake the tuna, and finely chop the waterchestnuts. Mix them all together, and place this mixture into the hollowed-out centres of each avocado half. Top with a generous helping of really lemony lemon mayonnaise.

Tomatoes Stuffed with Avocado

serves 8 as a starter, 4 as a supper dish

8 large ripe tomatoes

2 ripe avocadoes

juice and rind of 1 lemon

1 tablespoon onion juice

1 clove garlic, crushed with salt

4 tablespoons red peppers, finely diced

1 tablespoon parsley, finely chopped

Make a criss-cross incision in the skin of the tomatoes with a sharp knife, and then pop them into boiling water to loosen the skin. Leave them until the skin begins to peel away from the edges of the criss-cross, and then dip immediately into ice-cold water to arrest the cooking. I can't be precise about the length of time, as the firmer the tomato the longer it will need to shed its skin, but usually you need only count slowly up to 5 before taking the tomato out of the water to test if the skin will come away fairly easily. When this stage has been reached, remove all the skin and take a thin slice off the top of the tomato (by the top I mean the opposite side to the stalk). Using a parisian scoop remove all the inside from the tomato (tricky if you've over-cooked it). Put the tomatoes into the fridge, covered with foil, to stiffen up.

Cut round the avocado from top to bottom and break in two. Remove the stone, and take out the lovely light green flesh with a silver spoon and put into a china or plastic bowl. Using a wooden spoon, mash to a pulp, and incorporate the other ingredients. When ready to serve, spoon into the tomato cases. Serve, preferably with a large dollop of home-made mayonnaise (page 177).

I often do this and then surround the stuffed tomato with flakes of tinned tuna fish and make the dish do for supper – especially if accompanied by quartered softly boiled eggs with runny egg yolks.

per whole banana

1 tablespoon lemon juice

1 oz (25 g) butter

1 oz (25 g) onion, finely chopped

2 oz (50 g) fine breadcrumbs

teaspoon curry powder (page 55)

Emmenthal cheese

Tomato provençale (page 175)

Curried Banana with Emmenthal Cheese and Tomato

One weekend, some visitors went on about how odd my recipe for banana baked with bacon in puff pastry sounded (in *Entertaining with Tovey*), and suggested I'd gone a bit too far in my attempt to titillate people's palates. I hadn't any puff pastry in the house (it's *so* involved to make at a moment's notice), but made this similar, but different, dish for supper and it dispelled their doubts. (I've since heard they cooked, and liked the puff pastry version!)

As a starter, use a half banana per person. For a more substantial spread use a whole one per person.

Skin the bananas and leave to one side sprinkled with lemon juice. Melt the butter in a saucepan, add the finely chopped onion, and sauté until golden. Make the buttery onion to a paste with the fine breadcrumbs to which you have added the curry flavouring of your choice (see pages 55 to 59 for quite a few hints). Liberally coat the bananas with these crumbs and put on a baking tray. Cook at 350°F (180°C), Gas 4, for 10 minutes. Remove from the oven and sprinkle with finely grated Emmenthal cheese, and finish off under the grill. Serve with some tomato provençale (page 175), and lots of chopped parsley.

TROUT

Farm trout are easily available nowadays throughout most of the year in most parts of the country and they are, more often than not, an excellent buy. They vividly remind me of my first introduction to fresh fish when I was working out in what was then Nyasaland – one of the most beautiful countries in Africa. When I lived there from 1951 to 1958 times were relatively hard, with the country striving to be as self-sufficient in foodstuffs as possible. The role of the local African fishermen was important; freshly-caught *chambo* from Lake Nyasa would be packed on the back of bicycles, firmly wrapped in cool banana and palm tree leaves, tightly tied with sisal rope, and thoroughly watered; the Africans would set off from Fort Johnston as the sun was setting and cycle through the night along the plains, over the ponderous (and I always thought rather treacherous) ferry at Liwonde. The next step was the long haul up the escarpment through the tsetse fly control area, into Zomba, and then along the twisty strip road to Blantyre and Limbe where, early next morning, their wares would be sold. Sometimes I had these fish for breakfast and, being so fresh, they were always quite delicious. As it was virtually the only fresh fish available, we had to invent many different ways of cooking it, and each time I gut a farm trout now, I vividly recall those happy days in Africa.

The two recipes I mention are very similar to those in *Entertaining with Tovey*, but I shan't make any excuses as they are perhaps the easiest and most popular fish dishes in my repertoire, and the mere substitution of orange for lemon and grapefruit amply demonstrates how a tiny adaptation can create something deliciously different.

Baked Farm Trout with Orange Butter

per person as a starter

½ trout, filleted

1 oz (25 g) butter, melted

juice and rind of ½ orange

sprigs of parsley to garnish

Cut off the head and tail of each trout and run a sharp knife from tail to head through the middle, using the main bone as your guide. Discard this bone along with the guts, and rinse lightly under a slow-running cold tap and then pat dry on kitchen paper. Have to hand a well-buttered metal tray, large enough to take as many fish as you are serving. Half a fish, one fillet, is a generous portion for a fish course or starter.

Place the fillets of trout on your greased baking tray, and pour the butter over them. Grate the rind from the orange and squeeze out the juice. Pour the juice over the fillets, and then sprinkle with rind. Bake in a pre-heated oven at 350°F (180°C), Gas 4, for 20 minutes.

Garnish for serving with a twirl of orange butter.

Flavoured Butters

Whenever you have your mixer out and some butter over, make some flavoured butters. They add enormously to the taste and look of many dishes, particularly baked potatoes, and baked, grilled or barbecued meat and fish. You will soon become adept at recognizing which flavours complement what. Keep tasting to see how tasty or nasty the butter is becoming!

But it is economical to make the butter or butters in larger mixings, and then you can store in the fridge or freezer. I make orange butter with 1 lb (450 g) soft butter, and the juice and rind of 2 oranges. Beat together, turn out onto a strip of greaseproof paper, and roll up like a fat sausage. Label and put away in the fridge or freezer. It doesn't take long to defrost enough to enable you to hack off individual circles for your requirements.

Even the dullest dish can be transformed by a pat of flavoured butter, so experiment with tomato purée, apple purée, spinach purée, walnut oil with chopped walnuts, all kinds of fresh herbs, garlic in large or small quantities, lemons or limes, anchovy essence, left-over sardines, baked bean purée, peanut butter and chopped peanuts.

Baked Trout with Hazelnuts and Orange

per person as a starter

½ trout, filleted

1 oz (25 g) butter, melted

1 oz (25 g) ground hazelnuts

2 orange segments

A more 'up-market' dish, and so, so easy. Prepare the trout in the same way as above. Dip in melted butter, then coat liberally with ground hazelnuts and bake (again as above). Just prior to serving, having removed the fillets from the oven, garnish with segments or slices of fresh orange and flash under a hot grill.

Serve half a filleted trout as a generous starter. A whole fish, filleted, is an equally generous main course.

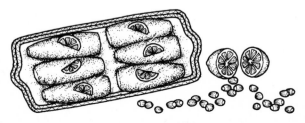

Main Courses

Grilled Spring Chicken

Eileen Spicer, my boss's wife, used to keep thousands of free-range chickens at their estate – Chipande, between Limbe and Zomba. Each day she would send the driver into Limbe and Blantyre loaded up with fresh eggs and freshly-killed chickens. Anybody who was anybody out in Nyasaland those days always, but always, ate Chipande fowl and produce.

I almost always got tiny chickens sent in on Saturdays as my prize for the week, and I used to like them simply grilled. Often nowadays, when entertaining at home, if I can get young baby chickens weighing about $1\frac{1}{4}$–$1\frac{1}{2}$ lbs (550–700 g) this is what I do with them.

Chop the chickens in half and sprinkle liberally with fresh lemon juice and, if you have it, some fresh tarragon (tarragon goes well with *any* chicken dish). Coat each half with 1 oz (25 g) melted butter. Light the grill and get it really hot. Place a double thickness of foil on the base of the grill tray, place the chicken halves in it, ribside up at first, and pop under the hot grill for about 10 minutes. Turn over, skin side up, and do for a further 10 minutes.

One half chicken of this size will easily satisfy any appetite, and they are enhanced by Curried Banana with Emmenthal Cheese and Tomato (page 49), or a heated half tinned peach with a pinch of curry powder.

serves 6–8

2 oz (50 g) butter or mutton fat

6 oz (175 g) onions, finely chopped

2 cloves garlic, crushed with 1 teaspoon salt

2 tablespoons tomato purée

2 tablespoons curry powder (page 55)

2–2½ lb (900 g–1·1 kg) shoulder of raw lamb, coarsely minced

4 oz (100–125 g) dried apricots, soaked overnight in 4 tablespoons cooking brandy

4 oz (100–125 g) nibbed almonds, baked brown

1 pint (600 ml) white sauce (page 174), thickened with 4 oz (100–125 g) ground almonds
or **see method**

Bobotie

This is a dish I first ate when I went out to Africa in 1949, and it often featured on the luncheon menu of South African Railways on the 3-day train journey from Cape Town to Rhodesia. The recipe was given to me by an old Cape Malay cook in Cape Town and it is an unusual and interesting way to use shoulders of lamb. I must admit though, that the addition of a rich egg custard at the end rather than the usual white sauce does rather transfer it to the up-market section of cooking (see the end of the recipe)!

Heat the butter or mutton fat and fry off the finely chopped onions with the crushed garlic. Add the tomato purée, the curry powder and the minced mutton, and cook, stirring from time to time, over a medium heat for about 40 minutes. Pre-heat the oven to 375°F (190°C), Gas 5. Mince the brandy-soaked apricots and fold them, along with the baked brown nibbed almonds, into the meat. Transfer to individual dishes or 1 large casserole. Top with the ground almond white sauce and re-heat in the pre-heated oven for 30 to 40 minutes.

Instead of the almondy white sauce, you could lash out on a rich egg custard made of 1 pint (600 ml) double cream with 4 eggs and 2 egg yolks. Season generously with freshly ground nutmeg and the merest touch of additional curry powder. When baking, allow this custard to cook until it sets naturally. It's *very* delicious and extra-special!

South African Sosaties

serves 6

3 lb (1·4 kg) shoulder of lamb, boned

2 large onions (see method)

36 dried apricots

for the marinade

juice and rind of 2 lemons

2 tablespoons ground coriander

$\frac{1}{4}$ pint (150 ml) red wine vinegar

$\frac{1}{2}$ pint (300 ml) red wine

1 tablespoon chilli

1 tablespoon turmeric

$\frac{1}{2}$ tablespoon freshly ground black pepper

2 tablespoons ground ginger

2 cloves juicy garlic

1 teaspoon mustard seeds

$\frac{1}{2}$ teaspoon ground cardamom

2 tablespoons brown sugar

2 teaspoons salt

$\frac{1}{4}$ teaspoon cayenne pepper

A 3 lb (1·4 kg) shoulder, boned, should give you approximately 2 lb 7 oz (just over 1 kg) of meat, once the fat has been trimmed off. Cut the meat into 1 inch (5 cm) cubes – you want 6 for each kebab stick. Divide the onions into 4, and separate the layers, roughly allowing 6 thick wedges for each kebab stick. Put the meat cubes, onion wedges and dried apricots into a large bowl.

Put all the marinade ingredients into a liquidizer and blend well. Pour over the meat, onions and apricots, and leave for at least 3 days, turning occasionally.

When needed, thread the cubes of meat/onion/apricots on to the kebab sticks, and cook over a barbecue or under a very hot grill, turning every so often, until cooked to your liking. Serve with baked potatoes and apricot chutney (page 60).

Minced Pork with Coconut

serves 8 generously

4 tablespoons tinned coconut cream, let down with 8 tablespoons water

2 lbs (900 g) shoulder of pork, boned and minced

¼ teaspoon salt

6 cloves garlic, finely chopped

2 tablespoons ground coriander

1 teaspoon ground nutmeg

10 peppercorns, finely ground

1 medium onion, finely chopped

lots of lovely fresh mint, chopped

I encountered the idea for this dish when cruising around Indonesia a few years ago. The food on board the Holland America ship, the 'Prinsendam', was absolutely superb and, in spite of vowing only to have fresh orange juice and black coffee for breakfast in my cabin, missing out on lunch and only having dinner in the evening, I'm afraid that each day spent on the various shore excursions found me invariably at a local native café – where a Balinese cook served me his version of this dish.

The tins of coconut milk are much more readily available now over here, particularly from Indian food shops, as are packets of creamed coconut which can be let down similarly.

In a thick bottomed saucepan (I often use my pressure cooker base), bring the reduced coconut milk to the boil. Combine all the other ingredients (except the mint), and add to the milk. Slowly simmer until the milk is more or less absorbed, which takes about 45 minutes. Stir from time to time to make sure nothing is sticking on the base of the pan. Should you prefer a much drier finished dish, cook for longer, but keep on stirring from time to time.

Pork can so often be fatty and rich, but this dish is dry and crunchy, and the fresh mint garnish, scattered over each portion, makes all the difference. If you're feeling extravagant, another nice garnish is sultanas soaked overnight in a little brandy. To enhance the dish still further, you can, prior to serving, sprinkle each portion with a tablespoon of toasted desiccated coconut, and garnish with a wedge of fresh lime or lemon.

Indonesian Pork

serves 4

2 lb (900 g) shoulder of pork, boned

12 whole cardamom seeds

12 whole cloves juicy garlic

12 black peppercorns

8 inch (20 cm) stick cinnamon

4 tablespoons plain flour, sieved

¼ pint (150 ml) soya or sesame oil

for the marinade

10 tablespoons peanut butter

1 pint (600 ml) coconut milk

2 tablespoons brown sugar

4 tablespoons soya sauce

Cut the pork into 1 inch (2·5 cm) cubes. Mix all the marinade ingredients together in a liquidizer, and pour over the pork cubes. Leave for about 48 hours, turning occasionally.

In a pestle and mortar, crush together the cardamom, garlic (seems a lot, I know), peppercorns, cinnamon and flour.

Remove the pork cubes from the marinade, dry on kitchen paper, and coat them with the curry/flour mixture. Fry them quickly in the hot oil to seal them, browning quickly on all sides, a few cubes at a time. Remove with a slotted spoon and drain on kitchen paper.

Put everything – the meat *and* the marinade – into a heat-proof casserole dish and bring to the boil on the top of the stove. Then put the casserole into a pre-heated oven at 275°F (140°C), Gas 1, for approximately 1¾ hours (but take a look at it after 1 hour to see that it hasn't dried out, and also check for tenderness at this stage). The end product does look slightly 'split' and I usually serve it with toasted desiccated coconut.

CURRIES

Curries were very much part of my life when I lived out in Africa, and I used then to think that the hotter and spicier the curry, the safer the cooked meat was! The butchers were Africans employed to slaughter twice weekly in the village markets, and first to come were served great hunks of meat – no such thing as posh joints, or civilised refrigeration.

It was only when I came to cook curries myself that I realized the fantastic medicinal properties many of the spices possessed. Cardamom warms the stomach and can be used to ease flatulence – in fact all over the East cardamom seeds are eaten after a meal (or mixed with the coffee) to aid digestion. Cinnamon is, believe it or not, an extremely powerful germicide. A warm cordial drink based on coriander used to be mixed to warm the stomach and ease pains caused by an upset stomach. Cloves refresh the weary and are also a highly antiseptic spice. Chilli is said to strengthen the heart, and turmeric is used often in the East and Africa for skin diseases and healing bad bruises or leech bites. A poultice of fenugreek is excellent for open wounds, and of course we all know how good garlic is for our health!

Curries are such stimulating dishes and if you go to the trouble of mixing your own curry spices, so much *more* stimulating will your curries be! I list below most of the things you need to have in the store cupboard to start mixing your own personal spices, but don't throw your hands up to heaven. You really don't have to have them *all* in, and I'm sure that if you look round your shelves this very minute you will find several items to hand already.

almonds	allspice	aniseed	cardamom
chilli	cinnamon	coconut	cloves
coriander	cummin	fennel	fenugreek
garlic	ginger	mace	mustard seed
nutmeg	pepper	poppy seed	turmeric

Your curry could be a mixture of anything from 8 to 20 different spices with the 'heat' coming from the amount of ground chillis used (perhaps the only thing you have to be really careful with). Experiment using any or all of the above – adding, subtracting, multiplying – grinding them gradually to a powdery paste in a pestle and mortar. You will soon find out what you do and don't like and what you want more or less of. Use your finished sieved powder by frying off with the onions in a recipe to make a buttery curry/onion paste, or by adding as instructed. It can also, of course, be added to casseroles, soups or mayonnaise to give them an unmistakeable curry flavour.

You could also put your selection of spices in a liquidizer, bringing them together with sufficient cooking wine to get a smooth paste which you then pass through a sieve. This can be added spoonful by spoonful to whatever you are 'currying' until by tasting, tasting, tasting, you get your desired result. By doing this, of course, you never ever get the same curry twice – which makes life much more interesting!

Buy your various curry spices as often as you can and in as small a quantity as you can, so that you always use them while fairly fresh. Small empty cream cartons can be used for storing your various assorted spices, provided you label them clearly and, after each use, re-seal them with a double layer of saranwrap or clingfilm.

And what do you drink with a curry? I personally always like to have a generous measure of gin in a large glass, topped with very, very cold milk. This combination seems to bring out the taste of the juniper, and is quite delicious with a curry. Otherwise serve beer, or a cheap and cheerful rosé wine.

But for me a curry is useless unless accompanied by dozens of little dishes of delicious delicacies. Onions finely chopped, some served raw and some fried. Finely diced red and green peppers. Toasted desiccated coconut. Any sliced fresh fruit such as banana, apple, pineapple, grapes, mango or passion fruit. Celery cut into thin strips marinated in soya sauce. Pickles. Chutneys. Tomatoes, skinned, seeded and chopped. Cucumbers, skinned and seeded and then diced very small, and combined with natural yoghurt and freshly chopped mint. Apple wedges left to marinate in fresh lime juice. Sultanas soaked overnight in cheap cooking brandy. Hard-boiled eggs chopped up together or with the yolks and white separated and passed through a fine sieve. Chopped fresh herbs to sprinkle on your bubbling casseroles of curries.

The art of giving a really successful curry party is to allow your guests to take a *small* portion of cooked rice or pulses, generous spoonfuls of the various curried meats, and then pile their plate of food high with teaspoons of this and that and t'other side dishes. Salted or plain cashew nuts or peanuts can be sprinkled on top of curries, and I am sure if you put your thinking-cap on you will come up with many more ideas. Serve the curries hot from the top of your cooker and also use the oven itself, and then the main dining table should be a mass of little dishes all ready for your guests to attack.

However, when re-heating curries, it is of the utmost importance to do this very gently indeed – better still to do so in the top of a double saucepan, although this can be time-consuming. Always, but always, re-heat your curries over the lowest light possible, and make sure that you do not allow them to burn. A pre-heated Hostess Trolley is an ideal way of keeping and then serving curries.

You can experiment with the combinations and quantities of spices, until you find something you like as much, or like more. The following recipes all make *very mild* curries, and if you prefer them to have more bite, simply increase the amount of spices, but *in the same proportion*.

When cooking curries you can, at times, use bay leaves for an added flavour. But for those of us lucky enough to travel far enough south to see citrus fruit growing, we can come back with a handful of orange or lemon leaves secured in dampened plastic bags. Adding these to a curry whilst cooking gives a wonderfully harmonious flavour.

Mild Beef Curry

serves 4 small portions

1 lb (450 g) stewing steak, cut into cubes

½ pint (300 ml) each natural yoghurt and red wine

2 tablespoons flour

5 tablespoons walnut oil (or other good oil)

1 medium onion, about 6 oz (175 g), chopped

1 teaspoon finely grated fresh root ginger

2 level teaspoons coriander seeds

1 teaspoon cummin seeds

2 teaspoons turmeric

4 cardamom seeds (out of the pod)

½ teaspoon paprika

3 cloves garlic

1 teaspoon wine vinegar

This is a very interesting mild curry which can be served immediately, re-heated the next day, or frozen when it's cold.

Marinate the pieces of stewing steak in the mixed yoghurt and red wine for 24 hours.

Remove the cubes from the marinade (which you keep), and dry well on kitchen paper. Coat them with the flour. Heat the oil and fry off a few cubes of the steak at a time, transferring them to a piece of clean kitchen paper. When all the meat cubes are fried off, fry the chopped onions until golden in the same oil. Place the cooked onion in a medium heatproof casserole, and cover them with the cooked meat.

Meanwhile mix all the ingredients from the root ginger to the wine vinegar vigorously in a liquidizer with the yoghurt and red wine marinade. Add this to the casserole.

Simmer slowly on top of the stove, covered (keep on looking in from time to time and stir occasionally with a wooden spoon to ensure nothing is sticking to the base), for 2 to 2½ hours.

Mild Curried Chicken

serves 6

1 chicken, at least 4 lb (1·8 kg)

3 teaspoons each fennel seeds, cummin seeds, coriander seeds

5 cardamom seeds (out of the pod)

2 cloves garlic

2 tablespoons flour

2½ fl. oz (65 ml) good oil

1 oz (25 g) ghee (or butter if you're not too particular)

2 medium onions, about 12 oz (350 g), chopped

8 oz (225 g) tomatoes, skinned and seeded

¾ pint (400 ml) double cream

sea salt, freshly ground black pepper

This is without doubt my favourite curry dish as it is on the sweetish side and is *so* tender. You can get ghee in Indian food shops, but clarified butter is a good substitute.

A fresh 4 lb (1·8 kg) chicken will yield approximately 1 lb 10 oz (725 g) of flesh off the bone, and you will need at least this amount for 6 people (although remember that all the accompanying garnishes and side dishes will help fill you and your guests up). Cube the chicken flesh, and save the bones of the carcase and the wings for the stock pot.

With a mortar and pestle pound away together all the seeds and the garlic, and then add the flour, making a light paste. Coat the chicken cubes with this, and then fry them off, a few at a time, in the hot oil. Remove the pieces from the frying pan when sealed, and put to one side on clean kitchen paper. Add the ghee or butter to the oil in the pan and fry off the onions until golden brown. Transfer to an ovenproof casserole dish. Place the cooked chicken cubes on top, and add the tomatoes, the cream, a little salt and generous pepper. Put in a pre-heated oven, set at 275°F (140°C), Gas 1, and bake for 1 hour.

Mild Curried Mutton

serves 6

3 lb (1·4 kg) shoulder of old lamb, boned

5 level teaspoons turmeric

4 cardamom seeds (out of the pod)

2 inch (5 cm) stick cinnamon

2 juicy cloves garlic

4 whole cloves

4 peppercorns

1 teaspoon cummin

1 teaspoon coriander

2½ fl. oz (65 ml) olive oil

2 medium onions, about 12 oz (350 g), chopped

4 large tomatoes, about 10–12 oz (275–350 g), chopped and seeded

¾ pint (400 ml) coconut milk

1 teaspoon salt

A shoulder of this size will give you approximately 2 lb (900 g) of fairly fat-free meat which should be sufficient for your 6 portions. Cut the meat into reasonably sized pieces.

In a liquidizer grind together the turmeric, cardamom, cinnamon, garlic, cloves, peppercorns, cummin and coriander. Coat the meat pieces with this, and heat the oil. Fry the meat off – about 6 pieces at a time – in the hot oil, removing with a slotted spoon to kitchen paper when sealed. Fry off the onions until golden and transfer to a large ovenproof casserole. Add the sealed meat, tomatoes, coconut milk, and salt, and cook at 275°F (140°C), Gas 1, for 2¾ to 3 hours. If it isn't as tender as you would like after this time, just cook for a little longer.

Cape Malay Pickled Fish

serves 6

1 lb (450 g) cod fillet

about 6 tablespoons oil, for frying

2 medium onions

¾ pint (400 ml) wine vinegar (*not* malt)

2 bay leaves

½ teaspoon allspice

½ oz (15 g) curry powder of choice

pinch turmeric and cayenne

½ oz (15 g) soft brown sugar

1 dessertspoon honey

This is a dish which is the better for keeping (in fact *has* to be kept for at least 5 days) and is just as popular in my house on a warm summer's day as when the ground outside is thickly covered with snow. I must admit, though, that I have found it is a dish that people have divided opinions on – they love it or they loathe it, and the ratio is 99·5 loving to 0·5 loathing!

Skin the fish, remove all the bones, and flake into pieces of about 1½ inches (3·5 cm) square. Heat through 4 tablespoons of the oil in a frying pan and lightly fry off the fish pieces in this, using a slotted spoon to remove the cooked bits to a tray lined with kitchen paper. Wipe out the pan and then put the other 2 tablespoons of oil in to warm through, and in this sauté off the onions.

Put all the other ingredients in a separate saucepan, and bring to the boil. Simmer for 5 minutes and gently spoon off any scum that comes up to the top.

Arrange the pieces of cooked fish in a shallow pyrex dish (or something similar) and cover it with the cooked onions. Pour into this the hot, unstrained vinegar mixture and leave for at least 5 days in either a fridge or cold-room.

A sprinkling of toasted desiccated coconut is a good side dish, and a robust rosé wine would accompany it perfectly. If you are feeling generous garnish with 2 tablespoons of sultanas soaked overnight in a similar amount of cooking brandy.

Lentil and Split Pea Curry

serves 8–12

½ lb (225 g) split lentils

½ lb (225 g) split peas

4 pints (2·2 litres) water for overnight soaking and cooking

2 knobs root ginger, walnut sized, speared through with 1 or 2 wooden cocktail sticks

5 level teaspoons turmeric

3 level tablespoons curry powder of your own choice

2 inch (5 cm) stick cinnamon

pinch of cummin

4 cloves garlic

1 teaspoon salt

4 tablespoons oil

1 medium onion, about 6 oz (175 g), thinly sliced

4 tomatoes, peeled, seeded and chopped

¾ pint (400 ml) natural yoghurt

A rather mushy dish to accompany any curry, something like the *dhal* without which no Indian meal is complete.

Place the lentils and peas in separate bowls and cover each with 1 pint (550 ml) cold water and leave overnight. Then strain and put into separate saucepans, each holding a further pint of water. Put one knob of ginger into each saucepan. Cook the lentils for approximately 30 minutes, and the split peas for approximately 45 minutes, over a slow simmering heat. Drain, and mix them together, removing the ginger.

With a pestle and mortar pound to a paste the turmeric, curry powder, cinnamon, cummin, garlic and salt. Heat the oil and fry off the paste in it, and then add the onions and cook until golden. Mix the curried onions gently into the lentils and peas. If serving at a later time, *stop here.*

Just prior to serving, re-heat the curried onion, lentil and pea mixture slowly, having added the chopped tomatoes and yoghurt. Do *not* bring to the boil, but re-heat *very* gently and serve as soon as possible.

Pickled Cauliflower

1 cauliflower, about 1½ lb (700 g) without its leaves

water to cover

4 tablespoons salt

2 cloves garlic

4 level teaspoons fenugreek

5 level teaspoons turmeric

5 level tablespoons curry powder

3 level tablespoons mustard seeds

about ¾ pint (450 ml) olive oil

Break up the fresh cauliflower into nice pretty flower-size pieces, cover with the water and salt, and leave overnight. Drain and then place on a cooling tray inside a roasting tin, and leave for at least 2 hours. Thereafter, put the fairly dry florets into sterilised jars (you'll need about 2 1 pint or 600 ml jars), packed about three-quarters of the way up.

Put the garlic, fenugreek, turmeric, curry powder, mustard seeds and olive oil into a liquidizer and blend. Put this cloudy mixture into a saucepan, bring to the boil and simmer for 5 minutes. Cool it slightly, then pour over the cauliflower in the jars. Cover with a double layer of greaseproof paper and seal when cold.

1 lb (450 g) dried apricots

1 pint (500–600 ml) cold water

6 cloves garlic

5 level teaspoons ground ginger

1 pint (500–600 ml) malt vinegar

1 lb (450 g) soft brown sugar

Cape Apricot Chutney

This recipe yields just over 3 lb (1·4 kg) of a chutney which is sweet, yet sharp, and much, much less expensive than the traditional mango chutney.

Soak the apricots overnight in the water and then cook slowly for about 20 minutes in a saucepan until the apricots are slightly mushy. Put the garlic, ground ginger and vinegar into a liquidizer, and whirl until well blended, then add to the cooked apricots along with the sugar.

Simmer slowly until the mixture thickens to *your* desired consistency. I usually do this for about 1½ hours. Put into sterilised jars.

If you can find them, you can use dried peaches instead of apricots.

Vegetables and Salads

Fried Mixed Vegetables

At first this may sound rather down-market and not quite you, but as you read on I think you will agree it is delicious, and good for you quickly cooked *al dente* for supper – or for that matter when entertaining. I did this once to accompany pan-fried sirloin steaks and the triple purée potted vegetables (see pages 164 and 165), and it was highly talked about.

The knack is to use as many different fresh seasonal vegetables as possible. You will require about 2 lb (900 g) altogether to give 8 good portions – onions, fennel, celery, turnip, swede, leeks, cauliflower, French beans, peas or broad beans (whatever you like). You must cut them all up into similar chunks or lengths, the smaller the better. Small florets of cauliflower; topped and tailed broad and French beans cut into 1 inch (2·5 cm) lengths; peas out of the pods (of course); and the root vegetables can be scooped into balls with a parisian scoop (with left-overs made into a cream of vegetable soup).

I must admit I have a small wok at home which I use for stir-frying, but *you* don't have to invest in one: a non-stick frying pan is good enough, or lacking that, a stainless steel dish. Use about 2 tablespoons of good olive oil and when this is beginning to smoke lightly add 1 oz (25 g) butter. When that's melted, throw in the vegetables, add salt, and simply stir-fry for 5 minutes at the very most, and serve as soon as possible.

Chopped mixed fresh herbs may be added at the end, or a generous sprinkling of celery salt, a pinch of nutmeg or curry powder, and serve a bowl of mayonnaise to be spooned over each portion if your guests like.

Aubergines with Cheese

serves 6

4 medium aubergines, about 1½ lb (700 g)

2 teaspoons salt

8 tablespoons olive oil

4 oz (100 g) butter

1 medium onion, about 6 oz (175 g), finely chopped

2 tablespoons concentrated tomato paste

6 tomatoes, about 14 oz (400 g), skinned, seeded and chopped

2 cloves fresh garlic, crushed

2 tablespoons parsley, finely chopped

generous pinch each of allspice, cinnamon and castor sugar

6 tablespoons white breadcrumbs

4 oz (125 g) Cheddar cheese, finely grated

I didn't mention aubergines in *Entertaining with Tovey*, as they're not on my personal list of likes, but this is a good vegetable accompaniment or supper dish.

Peel and dice the aubergines and lay them on a cooling tray on your sink draining board, and sprinkle with the salt. Leave for at least *1 whole hour*. Rinse the aubergine cubes under cold running water and dry thoroughly. Heat 4 tablespoons of the olive oil and 2 oz (50 g) of the butter in a frying pan, and sauté the onion until golden. Remove from pan and wipe the pan clean. Add the diced, dried aubergines and the remaining olive oil and butter, and sauté off until golden (you may well need a little more olive oil, as the aubergines seem to soak fat up). Add the tomato paste, the coarsely chopped tomatoes, and all the other ingredients (*except* the breadcrumbs and cheese), and combine. It will look like a stew.

Have to hand 6 buttered and seasoned 3 inch (7·5 cm) ramekins and divide the mixture between them. Top each one with a tablespoon of breadcrumbs. When you wish to serve the dish either as a starter, or as a vegetable, they take 10 minutes to cook through at 350°F (180°C), Gas 4. Top each with some of the cheese and brown quickly under the grill. These are also very nice served cold.

Avocado, Orange and Walnut Salad

serves 4

1 avocado

1 medium orange

4 lettuce leaves

French dressing, made with walnut oil

2 oz (50 g) walnuts, finely chopped

2 tablespoons chopped parsley

As with the recipe for Avocado with Fresh Pear (page 46), 1 avocado and 1 medium orange will serve 4 people as a starter, but be more generous if serving as a salad. Divide the avocado from stalk to stem into halves. Insert a large silver tablespoon close to the skin and scoop out the flesh halves in one fell swoop. Provided the avocado is ripe this is a simple task. Then with a small stainless steel knife cut each half into orange segment shapes. Segment the orange.

To serve, simply arrange the avocado and orange segments alternately in a half-circle shape effect on a wiped lettuce leaf, and pour on a small amount of French dressing. Scatter the finely chopped walnuts and fresh parsley on top.

This salad makes a good starter or is a good accompaniment to the baked trout dishes on page 50, if you want something different to the garnishes given.

Desserts, Cakes and Biscuits

serves 6

2 Granny Smith apples, peeled, cored and cut into 3 slices with holes in the middle

3 bananas, peeled and cut in half

6 slices fresh pineapple, just over ¼ inch (6 mm) thick

½ pint (300 ml) good oil, for deep frying

for the batter

4 oz (100 g) plain flour, sieved

pinch of salt

2 eggs, separated

8 tablespoons milk

1 tablespoon castor sugar

1 level teaspoon cinnamon

Apple, Banana and Pineapple Fritters

I don't really care if this sounds childish, because I know my tired and jaded palate wakes up at the thought of cooking and eating these – particularly if accompanied by a spoonful of lemon curd (page 180) or just plain straightforward apricot jam.

Put the flour, salt, egg *yolks*, sugar, cinnamon and milk into a liquidizer or Magimix, and whizz round until smoothly mixed. Transfer to a bowl. Stiffly beat the egg whites, and fold into the flour mixture.

Heat the cooking oil in a frying pan to smoking. Coat the pieces of fruit with the batter and deep-fry, separately, for about 2 to 3 minutes. Remove to a cooling tray and leave in a warm draught-free place until all are cooked. Sprinkle generously with further castor sugar and serve with single or whipped cream, lemon curd or apricot jam.

Lale's Brandy Fruit Pot

At Christmas, a Zimbabwe friend of mine always used to capture the true spirit of English Christmas pudding by serving, after a cold starter and hot turkey main course, this 'fruit pot' accompanied by a bowl of icecream. The texture was reminiscent of Christmas pud, but the flavour was much richer and stronger in booze, and the accompanying cream ice went down well on the hot Christmas days.

The first thing you need is a large, tightly-lidded earthenware pot (easily available at any pot shop, and some nowadays have very attractive designs). The fruit pot needs to be started at least 8 weeks in advance, but can actually be begun in mid-summer, when there are so many lovely fruits in abundance. You can use whatever fruit you have to hand – apples, pears, peaches, melons, raspberries, cherries or pineapple – and the whole idea is that the fruit pot develops *gradually* over the weeks leading up to Christmas, so don't panic at the thought of having to acquire all those fruits at the same time!

Put a layer or two of walnut-sized fruit in the bottom of your pot, scatter with demerara sugar, and cover, not *too* generously, with a marinade of half cooking brandy, half cooking sherry. The fruits absorb the booze, turn a brownish colour, and their flavours begin to intermingle. Each time you add further layers of fruit, repeat the sugar and alcohol additions, and always cover with a double layer of cut-out greaseproof paper, and the top of the pot with a double thickness of cling film prior to putting on the lid.

After 6 to 8 weeks the mixture rather resembles a chunky Christmas mincemeat. It is *so* good, and you only need a dessertspoon for each guest when you come to serve it with either home-made icecream (page 166) or lemon ice-box pudding.

TEAS

Tea-time was very important when, for a short time in 1961 I managed an inn – The Mountain Lodge – in the Vumba district of what was then Rhodesia. Queues used to form for afternoon tea from around 3 on Sundays and, being short of china and equipment, we had to perform conjuring tricks, timing exactly the taking of a finished tea tray, filling it up again with goodies, and presenting it to the next customer. With so many to serve in a short space of time, we had to cook our scones, cakes and loaves on the Wednesdays and Thursdays before, and therefore we learned the value of recipes with a good storage life.

Not so with a couple of elderly ladies who lived nearby. We were asked once to tea, and they welcomed us at 3.30 and rang the hand-bell. The tea trolley was brought in, but the cake was stale, the biscuits limp and soggy, and the scones were virtually mouldy. However *tea*, as it transpired, wasn't really the object of their sociability, as before we had time to even attempt to take any tea, they decided it was 'sundowner' time, and the drinks trolley was wheeled in. Glasses two-thirds full of brandy, with a splash of soda, were *much* more up their street!

I find most varieties of tea disappointing these days, and although I never seem to have less than 20 different kinds in my store-cupboard, very few of them would I serve straight from the packet. I don't know whether it's because the tea blenders are less skilful, or are using lower-grade teas, but gone for me are those fragrant real orange and lemon teas – Earl Grey, which used to have such a distinctive aroma and bouquet, is nothing like it used to be, nor the wonderful orange pekoe.

So I have resorted to my own kind of alchemy! I use a large 2 lb (900 g) tin tea caddy into which I put a few tablespoons of this and a few of that and shake it about until I fill two-thirds of the way up the tin. I then put in fairly thick strips of dried orange and lemon rind and disperse these liberally throughout the tea leaves. After a week the tea leaves are imbued with a lovely fresh orange/lemon flavour, and the brewed tea tastes delicious.

I get so depressed when I see people ruining tea in the making of it. Tea drinking is a wonderful entertaining occasion, but many don't bother to make tea properly. Once I saw warm water from the tap put into a glass jug, and then placed inside a microwave oven. When this bubbled, it was taken to the table and the cooling warmed water was poured over tea bags which were dunked away like fish at the end of a line until the right colour was reached. Warmed milk was then added (of the powdered type), and that was English tea!

The *proper* way is actually like a ceremony. Use a china teapot whenever possible, and fill this to the top with hot water just prior to actually brewing the tea. Use cold water for the kettle, and just as it starts to steam, empty the pot, and put in the amount of tea you like (I simply put 1 teaspoon for each person and *not* an extra one for the teapot). Take the teapot *to* the kettle and pour the boiling water over the tea leaves from a dizzy height. Serve (pouring through a tea strainer naturally) after about 4 minutes. By all means serve a second cup from the same pot of tea, but after 15 minutes a new pot must be brewed and the rigmarole gone through as before. The longer tea stands, quite apart from becoming colder, the more bitter it gets.

For afternoon tea, I like to serve thin cucumber sandwiches, bread with lemon curd (page 180) or jam, scones with lemon curd and cream (page 179). and lots of cakes and biscuits. Look also at pages 36–8, 86–7, 144 and 167, for further tea-time recipes and ideas.

Cucumber Sandwiches

Like Lady Bracknell in Wilde's *The Importance of Being Earnest*, I love to have cucumber sandwiches at tea-time, and I have seen them disappear quite as fast as hers seemed to go before the redoubtable butler, Lane, claimed cucumbers were unavailable 'even for ready money'!

Peel the cucumber and slice it very, very thinly indeed. Lay the slices, slightly overlapping, on a large plate, and sprinkle them with white wine vinegar (as you would your fish and chips from the chip shop). Leave to one side for at least an hour.

Cut fairly thin slices of brown bread (pages 35–6) and roll them even thinner with a wooden rolling pin. Spread soft butter liberally over the bread, and then fill with the cucumber slices after draining off their liquid. When the sandwiches are made, remove the crusts with a good serrated knife, and cut the sandwiches into triangles. They should be made at the last moment as they become rather soggy, but the wafer-thin morsels are a joy, particularly with the slight wine vinegar taste.

Rich Almond Cake

4 oz (100–125 g) butter

5 oz (150 g) castor sugar

3 eggs, lightly beaten

4 oz (100–125 g) ground almonds

1 oz (25 g) plain flour, sieved

2 tablespoons nibbed almonds

Cream the butter and sugar together and then gently beat in the eggs a little at a time. Combine the ground almonds and sieved plain flour and fold into the original mixture.

Have ready an 8 inch (20 cm) round sandwich tin, greased and floured, and turn the mixture into this. Sprinkle or arrange the nibbed almonds on the top. Bake in a pre-heated oven at 350°F (180°C), Gas 4, for 45 to 50 minutes.

Rich Afternoon Tea Biscuits

8 oz (225 g) plain flour, sieved

6 oz (175 g) soft butter

4 oz (100–125 g) ground almonds

2 oz (50 g) castor sugar

1 teaspoon vanilla essence

Combine all ingredients in the Kenwood bowl, and slowly mix to a dough. Line some baking trays with good greaseproof paper. Simply roll the dough into a long snake shape, and cut off the size of lump you require (about 1 inch or 2·5 cm in diameter approximately). Place on the lined trays, leaving enough space for spreading.

Bake at 300°F (150°C), Gas 2, in a pre-heated oven for 10 to 15 minutes, looking in from time to time to see that they are all baking evenly.

LEAH'S COTTAGE PIE (page 21).

ORANGE AND SYRUP SPONGE PUDDING (page 30). *Top.* Pour the warmed syrup and orange juice onto the bread or cornflake crumbs. *Centre.* Top the crumbs and sauce with the sponge mixture. *Foot.* Place the foil-covered bowl in the double steamer, put the lid on, and steam.

BASIC GRAVY (page 19). *Top*. With your
basic stock ready, fry off the vegetables,
and add the tomato paste, mustard and
flour. *Foot*. Add the stock, let the sauce
come to the boil, and simmer for 15
minutes.

Delicious Granny Smith apples used for a
starter or salad with grated root
vegetables and a yoghurt dressing (page
26); in Sausage and Apple Bake (page 27);
and for Toffee Apples (page 28).

A Wheatmeal Guinness Cake decorated
with whole almonds and cherries for
Christmas (page 87).

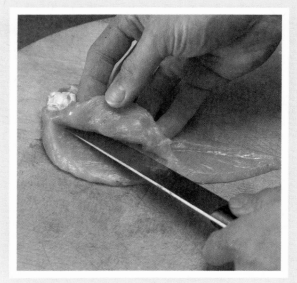

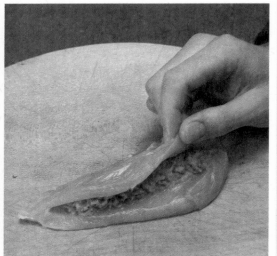

SUPRÊMES OF CHICKEN (pages 97 to 100). *Below*. A cooked stuffed suprême in its marinade. *Top left*. Taking the suprême off the bone. *Top right*. Making an incision in the suprême into which to pipe the stuffing. *Left*. Folding the flesh over the piped stuffing.

Happy Picknicking (pages 39 to 42) with
Casserole of Chicken, Liquorice Allsort
Sandwiches and Apricot Chutney.

AVOCADOES (pages 45 to 48). *Top*.
Healthfood Avocado. *Foot*. Avocado Pear
with Fresh Pear, Avocado and Smoked
Salmon, and Stuffed Avocado and Bacon.

Sesame Biscuits

makes about 50 biscuits

5 oz (150 g) sesame seeds

6 oz (175 g) butter

8 oz (225 g) soft light brown sugar, sieved

1 egg, lightly beaten

1 teaspoon vanilla essence

6 oz (175 g) self-raising flour, sieved

Roast the sesame seeds in a warm oven until nice and golden and allow them to cool. Beat together the butter and sugar and add the lightly beaten egg and vanilla essence. Fold in the self-raising flour, and browned sesame seeds.

Spoon teaspoon blobs onto a piece of greaseproof paper on a baking tray, leaving plenty of room around each blob (as they spread), and bake at 375°F (190°C), Gas 5, for about 10 minutes. Leave them on the paper to cool and harden for about 5 minutes. Store when cold in airtight containers or plastic bags.

Lime and Lemon Marmalade

makes about 10 lb (4·5 kg)

2½ lb (1·1 kg) lemons

1 lb (450 g) limes

6 pints (3·4 litres) water

6 lb (2·7 kg) preserving sugar

Wash the fruit, cut each one in half, then squeeze out the juice and pips. Strain this through a fine nylon sieve into a well-cleaned preserving pan. (To really clean your pan well, after washing and drying it, sprinkle the base and sides with salt and scrub with 2 halves of an additional lemon. Rinse again thoroughly with cold water, and dry well.) Put the pips and pulp into a piece of clean muslin measuring approximately 15 inches (38 cm) square. With a silver dessert or tablespoon remove as much pith as possible from the squeezed-out fruit halves, put into the muslin, and then, with a very sharp knife, cut the skin of the fruit into even fine strips. Add this cut peel to the pan of juice along with the water and then suspend the tied-up muslin bag in this.

Simmer for approximately 2 hours (or until the mixture is reduced by a little over half). Remove the soggy muslin to a sieve which should be held over the reduced liquid. Press down hard and firm on to the muslin with a wooden spoon in order to extract every single possible drop of liquid from the pulp.

Reduce the heat under the pan, and stir in the sugar a pound (450 g) at a time, never adding the next lot until the first is completely absorbed. Bring to the boil and, stirring from time to time, cook until the setting point is reached (about 15 to 20 minutes).

If you are the proud owner of a sugar thermometer this is the most accurate way of testing (but have no fear if you're not). A tip for those of you who *do* have a thermometer is always, at first, to place it in a jug of very hot water. When you think the marmalade is ready, half immerse the thermometer in the bubbling preserve. The magic point is reached when the thermometer registers between 220° and 222°F (104° and 107°C). In between testings, put the thermometer back into the jug of hot water and *never* plonk the base of the thermometer onto the base of the saucepan, and *never* put it directly into cold water after doing a test!

For those of you who don't possess a thermometer, put 3 small saucers in your fridge. Take one out when you think setting point has been reached, and remove the preserve from the heat. With a wooden spoon take out about a dessertspoonful and put this onto the cold saucer. If ready, the marmalade should crinkle when pushed with your finger, and feel tacky, but if it is still runny return the pan to the heat and continue boiling, and test after a while on one of the other cold saucers.

When the preserve is ready, remove from the heat and remove any scum from the top with a small sauce ladle. Have to hand some clean dry warm jam jars and, as the marmalade cools, ladle it out into these jars. Fill nearly to the top and then immediately place on a waxed disc and press it down gently to remove any air. Wipe the neck of the jam jar clean (and the sides if you're clumsy like me) and then, when cold, cover with a cellophane circle secured with a rubber band.

This is my very favourite marmalade, but once you have mastered the method ring the changes by using $3\frac{1}{2}$ lbs (1·6 kg) of any citrus fruit you like. Orange, grapefruit, and lemon in equal parts. Half and half of orange and grapefruit. Add stem ginger throughout the cooking time and remove before bottling. Experiment!

Seville Orange Marmalade

makes about 20 lb (about 9 kg)

6 lb (2·7 kg) fresh Seville oranges

4 lemons

12 pints (6·8 litres) cold water

12 lbs (5·4 kg) preserving sugar

Wipe the oranges and lemons and cut in half. Squeeze as much juice out of each half as you can and keep to one side. Using a silver tablespoon, carefully hack out as much pith and juiceless flesh as you possibly can and put this, with the pips, into the middle of a clean tea towel. Collect the 4 outside corners of the tea towel to the middle and tie up like the bag at the end of Dick Whittington's stick! Put the juice and water into a large mixing bowl, finely slice the skins of the lemons and oranges and put these into the bowl too. Plop the tea towel bag into the middle of this, and leave overnight.

It is essential that you use a perfectly clean saucepan for making the marmalade, and one that will give you plenty of room to put in the preserving sugar. See the previous recipe for instructions on how to get your pan spotlessly clean.

Put the rind, water and juice into the saucepan and tie the tea-towel bag to hang down into it suspended from a wooden spoon balanced across the saucepan. Bring to the boil, and then simmer away until the contents have definitely reduced by half (mark the saucepan on the outside with a marking pen at the beginning of your cooking time). Have your preserving sugar in the kitchen during the cooking time as you want it to be nice and warm when you add it to the thickening mixture. Add pound by pound, or 450 g at a time, stirring well after each addition.

Bring back to the boil and boil for a further 20 minutes, by which time the mixture should be tested for setting. Read the details in the recipe for lime and lemon marmalade, and follow the instructions thereafter when putting your marmalade into jars.

ENTERTAINING OCCASION

Barbecues

One of my very favourite ways of entertaining friends at home during the summer months is with a barbecue. The flavour of charcoal-grilled meat is unmistakeable and unbeatable and, like picnics, food eaten out of doors always tastes so much nicer. Even if cooked *out*doors and eaten *in*doors (the vagaries of our British weather often make the best-laid barbecue plans go awry at the last moment) the enjoyment is almost as great. I have been known to have the charcoal grill burning away in the car port at the front of the house, while the rain poured down outside, and my guests milled around happily in the lounge and dining-room. But the very nicest of occasions have been when the charcoal smouldered away beautifully, the meat crackled away appetizingly, and we all stood at the top of my hilly garden watching the sun set over Windermere.

If you aren't the proud owner of a portable barbecue don't rush out and buy one immediately until you have actually done a barbecue yourself. You might well ask what the devil I'm talking about as how on earth can you have a barbecue without a barbecue? *Improvize.* Get a galvanized iron dustbin lid and support it securely with bricks round the

edges on a flat bit of your garden, and line it with tinfoil. Balance a cooling tray or metal grid across the inside with the coals in the well at the bottom. Or, like the girl guide or boy scout you once were, build up house bricks and then make a bridge from an oven shelf to act as the grill!

Only then, after you've tried all these ways, and if you enjoy it – the smoke, the continual bending down, the charring, the occasional disaster – go and buy a proper barbecue. There are lots to choose from, some better than others, and they're not expensive. And always buy proper barbecue charcoal, and the packets of barbecue 'starters' which help you through that first awful stage when the coals just *will not* light!

There is something enormously satisfying about getting the barbecue itself ready, lighting it, waiting around for the coals to go white (with a drink in hand), and then popping the first of the meats to be cooked onto the grid. The sizzling, sensuous, 'charry' smell is a joy to the nostrils even if occasionally the smoke is an annoyance to the eyes. But you must, *must* leave the coals to develop a white ash before you start cooking. This is the most common mistake people make when barbecuing, but it is only at this stage that the temperature of the coals is high enough to grill the meat properly.

I start my preparations for a barbecue at least 4 days before, as meat grilled in this simple – and indeed primitive – way, needs the tenderizing ministrations of marination. And almost everything else, bar the making of the multitudinous salads and the actual grilling, can be done at least a couple of days in advance: if you want to serve a starter, most of those in the book can be made a day or two before they're eaten; if you want to serve a pudding, that too can be done beforehand (the American Wheatmeal Chocolate Rum Slice (page 141) is particularly delicious, although I usually just like to have bowls of fresh fruit and chunks of cheese. Bread is required to mop up any delicious juices and you *can* serve the savoury rolls on pages 145–6, but they are nicest straight from the oven which might interfere with your outside activities. Serve the spiced cobs or French bread instead, which can either be done in the oven at the last minute, or could be put at the side of the barbecue to warm through while the meats are grilling.

The following recipes are wonderful at barbecues, and I'm afraid that my particular brand of barbecue eating consists of munching my way through steaks, chops, chicken and sausages, with very little else apart from a salad or two, and a piece of fresh fruit to follow. These recipes are suggestions only of what you might prepare at a barbecue party, but many others throughout the book can be adapted to barbecuing too: the sosaties, for instance (page 58), the spiced spare ribs (page 79), the grilled chicken (page 51), the chicken drumsticks (page 81), and above all, the wonderful chicken suprême recipes with all their marinades on pages 97–100. The savoury mushrooms on page 84 are nice served alongside all the various salads, and you could bake potatoes in the oven first, and then just keep them warm in foil parcels at the sides of the barbecue along with the bread. Both the potatoes and all your meats will look wonderful and taste delicious adorned with a pat of savoury butter (page 50).

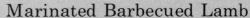

Marinated Barbecued Lamb

I will never forget a very special evening recently in Africa when, especially for the staff and me, some dear friends decided to barbecue a whole Karoo lamb, which they had marinated for days beforehand in a lemon herb mixture. They had dug a pit for the coals, and an electric spit moved slowly round with its appetizing cargo. After a busy day in the kitchen, at about 6 p.m. we had a swim in their lovely pool, immediately followed by large glasses of light, dry, white South African wine. That plus the wafting aromas of the barbecuing lamb were sheer bliss for me. But the joy of eating the flesh was even greater; the skin all crisp like a toffee apple, and the flesh slightly over-cooked, but oh, so good.

In a poor man's attempt to re-create this dish, I evolved this recipe. I like to use shoulder of lamb as I think it the tastiest part of the beast, even if a trifle more fatty. But you can use leg, of course. Bone the meat and then flatten it out to look like a clumsy butterfly.

serves as many as you like

1 shoulder or leg of lamb

8 oz (225 g) butter

juice and rind of 2 lemons

3 tablespoons fresh herbs, chopped

for the marinade

3 cloves garlic, crushed finely

4 tablespoons fresh lemon juice

$\frac{1}{4}$ pint (150 ml) dryish red wine

$\frac{1}{4}$ pint (150 ml) good olive oil

1 teaspoon oregano

2 tablespoons parsley, freshly chopped

2 teaspoons sea salt

1 teaspoon freshly ground black pepper

Place the boned lamb in a flat container which will just hold it and rub the garlic into and all over the meat. Pour on the mixed lemon juice, red wine and olive oil, and scatter the chopped parsley and oregano evenly over. Sprinkle on the sea salt and pepper. Cover tightly with foil and leave in the fridge for at least 3 days, turning each morning and evening and basting well.

When the charcoal fire is ready, remove the meat from the marinade (which you keep), and dry it thoroughly with paper towels. Set the cooking grid 4–5 inches (10–12·5 cm) above the coals and put the meat on the grid. Immediately start to baste with the marinade. Cook the meat for 5 to 6 minutes on each side (continuing to baste) and by this time – provided your charcoal is lovely and hot – the meat should be quite well 'charred'.

Raise the rack now to about 8 inches (20 cm) above the actual heat and continue cooking (turning at least twice) for a further 20 to 25 minutes. Put the meat on a plate and, just before you cut it, dab the butter all over together with the rind and juice of the lemons, and fresh herbs. Cut into generous portions and serve with a chopped salad dressed at the last moment with walnut oil.

Barbecued Sirloin Steaks

If I'm not pan-frying it, the next best thing to do with delicious well-hung sirloin is to barbecue it. Lay the steaks in a flat tray large enough to take them lying down in one layer. Mix all the other ingredients together in a liquidizer goblet and whizz them together for a few seconds. Put the marinade over the steaks and leave them for at least 3 days before cooking.

Place on the barbecue grid about 4–5 inches (10–12·5 cm) from the heat and grill for a few minutes each side, the length of time really depending on whether you like your steaks rare, medium or well-done.

A few minutes longer on each side is all that is required for grilling on your cooker grill, and you could even emulate the *look* of the barbecued steaks by using my trick with a hot coat-hanger (page 131).

serves 4

4 12 oz (350 g) sirloin steaks, 1 inch (2·5 cm) thick

1 medium onion, finely chopped

2 cloves fat juicy garlic

4 tablespoons bottled tomato sauce

1 tablespoon wine vinegar

4 tablespoons olive oil

1 tablespoon Worcestershire sauce

¼ teaspoon salt

1 teaspoon soft brown sugar

generous sprinkling of freshly ground black pepper

Barbecued Lamb Chops

serves 4

2 inch (5 cm) sprig fresh rosemary

2 cloves garlic

½ teaspoon salt

juice and rind of 2 lemons

4 1 inch (2·5 cm) thick lamb chops

Remove all the individual spikes from the sprig of fresh rosemary and pound them to a paste with the garlic and salt. Mix this with the lemon juice and pour this pungent and simple marinade over the chops in a dish large enough to hold them in 1 layer. Leave to marinate for at least 2 days, turning them once a day.

Cook on the barbecue grill about 4–5 inches (10–12·5 cm) from the heat for a few minutes each side, when they will still be nicely pink inside, basting continuously.

You could also cook them in a frying pan under the grill, surrounded by the marinade.

Spiced Cobs or French Bread

Making fresh bread for a party can be a bind, particularly if you wish to take it out of the oven just before your guests sit down, as we do each night at Miller Howe. The smell every evening around 8.30 is quite sensuous as the 90 odd rolls come out of the hot oven, are quickly painted with melted butter, placed into the covered basket trays and quickly whisked into the restaurant to be eagerly consumed. Bought dinner cobs or French bread can, however, be re-heated and served piping hot, in this simple way.

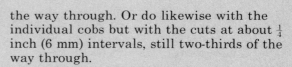

Per loaf of French bread or 12 bread rolls

½ lb (225 g) unsalted butter

2 juicy cloves garlic, crushed with ½ teaspoon salt

1 tablespoon parsley, finely chopped

4 tablespoons herbs of choice, finely chopped

With a sharp serrated knife, cut the long stick of bread at a 45-degree angle at 2 inch (5 cm) intervals two-thirds of the way through from the crusty top towards the base. Do *not* cut all the way through. Or do likewise with the individual cobs but with the cuts at about ¼ inch (6 mm) intervals, still two-thirds of the way through.

Melt the butter and mix in all the other ingredients, making sure the garlic is evenly distributed. Using a pastry brush generously daub the melted butter in between the cuts and then wrap each individual cob in a large square of tinfoil or the French bread in a large length of tinfoil, making sure the overlapping edges are *on the top*. When you wish to serve the hot bread or rolls simply cook in the oven at 350°F (180°C), Gas 4, for 10 minutes, and remove. Open up the foil on the top and bake for a further 5 minutes until the top of the bread is really crisp. Or you can put your foil parcels round the edges of your barbecue. Serve immediately. It's a little messy and sticky to eat, but so, so pleasant and tasty, and an ideal accompaniment to barbecued meats, particularly.

THREE

JUNIOR SCHOOL

JUNIOR SCHOOL

It was in the fifties, when I was working in Africa, that I first truly fell in love with the theatre. Every 15 or 18 months I used to come back to the UK with money to spend and an avid desire to 'do the London shows'. Whenever it was possible, a matinée and an evening performance was the order of the day, and I was even known to manage a matinée, early evening and then *late* evening show on certain Saturdays (much to the frustration of friends)! Such whole-hearted enthusiasm led to many slips, and I can clearly remember arriving at the Lyric, Hammersmith, when I had tickets for the Lyric, Shaftesbury Avenue (talk about the Americans and their 'If it's Brussels, it must be Tuesday').

For me to become actively involved with the theatre was very much removed from my mind at the time, but it happened – in 1959 – when a friend and I acquired an indefinite lease on Her Majesty's Theatre in Barrow-in-Furness, and I became Business Manager/Director. A gem of a Victorian theatre, it had been neglected for many years, but in our enthusiasm, we thought patrons would flock to see 'good' theatre and ignore the draughts, dust and drabness!

Despite the lack of money – and our poverty was prodigious – those years were the happiest of my life. Never had I laughed so much before – and I haven't laughed so much since! On reflection, I can't think why it *was* such fun as we were constantly going from one cash crisis to another. We used to walk by different routes to the theatre in the morning to avoid shopkeepers presenting us with bills; we used to take back empty bottles (sold but not paid for) from the bar to get the cash on them from an off-licence in order to get a few bob to buy something for supper; we used to go to incredible lengths – some humorous, some probably downright dishonest – in order to avoid paying bills (inventing a fictitious accountant, not signing cheques, dating them wrongly).

As the bank overdraft got larger so the size of the company got smaller, and in the end we were doing every 4, then 3, and finally 2-hander play ever written. I also learnt the knack of 'selling' myself and what I had to offer: once, during a newspaper strike, 3 of us toured the main streets of Barrow on market day holding up balloons and shouting out in sequence: 'Odd – Man – In Her Majesty's' (*Odd Man In* being the title of the play). And one lunchtime, the actress and I stood in the street in suave evening dress, just as thousands of workers were about to pour out of the shipyards, advertising *The Reluctant Debutante*; we literally stopped the traffic singing 'There's No Business Like Show Business'!

As I learned to sell my product, so I learned about a different kind of food and eating. We fed ourselves, in fact, surprisingly well – necessity breeds creativity – on economical vegetable soups and dishes, eggs, fish, the cheaper cuts of meat such as belly pork, all of which I would cook late at night as the actors learned their lines or relaxed from the strains of their performances. I became a dab hand at tarting up simple foods in different ways – I defy anyone to beat the number of inventions concerning plain and simple bought icecream!

Eventually, though, it became inevitable that one of us – me! – would have to bring in money from elsewhere. In desperation, I phoned Peter Campbell, the General Manager of the Old England Hotel in Bowness, saying that I was a fully qualified private secretary/accountant, and that

I would welcome the opportunity to work in any capacity provided I lived in (to avoid expense) and could learn a new trade. I was taken on, at the princely sum of £6.00 per week, as his Secretary and Assistant, and a new phase of my life had begun.

I still kept my hand in at the theatre for a few more years, but gradually my theatrical interests had to become secondary. That basic immersion behind the footlights had made its mark though, and the theatrical, the ideas of direction and careful production, have coloured my approach to life and cookery ever since. A *wonderful* time in which I learned to know myself and what life was all about. It was *people*, not material possessions that mattered, and I still regret . . .

Starters

4 oz (100–125 g) butter

2 medium onions, finely chopped

8 oz (225 g) good smoked bacon, finely chopped

1½ lb (700 g) firm white cabbage, very finely sliced

½ pint (300 ml) bottle beer or lager

1 pint (600 ml) beef stock

Beer, Bacon and Cabbage Soup

This was one of the 'fillers' during my theatre years, and I still like to serve it now at Miller Howe. It may *sound* a little less than 'oat' cuisine, but it's good basic cooking, and is a smashing dish served in substantial portions with fresh rolls for lunch, or in much smaller quantity at a dinner party with a small round crouton topped with brandied cheese (page 174) and lots of chopped parsley.

I personally prefer to use light ale instead of lager, but I have also used good strong Newcastle Brown Ale, and it has gone down a treat. Also try to find good smoked middle bacon, which makes all the difference, not being full of water.

In a 9 pint (5 litre) saucepan melt the butter and lightly fry off the chopped onion. Add the chopped bacon and cook with the onions until fairly well done. Add the finely sliced white cabbage and stir all the ingredients well so that each little shred of cabbage is coated with the delicious butter and onion mixture. Cook for about 10 minutes, stirring from time to time with a wooden spoon.

Add the bottle of beer or lager and stock, bring gently to the boil, and serve.

2 lb (900 g) smoked haddock, on the bone

2 pints (1·2 litres) milk

½ pint (300 ml) water

1 medium onion, roughly chopped

12 black peppercorns

3 large sprigs parsley

1 bay leaf

2 tablespoons brandy (optional)

8 oz (225 g) spinach, frozen

2 oz (50 g) butter

2 oz (50 g) split almonds, toasted

4 oz (125 g) prawns, defrosted (see page 96)

Smoked Haddock Soup with Spinach Cream

This sounds rather more posh, but haddock was cheap and tasty, and we ate it a lot, with milk, cheese, soup, bread etc.

Take the bones and skin from the haddock, and put the flesh into a saucepan with the milk and simmer slowly for 1 hour. Put the bones and skin into a separate saucepan with the water, onion, peppercorns, parsley and bay leaf, and simmer slowly for 20 minutes. Strain the water stock through a sieve and add to the milk and fish in the other pan. Liquidize thoroughly, pass through a sieve, and put back into a clean saucepan. Add the brandy (if using).

Meanwhile, cook off the spinach in the butter. Liquidize when cooked and pass through a sieve. This purée is used as a garnish by spooning it liberally into the centre of each bowl of smoked haddock soup. For a really wonderful dish, top off with a generous portion of toasted split almonds and a tablespoon of lightly warmed through prawns.

Omelettes

Because eggs were fairly cheap, we used to eat a lot done in a myriad different ways, moving round theatrical digs, cooking on Baby Bellings etc. I used to turn out the most rubbery and dull omelettes in those days, and believed that that was how omelettes should taste. It wasn't until years later, when I was at the Hydro, that Olga Hunter of the Yew Tree Restaurant in Seatoller showed me how to make them properly. Now I rustle them up at the drop of a hat, *but* there are several points you have to watch out for.

First you just *have* to have an omelette pan, and if you don't have one, put it on your next birthday, wedding anniversary or Christmas list. Buy a good one with a long handle. Take it home and put a smear of oil in the base and put it over a high heat until the oil smokes, jiggling the oil all over the base and up the sides, as high as you can. Discard the oil, and then, when it's cool, wipe the pan dry with plenty of kitchen paper. *Never, never, wash the pan.* Repeat this oiling and wiping process 4 or 5 times and then your pan is fit for use. *Do* please see that you have either worked the hot oil right up to the top rim of the pan or, when wiping, the sides have been rubbed well with the oily kitchen paper.

Omelettes *must* be served immediately, so before you start, get your fillings or accompaniments ready, your plates warmed and, preferably, your guests at the table. Many people like to have their omelettes filled with this and that. I don't. I prefer to have my tasty titbits – mushrooms, tomato provençale (page 175), warmed-up vegetables, sweetcorn, prawns, peppers, olives etc – served separately.

Eggs for omelettes in Olga's opinion – and mine – should always be warm (room temperature) and old. Put 3 medium-sized eggs into a small mixing bowl and add a pinch of salt and a generous turn of freshly ground black pepper. Lightly, oh so lightly, beat with a fork. Don't make an MGM production number out of this as all you want to do is break up the egg yolk and mix it gently into the white of the egg, bringing the eggs together as it were.

Place one dessertspoon of your favourite oil (I usually use olive, but corn oil is very good) into the omelette pan and heat. During this short spell of time vigorously shake the pan in order to coat it all over with the oil. Nearby have your warm serving plate ready.

When you think the oil is hot enough (lightly smoking) just put a teaspoon of the egg mixture into the pan over the heat and if it sets more or less immediately, you are ready to go to the next stage. Holding the middle of the handle of the omelette pan in your left hand (reverse all instructions if you're left-handed), shaking to and fro *constantly*, tip the lightly beaten egg mixture hurriedly into the pan. Grabbing your fork in your right hand, start to stir quite vigorously from the centre out towards the edges.

As the mixture starts to set, change the position of your left hand from a middle grip to one with your hand lightly and comfortably holding the extreme end of the handle. Now you have to tilt the pan to an angle of 45 degrees (leaning *away* from you) and by using the fork you can easily and quickly fold the cooked egg furthest away from you in towards the middle. Thereafter it is ever so easy to flip over the cooked egg *nearest* to you over the other turned-in section (so it's divided into 3, not just folded in half). Take the warmed plate in your right hand and simply slide the omelette over and on to the plate, so that the 2 folds are underneath and the top is smooth.

Go on, have a bash. On your fourth attempt you'll be quite pleased, and on your sixth, proper 'chuffed'!

COD

Cod nowadays is becoming more of a luxury item but, in my theatre days, like haddock, it used to be economical and good, and we ate it a lot. It's also a much under-estimated fish these days (except in fish and chip shops) for reasons I simply cannot fathom, as it can be baked, grilled, fried, boiled or stuffed, and served with a variety of pleasant sauces.

With regard to cod dishes (and other fish recipes in this book), I have had of late some complaints from diners at Miller Howe that the fish wasn't piping hot. I believe that to serve fish that hot completely ruins the texture and taste, and most of my recipes give timings that just cook the fish and no more. (You *can*, obviously, cook for longer, but I'm sure you won't like it so much.)

Scalloped Cod

per person

3 oz (75 g) cod, boned, skinned and cubed

white wine

salt, freshly ground black pepper

1 oz (25 g) butter

2 oz (50 g) coating of choice (mushroom pâté, tomato provençale, purée of spinach or apple)

A 3 oz (75 g) portion of fish will do each guest as a fish portion. If you wish to serve it as a main course, use about 5 oz (150 g) fish per person, and increase the other ingredient quantities in proportion.

Put your boned and skinned cod cubes into a bowl, sprinkle them with the white wine (as much or as little as you like), and leave to marinate throughout the day. Cod has quite a high liquid content which some people prefer to drain off, but I think this liquid quite tasty, so leave it in, with the wine marinade.

When you are ready to cook and serve, have ready a scallop shell or small dish per person on a baking tray. Set the oven at 350°F (180°C), Gas 4. Drain the cod cubes on a slotted spoon and put into the scallop shells. Salt and pepper the fish and place a knob of butter on top. Place the tray in the pre-heated oven and bake for 6 minutes (a 5 oz or 150 g portion of fish will take 8 minutes).

Meanwhile heat your choice of topping – mushroom pâté (page 173), tomato provençale (page 175), purée of spinach (page 133), or purée of apple (page 168), and as soon as the fish comes out of the oven, coat it, and serve it immediately.

serves 4–6

1 lb (450 g) cod fillet

salt

1 tablespoon plain flour

8 tablespoons olive oil

1 large fresh red pepper, about 4 oz (100 g)

about 6 oz (175 g) onion, finely sliced

$\frac{1}{2}$ lb (225 g) tomatoes, skinned, seeded and roughly chopped

$\frac{1}{4}$ pint (150 ml) dry white wine

1 tablespoon parsley, chopped

Sorrento-Style Cod

This is a good fish course for a dinner party, as it can all be done in the morning and then literally put together just 15 minutes before serving.

Remove the skin and any bones from the fish, then cut the flesh into about 1 inch (2·5 cm) cubes. Place on a cooling rack over a roasting tray, sprinkle with salt, and leave to stand for 30 minutes. Dry the fish on kitchen paper (discarding any liquor in the roasting tray) and toss in the plain flour. Fry the fish pieces in 6 tablespoons of the oil until golden brown. Remove from the pan, drain well and keep to one side on kitchen paper.

Cut the pepper into small pieces, blanch off in boiling water for 30 seconds and drain well. Heat the 2 remaining tablespoons of oil, and sauté the onions until lightly golden. Then add the tomatoes, cook for a further 10 minutes and then add the blanched peppers, cooking for a further 5 minutes. Season with salt and pepper. Add the dry white wine and simmer for 10 minutes. At this stage you can stop, and leave the rest until later.

When you wish to re-heat and serve this dish, simply portion out the cooked pieces of cod, coat them with the sauce, and put the individual dishes into a pre-heated oven, set at 325°F (170°C), Gas 3, for 15 minutes. Garnish with the chopped parsley.

Main Courses

BELLY PORK

The simplest, cheapest, richest, fattiest dish I know and one I never tire of (particularly if I raid my store cupboard for some tinned baked beans to go with it). I can remember one particularly nasty and harrowing brush with the then National Insurance Board in my theatre days. As we left, having handed over enough money to bring up to date our arrears on Insurance stamps – depressed and low, with nothing but 3/9d between us and starvation – we saw some belly pork in the window of a posh pork shop. We blew the lot on that roasting joint, and dined right royally that evening! And one of the weekly treats at Miller Howe is when the duck or chicken liver pâté is being made. We always cook about 3 times more belly pork than we actually need, for as soon as it comes out of the oven and the aroma wafts through the kitchen and restaurant, everybody seems to converge on the kitchen, nicking a bit of pork as they pass!

Roast Belly Pork

A piece of belly pork weighing 1 lb 4 oz (550–575 g) will give you, when cooked and carved, 6 generous thick slices. It needs no attention at all when being cooked and all you do is bung it in the pre-heated oven set at

350°F (180°C), Gas 4, and cook for 1¾ hours. But you can ring the changes and flavours by trying some of the following ideas, *before* roasting.

1. Make up some English mustard (or use Dijon mustard) and mix it with fried and dried breadcrumbs. Coat liberally over the skin side of the pork.

2. Make small incisions in the skin of the pork with a sharp pointed knife, and into these stick as many or as few peeled cloves of garlic and fresh sprigs of rosemary as you like.

3. A liberal scattering of curry powder on to the skin prior to putting it in the oven, provides a sharp or sweet flavour depending on the curry powder you use (see page 55).

4. Mix together some golden syrup, brown sugar and crushed garlic and daub on the joint.

5. Cooked on a liberal bed of the spice, star anise, the roasted meat has a lovely boozy flavour.

6. After 1 hour of cooking, coat generously with tomato provençale (page 175).

But *always* throw dignity and caution to the winds and give each belly pork dinner a hearty dollop of tarted-up baked beans (pages 159–60).

Belly Pork with Dijon Mustard

serves 6–8

4 tablespoons Dijon mustard

about 2 lb (900 g) belly pork, on the bone

3–4 tablespoons chopped mixed fresh herbs (chives, tarragon, parsley, watercress, mint)

8 oz (225 g) mixed root vegetables (onion, turnip, potato, carrot, swede), coarsely chopped

oil

salt

Spread the mustard thickly all over the flesh sides of the joint, and sprinkle with herbs, pressing them lightly into the mustard. Put the vegetables in the roasting tin and lay the joint on top, mustard side down. Prepare the skin for crackling with oil and salt. Roast at 450°F (230°C), Gas 8, for about 40 to 50 minutes. Reduce the heat to 375°F (190°C), Gas 5, for a further 40 to 50 minutes.

If you wish, purée the vegetables with a little stock, to serve with the meat.

Spiced Spare Ribs

serves 4–6

about 2 lb (900 g) belly pork

2 oz (50 g) butter

4 medium onions, finely chopped

4 tablespoons runny honey

½ pint (300 ml) wine vinegar

8 tablespoons Worcestershire sauce

6 teaspoons dry English mustard

4 teaspoons paprika

2 teaspoons salt

freshly ground black pepper to taste

Instead of cooking the belly pork in one whole piece, allow 2 or 3 individual 'chops' per person. Using a sharp knife cut the belly pork into about 12 thin slices, through crackling, flesh and bone.

Melt the butter in a frying pan and sauté the finely chopped onions until golden brown. Blend all the other ingredients in a liquidizer and stir into the cooked onions. Lay the 'chops' on the base of a shallow roasting tin and pour the sauce over them. Cover with a lid (or double thickness of tinfoil) and cook for 1½ hours at 300°F (150°C), Gas 2.

Eat conventionally, with knife and fork – or better still, with your fingers, dipping them into bowls of water from the hot tap with a thin slice of lemon and a sprig of fresh mint floating in them.

Moussaka

serves 8–12

2½ lbs (1·1 kg) raw shoulder of lamb, boned

2 oz (50 g) butter (or mutton fat)

6 oz (175 g) onions, finely chopped

2 fat cloves fresh garlic, crushed

2 tablespoons ground coriander

salt, freshly ground black pepper

3 medium aubergines, about 6 oz (175 g) each

½ pint (300 ml) fresh tomato cream (see over)

1 pint (550 ml) cheese sauce (see page 175)

Using a round 10 inch (25·5 cm) casserole, this is enough for 8 generous or 12 average portions. You could also divide it into small individual portions in foil freezer containers.

Chop the lamb into cubes and then mince it. Melt the butter or mutton fat in a large frying pan and lightly fry off the onions with the crushed cloves of garlic (if you are a fan, add more) and ground coriander. Add the minced lamb, salt and pepper, and stir thoroughly. Cook this over a medium heat, stirring from time to time, for 40 minutes. When cooked, transfer it to your casserole dish with a slotted spoon, in order to leave behind the lovely surplus fat. Fold in the tomato cream.

While the meat is cooking, slice the aubergines fairly thinly, sprinkle them with salt and leave them to 'sweat' for 30 minutes. Dry them thoroughly on kitchen paper. Fry the slices in the fat in the frying pan, and you'll be amazed at how quickly they absorb all the delicious lamb fat. There might not, indeed, be enough fat for all the aubergine – depending of course on how fatty your original shoulder of lamb was – so if you do have some unfried slices left over, simply blanch them for a few seconds in boiling water. (In fact, purists and goody-goodies might not want to have all this rich fat in the moussaka: they should blanch all the aubergine slices in boiling water.) Arrange the aubergine slices on top of the meat in the casserole and top off with the cheese sauce.

At this stage, when completely cold, the moussaka may be frozen, but if you are wanting to continue immediately with the cooking, simply transfer the casserole to a pre-heated oven set at 350°F (180°C), Gas 4, and cook for 45 minutes. Serve piping hot with a green salad.

makes ½ pint (300 ml)

2 lbs (900 g) tomatoes

2 cloves garlic, crushed

2 tablespoons wine vinegar

2 tablespoons demerara sugar

1 tablespoon each chopped parsley and mint

Tomato Cream
This tangy sauce is far better than any bought tomato sauce and will enhance a grilled pork chop, home-made fish and chips, baked egg in dinner cob, etc. It can also be used for flavouring stews and casseroles, and can also be frozen, so it's handy to do during the annual summer glut of tomatoes.

Wipe the tomatoes, cut them into quarters and place them (along with the stalks if they still have them) in a saucepan with the crushed cloves of garlic, wine vinegar, demerara sugar, parsley and mint. Simmer over a low light until the mixture is fairly dry (very difficult to define exactly, but at least 40 minutes). Remove the stalks, liquidize and pass through a sieve. If the sauce appears too thin for your personal taste return to a low heat and allow to evaporate further. When cold, freeze or store in a sterilised jam jar.

Boiled Bacon and Chicken

serves 8–10

collar of bacon, about 3 lb (1·4 kg)

2 oz (50 g) butter

2 medium onions, about 12 oz (350 g)

6 oz (175 g) carrots, finely chopped

3 oz (75 g) celery, finely chopped

2 oz (50 g) turnip, finely chopped

1 teaspoon dried tarragon

boiling chicken, about 3½–4 lb (1·5–1·8 kg)

1 small pig's trotter

salt, freshly ground black pepper

about 2½ pints (1·4 litres) inexpensive white wine or cider (or water)

During my time in the theatre, we used to go 'cadging' round the local market stalls as they were closing down around five on Wednesday and Saturday afternoons. By saying 'hello' to this person and 'how are you' to that person, and smiling sweetly, we often picked up some bargains. A good farm boiling chicken simmered away with a cheap collar of bacon would provide 2 hearty meals (the ham one, the chicken the other), *and* give us stock as well. *Never* turn your nose up at a boiler cooked this way, as it's such good, healthy and economical eating. (I must admit I have tarted the recipe up to give it even more appeal, but you can if you like use water instead of the cider or wine!) Be sure to use a casserole that will take both chicken and bacon comfortably side by side, with a small amount of room round the sides.

Submerge the bacon in cold water, and leave it overnight. In the morning, drain, re-submerge in water, and leave for another night to soak.

Melt the butter and fry off the onions, carrots, celery and turnip. Sprinkle on the dried tarragon. When partly cooked, place them in the bottom of the casserole, then put the chicken and bacon side by side on top, with the pig's trotter in between. Season well with ground black pepper and a little salt, and cover with the white wine or cider (or water). Bring to the boil on top of the stove, put the casserole lid on, and simmer slowly away for about 2 hours.

After 1¼ hours you should check that there is still plenty of liquid bubbling away in the casserole – if not, top up with a little more. After 2 hours, test with a sharp, pointed, stainless steel knife to see if the bacon and chicken are cooked. The bacon is usually ready first, and if it is, remove it.

If you are lashing out and serving both the meats at once, keep the bacon warm in the warming drawer of your oven, and carry on cooking the chicken until tender (usually a further 20 to 30 minutes). Take the chicken out, place it beside the bacon, and boil the liquid until reduced and tacky. Carve the chicken and bacon and place on the serving plates in alternate slices, and simply cover with the reduced liquid as a sauce, and serve with the vegetables.

I personally prefer to eat this dish cold. I simply remove the bacon after the 2 hours, turn off the heat, and leave the chicken to cool and finish cooking in the casserole. When cold, wrap them in tinfoil. I remove the pig's trotter, and the stock and vegetables left in the casserole turn to jelly when cold. I then slice the meats and serve the jellied vegetables with them as a salad.

Baked Chicken Drumsticks with Moutarde de Meaux

serves 4

4 chicken drumsticks

4 tablespoons oil

8 tablespoons fine breadcrumbs

4 tablespoons Moutarde de Meaux

1 egg, beaten

salt, freshly ground black pepper

4 oz (100–125 g) cheese and herb pâté (page 173)

As I cook so many chicken breasts, I invariably end up with a freezer full of drumsticks. They're tasty, filling and relatively inexpensive, and are now easily obtainable from butchers and poulterers, and supermarkets.

Skin the drumsticks and seal quickly in the very hot oil, even browning them. (If you're catering for more, don't try to do any more than 4 at a time.) In the fat and juices that are left fry the breadcrumbs lightly, then drain them and mix in the Moutarde de Meaux. Dip the drumsticks into the beaten seasoned egg, and then coat the drumsticks with the breadcrumb mixture.

Pre-heat your oven to 350°F (180°C), Gas 4, and cook the drumsticks on a baking tray for 45 minutes. Finish off under a hot grill to really brown the coating. Serve with a piped twirl of really cold cheese and herb pâté.

Chicken Drumsticks with Sparkling Wine Sauce

serves 4

2 oz (50 g) butter

2 cloves garlic, crushed

4 chicken drumsticks, skinned

plain flour

$\frac{3}{4}$ pint (400 ml) sparkling white wine (sweet *or* dry)

sea salt, freshly ground black pepper

$\frac{1}{2}$ pint (300 ml) double cream

Melt the butter, and add the crushed garlic to the pan. Sprinkle the drumsticks generously with flour from your flour-shaker, and brown them in the butter and garlic. Add the sparkling white wine, and be liberal with your freshly ground black pepper and sea salt. Cover and simmer on top of the stove for 40 minutes.

Remove the drumsticks from the juices and transfer to a plate and put in a warm oven. Add the cream to the winey juices in the pan and reduce to a coating consistency which will take about 15 minutes. (Take care the sauce doesn't catch on the base of the pan in the last 5 minutes.) Serve your drumsticks from the warm oven, coated with the sauce. Nice accompaniments are fried apple slices and toasted sesame seeds.

You can use ordinary white wine instead of sparkling wine, and if you don't feel like lashing out on double cream, simply remove the drumsticks to a warm oven, reduce the wine and juices, and fold in either some apple purée or tomato provençale (see pages 168 and 175).

Chicken Loaf Slice

serves 8–12

4 lb (1·8 kg) boiling fowl

8 oz (225 g) sausagemeat

4 oz (100–125 g) onions

2 oz (50 g) mushrooms, cleaned

3 cloves garlic

2 teaspoons dried mixed herbs

pinch of salt

generous twirl freshly ground black pepper

5 tablespoons white wine, dry cider or chicken stock

14 oz (400 g) smoked middle bacon, thinly sliced (optional)

When I was in the theatre, Robert Carrier was busily producing his superb weekly recipes for the new colour supplement of the *Sunday Times*. We avidly read each article every week although we could seldom afford to cook the dishes ourselves, but I will always remember his now famous articles on herbs and spices. Thereafter, we used to enhance our daily cooking by using some of his ideas with dried and fresh herbs, and this chicken dish – although not one of Mr Carrier's – used to be cooked on Sundays, when we were invariably at home, and as a delicious filling supper dish after the show one night mid-week.

We used to cook it in a dingy rectangular earthenware casserole we picked up for next to nothing at the cluttered second-hand shop run by Mrs Syd (who used to provide us with so many props, costumes and furnishishings for the weekly rep. shows). Nowadays I think it calls for a terrine mould, and the extra expense of the bacon for lining the terrine improves the flavour. Please read the section on terrines (pages 123–8) for details about lining the dishes, and bain-marie baking.

Remove all the meat and skin from the chicken (you should get about 1 lb 12 oz or 800 g of meat: discard the skin), and mince along with the sausagemeat, onions, mushrooms and garlic. Mix together with a spoon with the herbs, seasoning and chosen liquid.

Turn out into a terrine dish or 2 lb (900 g) bread tin, and cover with either the over-hanging bacon (see page 123), and the terrine lid or, if using the bread tin, with a double layer of foil. Bake in a pre-heated oven at 350°F (180°C), Gas 4, in a bain marie for 2 hours. Turn out and slice when cool. Serve with Poacher's Salad (page 107–8).

To give this dish a bit of style and to make it much lighter, use a Magimix (if you have one) instead of a mincer, and add 2 eggs and ½ pint (300 ml) double cream.

Vegetables and Salads

Baked Cauliflower Cheese

serves 4 generously

1 cauliflower, about 1 lb (450 g)

salt

1 pint (600 ml) cheese sauce (page 175)

1 oz (25 g) Cheddar cheese, grated

2 oz (50 g) flaked almonds, roasted

This is a favourite dish of mine at home, and one that is easy to do, economical, and quite filling. I normally serve this, accompanied only by onion marmalade (see the next recipe), as the main course for supper but, although easy, it is important to follow the method instructions very carefully.

Your cauliflower should weigh about 12 oz (350 g) without its outer leaves and its middle stalk. (To remove this, simply turn the cauliflower upside down and scoop out the thick stem with a sharp, pointed, stainless steel knife.) Leave the cauliflower to soak in cold, well-salted water for about 15 minutes and then drain. Have to hand a saucepan big enough to take the full cauliflower head, bring to the boil some salted water and place the cauliflower, head down, in this. When the water has come back to the boil, turn down the heat and simmer for about 10 minutes. You want the cauliflower to be *al dente* at this stage so don't, whatever you do, over-cook it.

Have your cheese sauce ready. Drain the cauliflower well, remove it speedily to a hot pyrex dish or serving platter which will just hold it, and pour over the lovely thick, hot, cheese sauce. Sprinkle with the grated Cheddar cheese, put under the grill (as far as possible away from the heat as you don't want the top and sides to burn.) When the sauce is browned, take to the table, the almonds sprinkled over the bubbling cheese sauce.

Onion Marmalade

6 tablespoons olive oil

2 lbs (900 g) onions, finely sliced

6 tablespoons demerara sugar

4 tablespoons sherry vinegar

Warm the oil through in a saucepan, add the finely sliced onions, and stir constantly until the onions are all finely coated with the oil. Stir in the sugar and leave simmering on the top of the stove. The onions will take at least 2 hours to shrink down to a rather tacky texture resembling a pickle. Beat in the sherry vinegar and gently cook on until this is completely reduced (about another 30 to 45 minutes).

The net weight of this resultant mixture is only a little over $\frac{1}{2}$ lb (225 g), but it is very sticky, sweet and rather delicious. It makes a wonderful accompaniment to cauliflower cheese as above, is ideal simply used as a chutney with cold meat or grilled meats, and is super served with a ploughman's platter of cheese and salad.

Vegetables à la Grecque

serves 8–10

1$\frac{1}{2}$ pints (900 ml) water

$\frac{1}{4}$ pint (150 ml) good olive oil

2 tablespoons white wine vinegar

$\frac{1}{4}$ pint (150 ml) fresh lemon juice, with the rind (about 4$\frac{1}{2}$ small lemons)

1 level teaspoon salt

4 tablespoons spring onions, finely chopped

12 sprigs of parsley

2 cloves garlic, crushed

2 sticks celery, finely chopped

1 level teaspoon each of fennel seeds and mustard seeds

24 peppercorns

12 coriander seeds

Practically any vegetable can be prepared and marinated in this tangy sauce, and then served as a starter, light lunch, or vegetable accompani-ment with a difference. I like it best served with 2 or 3 different mayonnaises, and lovely thick slices of well-buttered wholemeal bread.

Simply bring all these ingredients to the boil and then simmer over a low light for 20 minutes. Strain and then use this 'stock' for blanching off the vegetables of your choice – about 2 lb (900 g) *in all*. Bear in mind that mushrooms need the minimum of cooking, as do red and green peppers and button onions, but root vegetables cut into 2 inch (5 cm) length strips about the thickness of a pencil need a little more cooking time.

Put your chosen vegetables, separately, into the hot stock, and simmer until *al dente*. Take out with a slotted spoon, and mix them all together. When the stock has cooled, put the vegetables back in, and leave them for at least 24 hours to marinate.

serves 6

4 tablespoons good olive oil

2 small carrots, about 3 oz (75 g), finely grated

1 medium onion, about 6 oz (175 g), finely chopped

$\frac{1}{4}$ pint (150 ml) dry white wine

2 tablespoons white wine vinegar

12 coriander seeds, crushed finely

freshly ground black pepper

1 bay leaf

2 fat cloves of juicy garlic, crushed with 1 teaspoon salt

$\frac{1}{2}$ lb (225 g) tomatoes

$\frac{3}{4}$ lb (350 g) clean white small mushrooms, sliced

2 tablespoons parsley, chopped

1 tablespoon mint, chopped

Savoury Mushrooms

A lovely dish when served well chilled, and it's just as much at home at an outdoor barbecue as it is at the start of an elegant dinner party.

Heat the olive oil to smoking point and fry off the carrots and onion until soft and golden. Add the white wine, vinegar, crushed coriander seeds, pepper, bay leaf, garlic and salt. Skin and seed the tomatoes, chop roughly and add these to the mixture. Simmer uncovered for 10 minutes and pour it, while still hot, over the cold sliced mushrooms. Allow to cool and serve sprinkled with the chopped parsley and mint when quite cold.

serves 8–10

2 lb (900 g) mushrooms

4 oz (100–125 g) butter

juice of 1 lemon

¾ pint (400 ml) double cream

1 tablespoon white wine vinegar

4 tablespoons tomato sauce (fresh or bottled)

4 teaspoons Worcestershire sauce

2 teaspoons dry English mustard

freshly grated nutmeg

salt, freshly ground black pepper

1 tablespoon demerara sugar

pinch ground ginger

1 teaspoon soya sauce

Savoury Cream Mushrooms

This is another quick and simple dish but one that invariably causes lots of comment. I always feel I'm letting them down a bit when I explain to interested diners how simple the dish actually is – I feel they'd be happier if it was frightfully complicated. See what *you* think.

Remove the caps from the mushrooms, peel them if necessary, and trim the stalks. Sauté in butter, then pour the lemon juice over them. Distribute the lightly cooked mushrooms into buttered and seasoned ramekins and put them into a warm oven to heat through – about 10 minutes at 350°F (180°C), Gas 4. Combine all the other ingredients in a saucepan and, when you are just about to take the mushroom ramekins out of the oven and serve them, heat this sauce through (*don't* boil it). Coat the mushrooms liberally with the mixed warmed sauce and then sprinkle with plenty of chopped parsley. Serve immediately.

Desserts, Cakes and Biscuits

Icecream Magic

It was considered rather daring to remove the odd small tub of icecream from the freezer on the way out of the theatre after a particularly hard weary day, and to tart it up to resemble an 'haute cuisine' dish! Mind you, in those days icecream was considered much more of a treat than it is now and was, in my opinion, *much* better than some of the rubbish sold these days. Some makes are like blubber with the ghastliest of synthetic flavourings, and so many indifferent restaurants simply serve 'Icecreams, Various', and make a mint of money on their inflated mark-ups. With a little imagination they might make a little less, but certainly give the customer more satisfaction.

With a slice or scoop of bought vanilla icecream, serve one of the following:
    purée of fresh strawberries with a hint of Pernod;
    purée of fresh raspberries with a hint of Kirsch;
    a tablespoon of concentrated orange juice for each person with finely

chopped preserved ginger on top;

delicious soft peanut butter beaten up with a drop of rum, with some finely chopped dry salted peanuts scattered over;

the butterscotch sauce on page 33 is a *must*;

I can clearly remember once mixing some condensed milk with some strawberry jam and plonking this on a slice of icecream (I was quite sweet in the tooth then);

coarsely chopped chocolate mint crisps;

end bits of Blackpool spearmint rock bashed up into small pieces and scattered over, or better still, chopped-up aniseed balls;

a dollop of lemon curd topped off with toasted flaked almonds;

grated rind of 1 lemon with the juice warmed gently through with some runny honey;

any kind of chopped nut with the odd left-over bit of glacé fruit;

a dessertspoon of good old Camp Coffee mixed with soft brown sugar (very icecream-parlourish);

a banana, slightly over the hill, peeled and then mashed quite mushy, with a vinegar-bottle shake of rum!

Pancakes

makes about 24 pancakes

½ lb (225 g) strong plain flour

pinch of salt

½ tablespoon double cream

4 eggs, 2 of them separated

1 pint (600 ml) milk

1¼ oz (30–35 g) butter, melted

4 oz (100 g) butter, for frying

Sweet or savoury pancakes were a good filler when I was in the theatre, and they were fun to make – and not just on Shrove Tuesday!

Sieve the plain flour and salt into a large bowl and make a deep well in the centre. Lightly whip the double cream into the 2 unseparated eggs, add the other 2 egg yolks (leaving the egg whites to one side), and pour this into the well in the flour. With a wooden spoon slowly stir, gradually drawing in the flour from the edges. You will soon find that you require more liquid for the flour to absorb so add the milk in the centre little by little. Continue to stir, taking care not to beat the mixture as you want a thick batter at this stage. When all the flour has been incorporated and you have a completely lump-free mixture, slowly add the balance of the milk and beat in the 1¼ oz (30–35 g) melted butter. Cover with a tea towel and leave in a warm place for about 4 hours.

When just about to cook, beat up the 2 egg whites until very stiff and fold into the batter mixture. Fry the pancakes off in the remaining butter (remembering to just grease the pan and pour off the surplus). Stack the pancakes on one side, preferably on half of a tea towel, and after you add each cooked pancake, cover with the other half of the tea towel.

As a starter or main course, pancakes can be filled with mushroom pâté (page 173), cheese and herb pâté (page 173), spinach purée (page 133), with cream cheese, nuts and diced fruit, with white or cheese sauces (pages 174–5), with left-over minced meat, and grated vegetables.

As a dessert, pancakes can enfold apple purée (page 168), strawberry purée (page 140), icecream (page 166), whipped cream with nuts, chopped fruit, etc. The possibilities are endless.

These pancakes can also be used to line the dish for terrines, in particular the prawn and smoked salmon terrine on page 127.

8 oz (225 g) soft butter

8 oz (225 g) soft brown sugar

2 large eggs, lightly beaten

12 oz (350 g) wheatmeal flour

2 teaspoons baking powder

1 teaspoon mixed spice

6 oz (175 g) currants

6 oz (175 g) sultanas

2 oz (50 g) walnuts

2 oz (50 g) Brazil nuts

juice and rind of 2 oranges

¼ pint (150 ml) Guinness

2 tablespoons marmalade

For the topping

2 oz (50 g) demerara sugar

1 oz (25 g) whole almonds

glacé cherries to decorate

apricot glaze (see following recipe)

1 lb (450 g) good apricot jam

juice of ½ fresh lemon

2 tablespoons water (or brandy)

Wheatmeal Guinness Cake

Pre-heat the oven to 300°F (150°C), Gas 2, and line the base and sides of your 8 inch (20 cm) cake tin with 2 thicknesses of greaseproof paper. Beat the butter with the sugar until nice and fluffy and then slowly beat in the lightly beaten eggs. As with all cake-making, it is essential that you do not rush this process. The butter and sugar should really be beaten for 8 minutes if you are using an electric hand mixer, and the eggs should be added a little at a time and beaten well in before you add any more.

In a bowl combine the wheatmeal flour, baking powder, mixed spice, currants, sultanas and chopped nuts (you could use 4 oz or 100–125 g of walnuts instead of the mixture of walnuts and Brazils). Combine the juice and rind of the oranges with the Guinness and marmalade.

Add a little of the flour mixture to the light egg, butter and sugar mixture, mix gently, and then add a spoonful of the liquid. Mix again. Carry on doing this until everything is mixed together and ready for dropping into the prepared cake tin. Fill the tin and level the top. Do this gently without pressure.

Sprinkle over the demerara sugar and then arrange the almonds in a circle round the outside edge. Bake in the pre-heated oven for 2¼ hours and then test to see if the cake is ready (when it shows signs of shrinking away from the sides of the tin and the centre is firm and springy). Test with a long needle gently poked into the middle – it should come out completely clean. Remove from the oven but do not take out of the tin as it should continue to settle for another 30 minutes. When cool remove from the tin and decorate with apricot glaze and glacé cherries. Baking the almonds turns them brown, so you could just bake the cake without, and decorate afterwards, with the glaze, almonds and cherries. Store in an airtight tin, and it tastes better if kept for 4 or 5 days.

This is what we had at Christmas time: it's a good substitute for a more traditional Christmas cake.

Apricot Glaze

This glaze gives that added professional touch to any un-iced frangipane (see pages 110–11), or to an open apple or pear tart. Simply put the good clear apricot jam into a saucepan with the lemon juice and water (or better still, brandy). Cook over a slow heat until nice and runny, pass through a sieve and store in a sterilised airtight jar. Always re-heat before using and paint on to your cake or whatever with a pastry brush.

ENTERTAINING OCCASION

Before and After Theatre Suppers

The emphasis of this sort of entertaining must be on advance preparation and lightness (you don't want to eat too much before sitting for 2 hours in the theatre, or late at night not long before you go to bed). These six two-course suppers should feed you well, but not over-well, and are easy to do.

And do prepare the table, plates, flowers, garnishes etc *before* your guests arrive or before you go out. Even if there is 30 to 60 minutes of cooking once you get home (if you're entertaining *after* an evening out), the sight of a splendid table, and a nice chilled aperitif, will persuade everyone that all is totally in hand!

Supper Party
1

Breast of Chicken with Cherries (page 103)
Fresh Fruit Sorbet (page 141)
with Cigarette Russe Biscuits (pages 144–5)

Before you go out
Make the sorbet and the cigarette russe biscuits.

The breast of chicken casserole takes such a short time to cook that you could do everything when you come back – it will take 1 hour maximum. Leave everything in the heatproof casserole dish ready to start the moment you return.

Or you could pre-cook, taking it up to the stage when the breasts and trotter are removed from the dish (allow them to cool then cover carefully).

When you come back
Either cook the casserole from scratch, or uncover the breasts of chicken and put them in the warming drawer while you reduce the sauce and finalize the recipe.

Supper Party
2

Orange, Walnut and Pepper Chicken Liver Pâté (page 122)
Pork Chop with Honey and Pineapple (page 104)
with Spinach, Bacon and Apple Salad (page 166)

Before you go out
Make the pâté and leave to chill in the fridge. Prepare the garnishes and leave plates ready with their watercress base – but don't dress with the walnut oil until the last moment.

Prepare the casserole, and cook up to the end of the 45-minute stage. Take out of the oven and leave to cool.

Have ready your ingredients for the salad (you could dice the bacon before you go out, but don't shred the spinach or dice the apple).

When you come back
Heat the oven to 400°F (200°C), Gas 6, and put in the casserole for 20 to 25 minutes.

Dress the watercress with walnut oil, and put scoops of pâté on each and garnish.

Prepare the spinach, bacon and apple salad.

Just before serving the pâté pour the yoghurt over each portion.

Supper Party
3

Poacher's Salad (pages 107–8)
Sausage and Apple Bake (page 27)
with Baked Potato (page 22)

Before you go out
Chop up all the ingredients for the salad and leave in individual bowls ready to be dressed and tossed at the last moment.

For the bake, fry off the onions, sausages and apples as instructed in the recipe, and leave ready in the casserole dish. Make up the batter and leave in the fridge.

Prepare the tray with sea salt for the medium potatoes, and put the tray in the oven. Set the automatic timer to turn on the oven at 400°F (200°C), Gas 6, a little over an hour before you want to eat.

When you come home
Turn the oven down to 375°F (190°C), Gas 5, pour the batter over the sausages etc in the dish, and bake for 45 minutes on the top shelf. The potatoes and the bake should be ready together.

Dress the Poacher's Salad, and serve as a first course in the American style.

Supper Party
4

Minced Pork with Coconut (page 54)
Wholemeal Bread Cream Ice (page 109)

Before you go out
Make the wholemeal bread cream ice and freeze in ramekins.

Cook the pork in coconut milk until the milk is more or less absorbed – about 45 minutes – and then leave to cool. Have your garnishes to hand – the coconut ready to be toasted, the sultanas soaking in brandy, and any other curry garnish (page 56) you might like – the chutney on page 60 in particular.

When you come back
Re-heat the pork and stir constantly until it reaches the right texture and heat. You could also boil up some rice to serve with it. Toast the coconut, and shred the mint.

Take the ramekins of icecream out of the freezer and allow to come round for a while before serving.

Supper Party
5

Healthfood Avocado (page 47)
with Rich, Easy Brown Bread (pages 35–6)
Cold Boiled Bacon and Chicken
with jellied vegetables (page 80)

Before you go out
Make the healthfood avocado up to the stage of incorporating the beaten egg whites, and store in the fridge.

Make the brown bread.

Cook the bacon and chicken and allow to go cold. (Do remember that the bacon needs soaking for at least a day and night beforehand.)

When you come back
Slice and butter the brown bread, and toast the sunflower seeds. Beat the egg whites, fold them into the avocado mixture and portion into glasses. Top each one with yoghurt and garnish with the sunflower seeds.

Carefully remove any fat from the top of the jellied vegetables in the casserole dish, remove the chicken and the bacon, and slice the meats. Portion the meats out, in alternate slices, and serve with a scoopful of jellied vegetables as a salad.

Supper Party
6

Caesar Salad (page 134)
Bobotie (page 52)
served with Cape Apricot Chutney (page 60)

Before you go out
Make the chutney. Cook the bobotie on top of the stove for the 40 minutes of the recipe. Remove from the heat, transfer to a casserole dish, and allow to cool. Mince the apricots and leave on one side with the almonds. Make the almondy white sauce, or mix together the rich egg custard ingredients, and leave either on one side, covered.

Wipe the lettuce leaves for the salad, and store them in the fridge. Prepare the dry croutons and the garlicky oil ready to fry off when you return.

When you come back
Heat the oven to 375°F (190°C), Gas 5, and put the bobotie casserole, coated with whichever sauce you have chosen, into the oven to cook and set for 30 to 40 minutes.

Toss the lettuce for the salad in the olive oil and lemon juice, and add the Parmesan cheese. Fry off the croutons quickly in the oil, watching them carefully all the time.

FOUR
SECONDARY SCHOOL

I started work at the Old England Hotel in Bowness between Christmas and New Year in 1960, and after the months of living on the smell of an oil rag, and our happy Dickensian theatre Christmas, the opulence and luxury of the hotel was like a dream. Relieved as I was to have got a job, the first problem was what I should wear. Peter Campbell's parting remark after our first interview was 'You do have, don't you, black tails and grey pinstripes?' 'Of course,' I haughtily replied, and immediately panicked. After pawning a cine camera (left over from my more affluent days in Africa), I bought a North Country Club cheque and had a suit tailor-made. People today in the Lakes still recall the penguin figure rushing along the corridors of the Old England, black tails flapping behind!

Very soon, Mr Campbell suggested I join his Management Trainee scheme to which I agreed enthusiastically (to realize later that he had only just invented it). For the next year or so, therefore, I did all his secretarial work, ran the reception office, filled in where they were short-handed – the floors, the restaurant, bar or still-room. It was a hard and exhausting training, but eye-opening in that it showed me I had both the inclination *and* stamina to withstand the rigours of hotel work.

The bar was run by Bella, the terror of the hotel, feared by all and sundry. She ran a very tight ship, topping up bottles here, under-measuring there, and she made a small fortune for the hotel and a tidy profit for herself. Bella could draw the last drop of draught out of the keg and the last splosh out of a soda syphon; her wonderful flower arrangements discreetly hid the list of bar prices; her smile was infectious and her tongue vicious (to the staff) – but in every way her work was to be admired and, by gum, she earned every penny of her weekly basic three pounds ten shillings. She knew the likes and dislikes of all the regular customers, and occasionally some of their indiscretions. Mr B, who came every year, would wink his right eye which meant a double for him and a single for his wife before dinner; after dinner the wink of the left eye meant another double for himself and an offer to the single lady sitting at the bar now that his wife was bedded down! From Bella I learned the basics of bar-work – even if once (never again) I was flummoxed by an order for a 'Gin and It' – and also how relatively simple it was to truly please people. She also taught me what grand 'troupers' the catering profession is full of. For her the show always had to go on and even today, she appears three times a week at Miller Howe to prepare the vegetables. She's a lovely friend, even though on off days her tongue is still as sharp!

I was a quick learner and progressed swiftly. There really was no formal training programme, and there was no such thing in those days as a manual for the hotel trainee; I just had to use my basic common sense and my wits to survive and prosper. Not that everything went entirely smoothly. I once nearly set fire to the hotel by putting a serving plate on top of a burner; the overhanging doyleys caught fire and licked greedily at the nearby curtains! And when I was made Assistant Manager after 6 months, my first night in sole charge was a disaster. Considering we only had 2 couples in for dinner, the manager must have thought absolutely nothing could go wrong. But, for some reason, the earthenware casserole of poulet en cocotte blew up – scattering sauce up the walls, chicken pieces into the chandeliers, and stains all over the customers. Those people will never forget that evening – neither will I – and we were more than a little like Fawlty Towers that night (Spanish waiter and all, as I have a vivid mental picture of him prodding away at the chicken-festooned chandeliers with a mop, completely ignoring the dripping diners).

After a happy and hard-working couple of years, I was offered the management of the Hydro Hotel in Windermere at the annual salary of £720. I thought I had arrived, managing this 93-bedroomed, vast, characterful, antiquated hotel. The 7 years spent there were my senior years in hotel management, and I learned the intricacies of looking after and bringing out the best in staff, directing full-scale banquet performances entirely by myself, organizing the entire day-to-day running of the place. I doubled the business in 2 years, and came to look upon it as my own (the owners had entered upon a kind of semi-retirement, only ringing through for basic room service from their large house behind the hotel).

I collected a marvellous team around me, and eventually all the big Lakeland do's were held at the Hydro, as well as the daily operations of catering for 150 breakfasts, 500 lunches, 400 high teas, and at least 150 dinners. All the detailed planning, organizing, food buying, rotas, costings, timings, etc, gave me an incredible sense of fulfilment. I thrived on it, and started to discover that mass cooking and entertaining could be inventive, creative and clever.

But in 1968 I plunged all my energies into a new venture – the 'Tonight at 8.30' restaurant. After the mass catering of the day the pleasuring of 18 to 24 people in one small room, with the blue glass, blue and white china, and Victorian theatre menus, seemed restful and very stimulating (although it seemed madness to the owners). By this time I was also looking after two other hotels, but 'Tonight at 8.30' was the main excitement. We had such fun, made a lot of mistakes, but had lots of satisfied customers. Then it was that I really started to cook, beginning with the puddings.

The 1969/70 edition of the *Good Food Guide* was full of praise for our new venture, and I started to hanker after a ship of my own to run. In early 1971, I saw an advertisement for Miller Howe, a large house overlooking the lake. . . .

Starters

Cowboy Tomato and Orange Soup

When I started the 'Tonight at 8.30' restaurant at the Hydro, I was determined to do a set five-course production, changing the programme weekly. It was fun, exciting and, in those days, unique. But now, on reflection, I occasionally groan about what we did (as I do quite often about what we have done or still do at Miller Howe – one can become blind through being so close). One good old stand-by that used to elicit much comment and cries of appreciation, was a portion of tinned tomato soup with a dessertspoon of frozen concentrated orange juice added. It's really not at all bad, though I do blush about it a little now. . . .

Leek, Lemon and Lime Soup

serves 10 generously

4 oz (100–125 g) butter

8 oz (225 g) onions, finely chopped

2 lb (900 g) leeks, cleaned and diced

2 tablespoons castor sugar

¼ pint (150 ml) sweet sherry

1 lemon

½ fresh lime

1½ pints (900 ml) milk

I find this soup equally delicious served hot on a cold winter's evening, or cold in early summer or late autumn. The 3 different flavours come through clearly, and it is lovely and smooth.

Melt the butter in a large saucepan and gently fry off the chopped onions until golden. Add the washed and diced leeks, followed by the sugar and sherry. Cut the lemon into half and then each half into 4, cut the half lime into 4, and add all the pieces to the pan.

Cover the contents of the pan with a double thickness of good, well-dampened, greaseproof paper, large enough to just come up the sides of the saucepan. Put the lid on the pan and simmer very slowly over a low heat for at least 1 hour. After 30 minutes take a peek at the contents and gently stir with a wooden spoon in order to make sure that there is still some liquid there (a lot comes out of the leeks), but if you have had the heat too high and your mixture is beginning to dry out, add ½ pint (300 ml) of the milk and continue to cook.

After the hour's cooking, add the milk (or the remaining milk) to the pan, then liquidize (remembering to fill the liquidizer no more than two-thirds full each time, and always with equal parts of liquid and solids). Pass the mixture through a fairly fine sieve as leeks tend to be rather stringy and, of course, you don't want to impose any of the citrus pith or pips on your guests!

The soup can easily be made the day before and gently re-heated in a clean saucepan (about 20 minutes over a medium heat) when you wish to serve it. At this stage you *must* taste the soup. If too sharp add a little more sugar; if too sweet, add a little salt. Serve the soup generously sprinkled with flaked almonds that have been toasted in a warm oven, top with a whirl of whipped cream and some finely chopped parsley. It is also quite delicious well chilled, with the same garnish.

Pear, Stilton and Port Cream

fills 12–15 3 inch (7·5 cm) ramekins

½ oz (15 g) gelatine

5 tablespoons port wine

1 lb (450 g) plain digestive biscuits

4 oz (100–125 g) butter, melted

pinch curry powder

3 eggs

2 egg yolks

½ oz (15 g) castor sugar, sieved

1 teaspoon onion salt (or ordinary)

½ teaspoon paprika

8 oz (225 g) soft Stilton cheese

½ pint (300 ml) double cream

1 lb (450 g) pears, peeled, cored and finely chopped

Sprinkle the gelatine onto the base of a small saucepan and pour in the port wine all at once. Liquidize the digestive biscuits, mix to a paste with the melted butter and curry powder. Line the ramekins with this biscuit paste and bake them off in the oven at 350°F (180°C), Gas 4, for about 20 minutes. Leave to cool.

Put the eggs and egg yolks into a warmed bowl, and whip them up until white and fluffy (about 10 minutes). Then beat in the sugar and salt along with the paprika.

Cream together the soft Stilton and the double cream, mix into the egg mousse, and then gently fold in the chopped pears.

When the port has absorbed the gelatine, *very*, very gently heat the mixture (*at all times* you should be able to take the saucepan off the heat and place it on the palm of your hand without discomfort). When the gelatine has melted, pour it through a warmed sieve onto the mixture, and fold together.

Portion out into the individual lined ramekins, making sure you tap the filling down well. Refrigerate. To get them out for serving, run a knife sharply round the inside edge of each ramekin and stand the bottom momentarily in a bowl of very hot water. Turn out into your hand and then place on the serving plate base down.

Cheese Cucumber Prawn Loaf

½ oz (15 g) gelatine

5 tablespoons dry white wine

1 large cucumber

¾ lb (350 g) cream cheese

2 eggs

¾ pint (400 ml) double cream

1 tablespoon grated onion

juice and rind of 1 lemon

1 tablespoon chervil

1 tablespoon horseradish cream

¼ pint (150 ml) home-made mayonnaise (page 177)

1 lb (450 g) net weight of defrosted prawns (see method)

This mixing fills 2 1 lb (450 g) bread tins, which slices into 16 to 20 portions, depending on how generous or mean you wish to be.

Put the gelatine into a small saucepan and add the dry white wine in one fell swoop. Wipe the cucumber clean, and grate it into a bowl, taking care to retain all the juice. In a separate large plastic bowl beat the cream cheese with the eggs until smooth and then beat in the double cream. Mix together the onion, juice and rind of the lemon, chervil, horseradish cream and the mayonnaise. Finally fold together the mayonnaise and cream mixtures with the grated cucumber.

Almost the last step is to fold in the prawns but, in spite of the so-called trade descriptions act, it is very difficult indeed to purchase one pound (450 g) pure net weight of any brand name of frozen prawns. Some packs have practically 4 oz (100 g) of chipped ice or frozen brine making up the pound weight. As this recipe really needs the *whole* pound of prawns, you will have to shop around for the best, and you will have to defrost your prawns very carefully – first of all overnight in the kitchen, then in a strainer to drip further. Leave them for as long as you can, a couple of hours at least, to allow every drop of brine to drip away from the prawns. Put on a baking tray in the warming drawer of your oven for about 10 to 15 minutes. Brine will *still* come out!

Anyway, once your prawns, the whole pound of them, are well and truly defrosted, chop them coarsely and fold them into the mixture. Reconstitute the gelatine as described in the last recipe, and pour through a warmed sieve into the mixture. Combine everything together, and turn into the 2 greased bread tins. Put in the refrigerator to set, and when ready to serve, remove from the tins, and slice as you would a loaf of bread. Serve on cucumber, kiwi fruit, yoghurt herb salad (page 134), or with any other salad of your own choice.

You can also make the loaf slice with smoked mackerel, trout or crab, which are all equally pleasant. If you are feeling adventurous, add a generous tablespoon of red lumpfish caviare roe to the recipe, which adds to the dish's attractiveness.

Gravadlax

serves 6

about 1½ lb (700 g) tail piece of fresh salmon

3 tablespoons brandy

4 tablespoons sea salt

3 tablespoons demerara sugar

1 teaspoon black peppercorns, crushed

4 tablespoons fresh dill, chopped (or 2 tablespoons dried dill weed)

Remove the bones from the salmon, dividing it into 2 pieces. Leave the skin on. On a large double thickness of oiled tinfoil, massage the brandy into each of these pieces. Then mix all the other ingredients together, and coat each tail evenly with them. Bring the tail pieces together so that it looks like the original tail, and wrap the tinfoil around the fish tightly. Place the packet in a small tray, and cover it with another small tray which actually rests on the top of the fish tail. Weigh down with either scale weights or tins from the store cupboard, and leave in a cold place for 5 days. Each morning and evening turn the salmon.

When you want to serve this as a starter, simply cut as if you were thinly slicing smoked salmon, and accompany it with brown bread and a sweet and sour mayonnaise (page 177). I have also eaten this dish cut into thick thumb-like strips, and found it just as digestible!

Main Courses

SUPRÊMES OF CHICKEN

If you are fortunate enough to find the relatively scarce free-range farm chicken, there is nothing simpler or tastier than baking the breasts with a little oil, butter, wine and seasoning. No sauces, no dressings, no nothing – just a marvellous simplicity and taste.

But most of us have to make do with battery farm products which, if fed well, *can* have good flavour and texture, but so often produce flesh that looks rather jaundiced. Luckily, I've found a constant and fairly reliable source of breasts of chicken which, as a main course, are very good value for money. I always buy them still on the rib cage which, as well as being cheaper, leaves me with ample bones for making a good stock. If you buy the whole chicken, it's just as economical, as you have the carcase and wings for stock which you can freeze, and the drumsticks, which you can use as outlined on page 81.

I wrote a lot in *Entertaining with Tovey* about breasts or suprêmes of chicken, and I can offer no excuses for writing about them again, except that they're fairly economical, tasty, unusual, and surprisingly easy to do. One thing I didn't explain, and many people have asked me since the first book was published, was how to take the suprêmes off the bone. It's not at all difficult, but you must use a good small sharp pointed knife. Starting from the top point of the wishbone (you could remove the wishbone first), keep the knife resting against the bone of the rib-cage and slowly ease the flesh away. Thereafter it is quite simple to remove the skin. Take hold of the end piece of skin (opposite to the wing-bone) between your thumb and first finger, and tear the skin away from the flesh in an upward motion towards the wing-bone. Finally, make a vertical slice through the skin surrounding the wing-bone.

Lay the breast down on a cleaned board with the small wing-bone underneath. Curl your fingers underneath the breast and let your thumb feel out the strip fillet. Ease this back a little to give you the section you stuff with the appropriate filling (see later for some ideas). Some people remove these tender fillets and deep-fry them like goujons for cocktail canapés (see page 107). If you do this, you will have to make a 2 inch (5 cm) long incision about $\frac{1}{4}$ inch (6 mm) deep into the flesh, using a sharp pointed small knife, into which to pipe the filling.

Marinades

At this stage I marinate the breasts of chicken for at least 36 hours. When cooked – baked or barbecued – they are very juicy and succulent, and the marinade gives them extra flavour. Do remember to turn the breasts over in the marinade every 8 hours or so.

The following marinades all have their particular flavour – choose the one you prefer. I whizz all the ingredients together in a liquidizer or blender for a minute or so.

Marinade Number One

1 cup dry white wine
1 cup olive oil
1 clove garlic, chopped
$\frac{1}{2}$ teaspoon salt
1 tablespoon fresh tarragon, basil or rosemary

Marinade Number Two

1 cup medium sherry
1 cup soya sauce
$\frac{1}{2}$ teaspoon ground ginger
1 clove garlic, chopped
2 tablespoons soft brown sugar

Marinade Number Three

$\frac{3}{4}$ cup redcurrant jelly
$\frac{1}{4}$ cup red wine
juice and rind of 1 lemon
juice and rind of 1 orange
1 teaspoon dry English mustard

Marinade Number Four

$\frac{1}{2}$ cup brandy
$\frac{1}{4}$ cup sherry
$\frac{1}{4}$ cup olive oil
$\frac{1}{2}$ medium onion, roughly chopped
$\frac{1}{4}$ teaspoon fresh thyme
$\frac{1}{4}$ teaspoon sea salt

Marinade Number Five

$\frac{1}{4}$ cup white wine vinegar
$\frac{1}{4}$ cup olive oil
1 teaspoon Worcestershire sauce
$\frac{1}{4}$ teaspoon Tabasco
1 teaspoon onion, grated
$\frac{1}{4}$ teaspoon garlic, crushed
1 teaspoon tomato purée
$\frac{1}{4}$ teaspoon dry English mustard
1 teaspoon sea salt
2 teaspoons soft brown sugar

Marinade Number Six

$\frac{1}{4}$ pint (150 ml) wine vinegar
$\frac{1}{4}$ pint (150 ml) olive oil
$\frac{1}{2}$ tablespoon Worcestershire sauce
2 cloves juicy garlic
1 teaspoon salt
1 teaspoon paprika
$\frac{1}{2}$ teaspoon dry English mustard
2 teaspoons cayenne pepper

Marinade Number Seven

$\frac{1}{2}$ pint (300 ml) white wine
4 teaspoons wine vinegar
4 teaspoons fennel seeds
2 teaspoons coriander seeds

Stuffings

A generous stuffing for a chicken breast weighs about $1\frac{1}{2}$ oz (40 g). I enjoy experimenting by bringing various flavours together, and the following few have been well and truly tested and fully justified!

Mushroom pâté or cheese and herb pâté (page 173);

equal parts of finely chopped walnuts, mashed banana and finely diced preserved ginger;

equal parts of finely minced tongue and finely diced smoked bacon;

a little onion fried in salted butter, with finely diced dried apricots, brought together to a paste with ground hazelnuts and finely chopped watercress;

rather strange, although it works, is equal parts of smoked salmon pieces and avocado brought together in a liquidizer. Garnish with fanned-out quarters of ripe avocado baked for 5 minutes on a well-greased tray.

Baking

Cut pieces of foil large enough so that when you place the stuffed or marinated breast on them, the sides can easily be brought together to resemble a Cornish pasty. Coat each piece of foil liberally with melted butter on its dull side, and lightly season with a little salt and freshly ground black pepper. Place the breasts of chicken (filling upwards) on the pieces of foil, coat them liberally with more melted butter, and season. Turn up the corners of the foil, then generously pour over whichever marinade you have used, and gently and lightly make the Cornish pasty shape, enclosing the breasts loosely but firmly. The chicken breast is then ready for cooking and can, at this stage, be frozen.

When you want to cook them, put an appropriately sized cooling tray in a roasting tin. Fill the roasting tray with boiling water up to the base of the cooling tray, place the parcels of chicken breasts on to the cooling tray, and cook in a pre-heated oven at 350°F (180°C), Gas 4, for 35 minutes.

You could also, of course, bake your foil parcels of chicken breasts, with marinade and stuffing, on your barbecue.

Yoghurt Baked Chicken Breasts

serves 4

4 chicken breasts

2 limes

10 fl. oz (300 ml) natural yoghurt

½ tablespoon fresh chopped herbs (optional)

Chicken breasts marinated in flavoured yoghurt for 48 hours are succulent, moist and tasty. Place the breasts in a pyrex dish or earthenware tray and cover them with the yoghurt and juice and grated rind of the limes. You can also sprinkle half a tablespoon of fresh chopped herbs into the marinade to add more flavour. They only take 25 minutes to cook (see method) in a pre-heated oven at 300°F (150°C), Gas 2, after the tray of breasts is put in. They are extremely moist when served, and slightly pink.

For those of you who can get hold of buttermilk, use this too for marinating, in much the same way as above.

Pineapple is not my favourite fruit by any means, but last winter in the Cape I had a tasty piece of chicken that had been marinated overnight in the liquidized pulp of a 'well advanced' pineapple, served with a touch of fresh curry powder both in the stuffing and sauce.

Casserole of Chicken Breasts

serves 4

1½ pints (900 ml) strong chicken stock

¼ pint (150 ml) dry white wine

¼ pint (150 ml) dry sherry

¾ lb (350 g) root vegetables and onions, finely diced

4 chicken breasts, on the bone

1 pig's trotter

Similar to the whole chicken dish on page 42, breast of chicken can be casseroled with wine and vegetables, left to go cold, then taken on a picnic, with the jellied vegetables as an accompanying salad.

Place the stock, wine, sherry and vegetables into a suitably sized casserole dish along with some chopped fresh herbs if available. Then place the 4 chicken breasts face down in the casserole with the pig's trotter. Cover and cook for 1 hour in an oven pre-heated to 350°F (180°C), Gas 4.

At the end of the hour, turn off the oven but leave the casserole in until quite cold. Transfer to the fridge to chill. The tender juicy breasts are surrounded by partly cooked vegetables set in a soft, tasty jelly.

CASSEROLES

At the end of every season at Miller Howe, after another year of what seems like penal servitude – racking my brain for new dishes to cook, working anything up to 72 hours a week, travelling (this year, over 160,000 miles working with British Airways), trying hard to establish and maintain a good team, please and humour guests – I look at my ageing, sagging waistline and larger posterior, and feel nothing short of utter, manic depression. Then, for a few weeks, I take to the diet which makes me a trifle thinner and those around me a trifle fraught – without food and booze, I may lose 2 inches, but I also seem to lose my sense of humour! I virtuously sup my morning cup of hot water and lemon, force down all the segments of a fresh grapefruit followed by 2 poached eggs with lots of freshly ground black pepper, and then fast until I eagerly devour a huge steak, pan-fried (yes, I know it should be grilled, but for God's sake allow me some vices) by Bob or Tom, and in the end lose about 10 pounds, knowing only too well that I shall put on at least double that during the closed season.

For it's then that I turn to fattening, easily-prepared readily re-heatable casseroles, divine, sticky steamed puds, and lots and lots of lovely fruit cakes etc. When I'm at home at Brantlea, I find it far too much of a chore doing haute cuisine just for me, so I have a weekly cooking session when I make several casseroles, a few fruit cakes and then on odd days, prepare, cook, and devour the worst enemy of the waistline, steamed puds. But after all the hassle of trying to keep up culinary standards, it does my spirit a power of good and my figure a power of damage!

In fact if I were to change the course of my career in catering, I think my next venture would be a café where I served lovely home-made soups, basic casseroles with mushy wind-developing marrow-fat peas, followed by piping hot, fattening steamed puds. There must be in this diet-conscious slim-figure day and age *some* people who can throw caution to the winds, and return to more *comforting* food.

Casseroles are invariably the better for cooking the day before (at least) and then being re-heated – particularly so if you've used beer, cider, wine or spirits as the liquid. They are also ideal for storing in the freezer for that last-minute rush occasion, and can easily be prepared in a quiet time in your working period, or while you are cooking something else. We often served casseroles, in one form of another, during the years in catering before Miller Howe, for precisely the same reasons. They're easy, can be prepared well in advance, and can be re-heated.

Herb Beef Casserole

serves 6

2 lb (900 g) stewing beef

3 oz (75 g) seasoned flour

2½ fl. oz (65 ml) cooking oil

3 oz (75 g) butter

6 oz (175 g) smoked bacon, finely chopped

8 oz (225 g) button onions

4 oz (125 g) each of carrots and turnips, finely diced

4 cloves juicy garlic, crushed with 1 teaspoon salt

2 tablespoons cooking brandy

12 juniper berries

3 teaspoons dried thyme

2 tablespoons fresh chopped parsley

1½ pints (900 ml) red wine

4 oz (125 g) mushrooms, finely sliced

Cut the beef into 1 inch (2·5 cm) cubes and then lightly coat with the seasoned flour. Heat the oil in a frying pan, then melt the butter, and seal off 8 pieces of meat at a time. Transfer the sealed meat to a tray lined with kitchen paper. Add the chopped bacon to the remaining fat in the pan and cook for a few minutes. Using a slotted metal spoon, transfer the bacon to the tray with the meat.

Fry off the button onions, turnip and carrot cubes, and drain. Transfer to another tray lined with kitchen paper. Finally cook off the crushed garlic and salt and remove to the tray with the other vegetables.

There should be hardly any fat left in the frying pan now, so turn up the heat and throw in the brandy. Swirl around the pan, scraping up the bits, and transfer to a liquidizer goblet. Add the juniper berries, thyme, parsley and red wine and liquidize.

Coat the base of a large heatproof casserole dish with some of the meat and some of the cooked mixed vegetables and onions, and pour over some of the liquid from the liquidizer. Repeat this operation until everything is used up. Bring to the boil on top of the stove and then cover and cook in a pre-heated oven at 325°F (160°C), Gas 3, for approximately 2 hours. Fifteen minutes before the end of the cooking time stir in the finely sliced mushrooms and test for liquid, seasoning and tenderness.

Tomato and Orange Lamb Casserole

serves 6

2 lb (900 g) fat-free shoulder or middle neck of lamb

3 oz (75 g) seasoned flour

2½ fl. oz (65 ml) oil

2 oz (50 g) butter

1 clove garlic, crushed with 1 teaspoon salt

8 oz (225 g) onions, finely chopped

10 oz (275 g) carrots, peeled and roughly grated

rind and juice of 2 oranges

18 fl. oz (500 ml) tomato juice

½ pint (300 ml) water

2 tablespoons chopped parsley

2 sprigs fresh mint (optional)

Cut the lamb into 1 inch (2·5 cm) cubes and coat with seasoned flour. Heat the oil in a frying pan, then add the butter, and when combined seal off the lamb cubes, 8 at a time. When sealed, transfer to a tray lined with a double thickness of kitchen paper. Fry off the crushed garlic and onions as well as the roughly grated carrots and the orange rind.

Transfer everything to a casserole dish, cover with the tomato juice, orange juice and water mixed together, and bake in a pre-heated oven at 325°F (160°C), Gas 3, for 1¼ hours. Serve garnished with chopped parsley, with chopped mint too, if you like.

serves 6

6 breasts from 3 chickens

salt, freshly ground black pepper

1 pig's trotter, about 8 oz (225 g)

1 large sprig parsley

1¼ pints (700 ml) white wine

3 teaspoons cornflour

2 tablespoons water

36 red pitted tinned Italian cherries

2 tablespoons fresh parsley, chopped

Breast of Chicken with Cherries

Place the seasoned breasts of chicken in a casserole along with the pig's trotter, the large sprig of parsley and the wine, and bring to the boil on top of the stove. Pre-heat the oven to 350°F (180°C), Gas 4, and cook the casserole, covered, for 35 minutes.

Remove from the oven and take out the pig's trotter, the chicken breasts and the parsley, and leave to one side in a warming drawer while you put the casserole back on the top of the stove over a high heat in order to reduce the wine. As you start doing this, mix the cornflour and water together in a small cup and when smooth add to the hot wine and stir from time to time in order to reduce and thicken. Then fold in the 36 red cherries, re-heat the chicken breasts in the sauce, and serve immediately with the chopped parsley.

serves 6

3 pig's kidneys

1 lb (450 g) potatoes

3 medium apples, about 5 oz (150 g) each

3 medium onions, about 1 lb (450 g)

6 pork chops (minus skin), about 6 oz (175 g) each

salt, freshly ground black pepper

1 bottle cider, 35 fl. oz or about 900 ml

2 oz (50 g) butter

Pork Chop and Kidney Casserole

This is a dish that can be prepared and then left completely alone for 2 hours.

Skin and clean the pig's kidneys, removing the tubes, and cut into thin slices crossways. Peel and thinly slice the potatoes and apples, and chop the peeled onions fairly finely. Wipe the pork chops dry with a cloth, and season them.

Butter a casserole dish big enough to take the chops in 1 layer, and line the base with a layer of sliced potatoes and season. On top of this place a layer of apple slices and then onions. Season again and then put in the chops, with approximately 2 kidney slices on top of each chop. Then sprinkle with some more of the onion and a layer of apple, season for the last time, and finish off with a layer of potatoes. Pour over the bottle of cider. Spread the butter in knobs over the top of the potatoes. Bring up to simmering point on the hob and then bake in a pre-heated oven, covered, at 325°F (170°C), Gas 3, for 2 hours. Remove the lid and return to the oven for a further 30 minutes with the heat turned up to 375°F (190°C), Gas 5. Serve hot, with something delicious like a red cabbage casserole.

serves 8

8 thick pork chops

2 tablespoons oil

2 oz (50 g) butter

2 tablespoons dry English mustard

½ oz (15 g) cornflour

½ pint (300 ml) dry red wine

2 tablespoons red wine vinegar

10 oz (275 g) fresh pineapple (or the same net weight, canned)

4 tablespoons runny honey

salt, freshly ground black pepper

Pork Chops with Honey and Pineapple

This is a dish that will make Escoffier turn in his grave, but I really love it as the sauce literally thickens and makes itself during the cooking period! It's a dark-coloured, gooey sauce which to the professional reeks of cornflour and amateurism, but tell them to go pick flowers in a field as the taste is of honey, slightly tangy pineapple, and is lovely and tacky thick.

Remove the skin from the pork chops, and dry them. Heat the oil, add the butter and then seal the dry chops on both sides and ends and transfer to a casserole dish. Put the mustard, cornflour, wine, vinegar, the pineapple (cut into chunks), honey, salt and pepper into a liquidizer and blend together and then simply pour this over the chops.

Put the lid on the casserole and bake at 350°F (180°C), Gas 4, for 45 minutes. Remove the lid and turn the temperature of the oven up to 400°F (200°C), Gas 6, and cook for a further 20 minutes. Serve garnished with sprigs of watercress. The pork simply falls apart and is quite delicious.

serves 8

8 thick pork chops

2 tablespoons olive oil

2 oz (50 g) butter

1 large onion, finely chopped

4 medium tomatoes

4 cloves fresh garlic, crushed

½ pint (300 ml) dry white wine

generous pinch ground cinnamon

4 hard-boiled eggs, finely chopped

32 strips of anchovy fillets, soaked in milk for 1½ hours

4 oz (100 g) parsley, chopped

Pork Chop with Tomato and Anchovy

Remove the skin from the chops and dry them with a kitchen cloth. Heat the olive oil and then add the butter. Seal the chops and put them in a casserole dish. Lightly fry the onion, and while this is cooking, skin and seed the tomatoes and chop up along with the garlic. Add the tomatoes and garlic to the cooked onions and pour on the white wine along with the ground cinnamon. Simmer for about 5 minutes with the lid off the pan.

Cover the chops in the casserole dish with the tomato sauce, and cook in the oven, covered, for 45 minutes at 350°F (180°C) Gas 4, and then remove the lid. Turn the temperature up to 400°F (200°C), Gas 6, and cook for a further 20 minutes.

Garnish the finished dish (on each plate) with finely chopped hard-boiled egg, a criss-cross of anchovy fillets on each chop (discard the soaking milk), and sprinkle generously with the chopped parsley.

Pork Chop in Ginger with Water Chestnuts and Fried Beansprouts

serves 6

6 well-trimmed pork cutlets, about $\frac{3}{4}$ inch (18 mm) thick

salt, freshly ground black pepper

1$\frac{1}{2}$ pints (900 ml) dry white wine

3 tablespoons olive oil

2 oz (50 g) butter

3 circles root ginger in sherry

12 water chestnuts

6 tablespoons beansprouts, fried in 2 oz (50 g) butter

Root ginger is a most versatile spice, said by some to have aphrodisiac properties and, more mundanely, to keep out the cold of our English winters. I like the knobbly root ginger which I buy, peel and cut into $\frac{1}{4}$ inch (6 mm) round pieces and steep in jam jars of sherry. Like garlic, it is a very personal taste: some people can take much more than others, but in this recipe the ginger is distinct but doesn't, in my opinion, take over the dish. The water chestnuts added at the end of the cooking provide a contrasting crispness which is pleasant and if you are lucky enough to be able to buy beansprouts (even here in the Lakes they are occasionally appearing in vegetable shops, which means they should be more readily available elsewhere) they are an ideal accompaniment. The secret of the success of this dish is purely and simply the length of time you leave the pork cutlets marinating in the white wine. Two days is a must, 4 days preferable, and after a week the meat literally melts in your mouth.

Coat the cutlets generously with salt and pepper, and put them into a roasting tray or casserole dish that will allow them to lie separately on its base. Pour the wine over, cover, and leave to marinate, turning from time to time.

Remove the cutlets from the marinade and pat dry with paper towels, and then quickly seal in the heated oil and butter (remembering to put the oil in first to get hot and then the butter). Pat the cutlets dry again and return to the casserole of wine. Push a wooden cocktail stick through the 3 circles of root ginger and add to the casserole.

Cook in a pre-heated oven set at 325°F (170°C), Gas 3, for 2 hours (a double check on the temperature with a separate oven thermometer is vital in this recipe as ovens can vary by up to 30°, and a hotter oven will dry out your casserole).

After the cooking time, take the casserole out of the oven and remove the pieces of ginger (the cocktail sticks are clearly visible), and add the chopped water chestnuts to warm through. Fry off the beansprouts in the butter, and serve with the flavoured pork and warm water chestnuts.

If you plan to freeze all or some of the cutlets, only cook them for 1$\frac{1}{2}$ hours and continue the cooking when you re-heat from the freezer. If the dish is going to be left overnight and then cooked again the following day allow 1$\frac{3}{4}$ hours for the initial cooking time.

GOUJONS AND DEEP FRYING

I first realized that there was more to chips than just devouring them to fill an empty tummy when, at a very early age, I suddenly tasted chips that were *different*. They had been cooked in a large witch's cauldron on an open fire, but *beef dripping* had been used for the deep-frying. *What* a difference this makes, and the few decent fish and chip shops left go to endless trouble to secure beef fat for their fish fryers. (I would drive up to 30 miles to avoid having to eat the limp, insipid, fatty-tasting, pale things some fish and chip shops call chips.) Beef fat can be heated to a very high temperature without burning, and can be used more times than any other type of fat, as well as having a certain classy flavour.

You don't necessarily have to sport the luxury of a built-in deep-fryer, or one of the many electric free-standing ones now available, to deep-fry successfully. But before you attempt to make proper chips or any other deep-fried dishes, you must invest in a 'fat' thermometer. This is most important, and much more reliable than the 'throw in piece of bread or raw potato' method, ensuring that your fat pan doesn't catch fire, as the rising mercury tells you immediately when the frying can start. The correct temperature is also important as if it's too low when you put your food in, it doesn't seal quickly and thus absorbs a certain amount of the fat. Likewise if the temperature initially is too hot the outside gets overcooked long before the actual inside of the food is ready.

Most foods can be deep-fried in a deep saucepan kept especially for this purpose, but *do* remember never to leave the handle poking out when cooking, as a knocked-over pan of hot bubbling fat causes more harm and injury than anything else in the kitchen. The ideal range of temperature is from just over 355°F, around 360°F, to no hotter than 375°F (180°C to 190°C).

Coating food for deep-frying should be done with care, and you should use 3 deep old-fashioned soup plates (rather than those consommé-type bowls used these days) or 3 large concave dinner plates. On the first plate put sieved plain flour mixed with a generous sprinkling of salt and freshly ground black pepper. The second plate holds 2 well-beaten eggs, and the third has the dry breadcrumbs, desiccated coconut, sesame seeds, chopped salted peanuts or whatever.

Dip your food for deep-frying first in the flour and then immediately in the beaten egg. Ensure that the piece of food is evenly coated with the egg wash, and occasionally I resort to using a pastry brush for this. Then transfer to the third dish and turn your piece of wet food constantly until coated evenly all over, pressing firmly to make sure the coating sticks if necessary.

You can if you like do all this some hours ahead of when you intend to fry your food off, and leave the coated goujons on greaseproof paper, *uncovered*, in the fridge or larder. Before frying, do make sure that they haven't acquired a 'dampness' from the fridge, and if so, add further crumbs or coating.

Goujons need no more than 5 minutes to cook in fat of the right temperature.

Goujons of Sole

You will need approximately 3–4 oz (75–125 g) sole per person. Cut your skinned fillets of sole into pieces about 3 inches (7·5 cm) long and as thick as your middle finger. Proceed as in the introduction, using breadcrumbs as the coating, and serve at once accompanied with some mayonnaise into which you have folded some small capers.

Goujons of Turkey Breast

You will need approximately 3–4 oz (75–125 g) per person. I really do like this dish as you coat the fingers of prepared turkey breast with desiccated coconut rather than breadcrumbs (after flouring and egging naturally). Serve the goujons with the sweet and sour sauce on page 176.

Goujons of Pork Fillets

Allow 3–4 oz (75–125 g) per person. Cut pork fillet into finger lengths, but after flouring and egging, coat with finely crushed salted peanuts and serve with an apple purée (page 168).

Deep-Fried Fillets of Chicken Breast

On page 98 I tell you how some 'mean' people remove the fillets from the chicken breasts and use another time. This is how you use them! It's not strictly speaking a goujon, but so similar in size, and 8 fillets will serve 4 as a starter (or they're good as cocktail finger food).

Simply flour, egg wash and then coat each fillet in sesame seeds, deep-fry, and serve at once sprinkled with some soya sauce.

Deep-Fried Fillet of Lamb

Allow 3–4 oz (75–125 g) lamb per person. The fillets should be cut into cubes and then left to marinate in fresh lime juice and finely grated rind for at least 1 day. Dry off the cubes, coat with flour and egg wash and cover with breadcrumbs to which you have added a touch (as much or as little as you want) of curry powder. Deep-fry and serve with a spoonful of peanut butter.

Vegetables and Salads

Poacher's Salad

Virtually anything you can scrounge from left-overs of fruit and vegetables can be put into this, and all the different textures and tastes add to the pleasure of eating it. Just go into your store cupboard and fridge now, and I am sure you will be able to find some of the following:

walnuts
hazelnuts
apples
celery
radish
olives
gherkins
hard-boiled egg

any kind of fresh fruit
(peach, pear, orange,
apricot, grape, mango,
kiwi fruit)

vegetables (carrot, parsnip,
turnip, leek, spinach,
broccoli, cauliflower)

I prefer to serve individual poacher salads, and if you don't sport the luxury of small individual wooden salad bowls, use soup bowls or even large tea-cups. Rub a peeled clove of garlic round the edge of the container to be used. Shred lettuce leaves finely and put these on the base. Then all you do is painstakingly chop away at your conglomeration of ingredients and keep piling them on, building quite a pyramid: florets of cauliflower or broccoli, grated root vegetables, finely diced leeks, skinned fruit mashed or chopped up, nuts, chopped olives, diced radishes, finely sliced this or that.

It is an hors d'oeuvre salad or the knickerbocker glory of salads, and always topped off at the last minute with your favourite French dressing (see page 176). You will be surprised how delicious, tempting and satisfying this can be. Served with left-over cold meat, terrine, or some fish dishes, it makes a filling main course for a supper and you will be amazed at how light the ingredients are on your purse and how effectively they fill up a hungry tummy!

Desserts, Cakes and Biscuits

Pear Hazelnut Coffee Cream Gâteau

serves 8–12

3 eggs

4 oz (100 g) castor sugar, sieved

2 tablespoons Camp Coffee

3 oz (75 g) plain flour, sieved

2 oz (50 g) hazelnuts, coarsely chopped

As much fruit, chopped, as you like folded into as much double cream, whipped with a little sugar, as you like

This is an extremely light, easy to make, gâteau – the perfect sweet for the ending of a dinner party, particularly as it comes to no harm if made the day before and stored, when cool, in an airtight tin. This was the first sweet I made myself for the 'Tonight at 8.30' restaurant at the Hydro. To ring the changes, you can substitute walnuts for the hazelnuts and have any filling you prefer that is in season at the time – apples, raspberries, blackberries, strawberries, or kiwi fruit.

The only points to watch are:
1. Your mixing bowl should be nice and warm when you break in the eggs and these themselves should be at a nice, warm, room temperature.
2. Whatever you do, add the sugar just a little at a time, remembering that the more air and volume you get into the mixture at this stage the lighter your gâteau eventually will be.
3. Sieve in the plain flour from a dizzy height to add more lightness.
4. Fold in the chopped nuts carefully at the end with a large metal spoon.

Line the base and sides of a round 8 inch (20 cm) loose-bottomed cake tin with greaseproof paper and set your oven to 350°F (180°C), Gas 4. Break the eggs into the warmed mixing bowl and beat the living daylights out of them until they come light and fluffy (this takes at least 8 minutes with an electric beater) and then, little by little, add the castor sugar. The end mixing will be very much increased in volume and quite pale in colour. Beat in the Camp coffee, then fold in the plain flour and the chopped nuts. Pour into the prepared cake tin and bake for approximately 45 minutes.

The cake is done when it is springy to the touch and a sharp pointed knife, pushed into the middle, comes out perfectly clean and dry. Leave to cool and then store, *or* cut into 3 sections and layer with the whipped cream and fruit, and eat immediately.

Chilled Apricot Cream

serves 10–12

1 pint (600 ml) double cream

rind and juice of 1 lemon

12 oz (350 g) apricot jam

8 eggs

2 oz (50 g) castor sugar

This is a very handy pud to have in the freezer for those sudden unexpected guests, or as a godsend on a fraught day when you can't think of what to give the family to eat. They last for a few weeks in the freezer so can be made at any time.

Bring the double cream and rind of the lemon to a gentle boil, remembering to use a rather large saucepan, as cream has the rotten habit of swiftly and suddenly bubbling up and over sides! Melt the apricot jam over a low heat in a separate saucepan.

In a warmed bowl, beat the eggs vigorously for about 8 minutes if you're using an electric whisk, or about 12 to 15 minutes if you're doing it by non-electric means. Slowly add the sugar little by little until you have a lovely mousse-like texture.

Turn the slightly cooled double cream into a large plastic bowl and fold in the mousse mixture along with the juice of the lemon and the melted apricot jam. Pour the blended cream into individual pots or bread tins (to be spooned out). When serving, a dash of cooking brandy splashed on each portion certainly enhances it!

Wholemeal Bread Cream Ice

serves 10

6 oz (175 g) wholemeal bread, stale

6 oz (175 g) demerara sugar

1 pint (550–600 ml) double cream

2 oz (50 g) castor sugar

4 tablespoons brandy

This is a good and easy party piece which always goes down well, with no custard to make, no freezing and re-freezing with messy churning around.

Make the stale wholemeal bread into breadcrumbs either in a liquidizer or by the old-fashioned method of rubbing up and down against a grater. Mix the breadcrumbs and demerara sugar together and then pat out onto a lightly greased baking tray. Have your oven set to 400°F (200°C), Gas 6, and put the tray in for 10 minutes. Keep on looking at the tray as you want the sugar to caramelize and mix with the breadcrumbs to become sharp and crunchy. Stir it occasionally, as it often cooks first on the outside. When the mixture is tacky and caramelized, take out of the oven and leave to cool. Break up again into crumbs.

Lightly beat up the cream and sugar with the brandy and simply fold in the sugared breadcrumbs. Pot and freeze in 10 3 inch (7·5 cm) ramekins.

serves 8–10

pre-cooked 11 inch (28 cm) pastry flan case (page 178)

apricot jam

fruit (see methods)

2 tablespoons castor sugar

apricot glaze (page 87)

for the filling

4 oz (100–125 g) butter

4 oz (100–125 g) castor sugar

2 small eggs, beaten

4 oz (100–125 g) ground almonds

2 tablespoons self-raising flour

Frangipanes

Frangipanes are rich, filling, luscious, fattening, tempting, moreish and, more important still, relatively simple to make and not all that expensive.

When baking the pastry flan case (page 178), do, *do* make sure that the base is cooked firmly, without the slightest sign of sogginess. I always line my uncooked flans with tinfoil, bringing the foil up the sides of the flan and wrapping it gently over the edges, before filling with beans and baking blind in an oven pre-heated to 325°F (160°C), Gas 3, for 45 minutes. I know this seems a long time but you always get crisp pastry.

When the flan case is cool, coat the base liberally with lump-free good-quality apricot jam and then prepare the fruit of your choice and the almond filling.

To make the filling, cream the butter and sugar together and then beat in the beaten eggs little by little. Fold in the ground almonds and self-raising flour. Spread this floppy mixture on top of the apricot jam in the cooked pastry flan.

The next step is to put in the fruit of your choice and push down into the filling in the flan case. Then bake at 350°F (180°C), Gas 4, in a pre-heated oven, for at least 30 minutes. Test carefully after this time to see if it is cooked by using a small stainless steel knife: if it comes out clean, all is well, but if showing any signs of sogginess keep on cooking. You may think I sound rather vague on this point, and I have to be – the cooking time really depends very much on the size of the fruit you have used. When you test the frangipane, sprinkle over it the 2 tablespoons of castor sugar, and always return to the oven for a few minutes allowing time for the sugar to caramelize a little.

Just prior to serving these frangipanes, I paint the top caramelized surface liberally with apricot glaze (page 87), and I sometimes top the cherry one with plain white icing.

All frangipanes are best eaten on the day they are cooked, but they can last for up to a week. If you have made your frangipane the morning of your dinner party, as you serve the main course, pop the frangipane back into the now turned-off oven to heat through slightly. Don't, however, do this with an icing-topped cherry one!

Red Cherry Frangipane

Use the tinned pitted cherries, as fresh cherries, although tasting much better, seem to go mushy in frangipanes. All you have to do is take them out of their tin and drain well. Put on top of the filling in the flan case, and push down into it.

Pear Frangipane

Peel 3 fairly ripe pears and cut them lengthwise in 2 and scoop out the core and stems. Lay the 6 halves flat side down on your chopping board and then cut across each half lengthwise at thin intervals with a sharp stainless steel knife, and push the slices down flat (think of when you were a kid and used to stand dominoes up in squiggly lines, and then with bated breath push one down, thus toppling them all).

With a palette knife take up each sliced and 'flattened' portion of pear and transfer to the top of the frangipane filling. Put the stem end towards the middle and the fatter end running around the outside edge of the flan. Using the tips of your fingers gently press the pear pieces down through the sponge-like mixing onto the jammed base of the flan. Repeat this round the flan using up all the pears.

Apple Frangipane

Prepare in a similar way to the pear frangipane.

Pineapple Frangipane

Use fresh pineapple if you can, but if this is impossible, small tinned Hawaiian pineapple rings are almost as good. Simply cut your fresh pineapple into $\frac{1}{4}$ inch (6 mm) rings, take out the core, and push the rings through the frangipane filling down on to the jammed base of the flan.

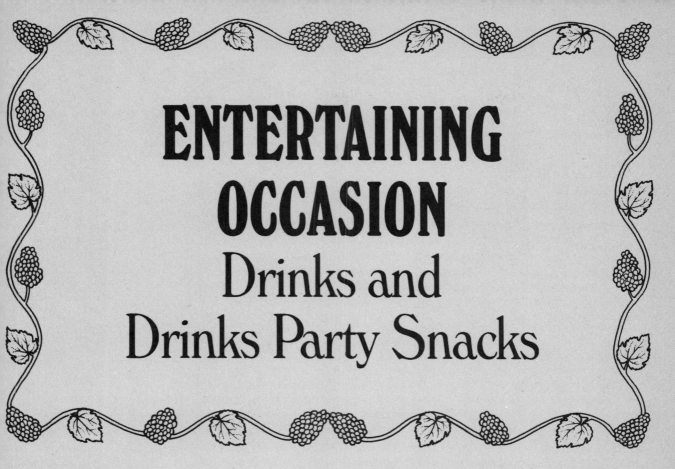

ENTERTAINING OCCASION
Drinks and Drinks Party Snacks

Drinks

If you were to get a dozen 'wine and food' people trapped together in a room for 24 hours they would never stop talking about the subject of wine and food and would never agree – but in the nicest possible way!

Buying wine depends mainly on 2 things these days, your own personal palate and the state of your pocket and purse. French wines are soaring in price both in wine stores and restaurants and so, over the last year or so, I have been seriously looking around for good, basic, clean, tasty cheap wines and have learnt a great deal. I use a system which I feel is fool-proof, but which annoys some wine suppliers. I carefully select 2 bottles each of 12 different wines from the supplier's list, and ask them to go to the trouble to make up the split order. (Once they would have politely told me where to go but, in these relatively hard times, aren't we all bending over backwards to see the customer gets exactly what he or she wants?) When these 2 cases of 12 different wines arrive, we open one each lunchtime and make

our own personal comments. Ugh, awful. Quite nice. Pleasant little wine. Oh yes, good, clean, I like that. I wouldn't water my peonies with that. What will they send next. Gut rot. When we think we have found a 'winner' (and I'd be happier if it happened more often) I have the task of taking the second bottle back to my house. On my night off I slowly but surely devour the whole bottle, eating a bit of this and a bit of that, but drinking *nothing else*. The next morning I give my blessing or curse to the wine. If I have a queasy stomach or thick head, I know that the wine might have appeared good but is decidedly not for us at Miller Howe. Put it on the wine list and a customer purchasing and drinking it would probably feel the same as you the next morning. And the horrifying thing is that – believe you me, I *know* – they wouldn't think for one single moment that the wine had made them ill but would condemn the food. 'Imagine paying those fancy prices for those fancy dishes and ending up with gut rot – shan't go there again.' Oh no, the wine never seems to be the cause of the trouble! So if you do discover an inexpensive wine that you particularly enjoy by the glass, do repeat my experiment before you attempt to show off in front of your dinner guests.

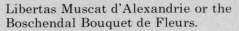

However, the wines that I have literally gone overboard about, due to their consistency, clarity and class, are those from South Africa. Having spent several winters working out in the Cape and the Transvaal, I have realized that over the last few years South African wines have changed remarkably and now taste as good in this cold climate as they do under the sun of the south. On 1 September 1973 – when Britain became a member of the Common Market – strictly-enforced legislation came into force in South Africa with regard to wine production and selling, and it is regarded today as probably the most comprehensive legal wine-control system in the world.

There are 5 various certifications:
Estate: the wine must be made from grapes grown and produced on a proclaimed wine estate;
Origin: a wine may only have this labelling if 75 per cent of it actually comes from the specified area;
Cultivar: 75 per cent of the wine must be made from the grape variety stated on the label;
Vintage: 75 per cent of the wine in the bottle must have been produced in the specified year;
Superior: wines of exceptional quality are occasionally granted the 'Superior' category by the government-controlled wine board.

When buying South African wines you might think that the vintage is too young to be good, but do bear in mind that the harvesting of the grapes can cover an 8-week period commencing towards the end of January, and so each vintage year shown on a list of South African wines is a good 8 months older than those wines produced in Europe! I have had quite a few South African wines that haven't appealed to me, but I think I can honestly say I have never ever had a bad one.

One of my favourites is Nederburg Premiere Cuvée Brut, which is a delightful sparkling white wine, good value for money, and ideal for Buck's Fizz (next page). For a summer's day or a barbecue party, I like the Nederburg Rosé Sec which is dry and smooth with the merest tingle to the palate. The Dry Steen from Oude Libertas is without a doubt my favourite full-bodied dry white wine; and one that I never tire of is the Nederburg Paarl Riesling. This is a very clean, fresh wine, dry and lively with a joyful fruit acid content. A wine that is similar to those from Alsace but only half their price is the Nederburg Fonternel and, to go with any puds you serve, do search out the Oude

Libertas Muscat d'Alexandrie or the Boschendal Bouquet de Fleurs.

It is the reds, however that I really like, and I do find it difficult to select between a Zonnebloem Cabernet Sauvignon or KWV Cabernet Sauvignon and the Oude Libertas Pinotage. The Cabernet Sauvignon grape originates from the Bordeaux region of France, where it is the mainstay of the Médoc and St Emilion areas. This grape has proved very successful in the Cape. Full bodied, with a fruity, slightly acid taste, the wine is matured for at least 18 months in seasoned French oak casks. The Pinotage from Oude Libertas is made from a cross-pollinating of the Pinot Noir from Burgundy and the Cinsaut (originating from the South of France, and imported to the Cape in 1880) – a soft, round flowery wine.

The chain grocery stores often sell remarkably good table wine and don't, whatever you do, turn your nose up at such bottles. If the pocket doesn't stretch to a glass of wine a day, do try to budget for such pleasure at the weekend, and, if you discover a wine that gives you satisfaction, by all means serve it to guests at a dinner party. Don't be put off by the cheapness of such wine: impress your guests with the fact that you have taken the trouble to find the wine and, of course, you must tell them where they too can obtain it.

The general rule is red with red meat and white with fish and white meat, but for goodness sake don't let this worry you. If red does something to your liver, serve your guests white. Don't become too holy-holy about your approach to wine. The most important thing is a basic honesty to yourself and others. You have no idea what embarrassment I occasionally endured when I blurted out to those much more professional than I what I thought about a wine. But now I stick to my guns: there is nothing more personal in the world than the saliva in your mouth, what *you* taste as the wine swills around your palate, slips down your throat, and hits your gut! Whether it's Sainsbury's plonk or Louis Latour, take in the wine, swill it around on the edge of your tongue and then slowly swallow and immediately note down, mentally or actually, *exactly* what you think. Sweet, dry, sharp, mellow. Tingly, smooth. Gooseberries or blackcurrants. Yes, really! I can clearly remember once saying 'brown boot polish', after tasting one wine from the Rhône, and in spite of what anybody says it still, today, tastes to me of brown boot polish!

The one thing I invariably steer clear of at a party is any form of punch cup, as I find it literally punching me drunk! I don't care whose auntie or great-uncle handed down the recipe, I simply cannot stomach them. I can't help thinking of all the ingredients they might have put in the wretched thing and work myself up into such a state that I can't possibly drink a luke-warm drop!

At a party it is much easier and much more pleasant to simply serve a choice of wines before the meal: or, if you are sure of your wine and guests, just one wine. If you try to set up a bar, you will invariably find somebody asking for something you haven't got and, even worse, find yourself without their second choice (making you feel inadequate right at the *start* of the party). Look after the bottles you have opened, making sure the red is at the correct room temperature (and that doesn't mean a room with a roaring log or coal fire or one with the central heating switched up to full), and chill your whites.

You must also take care with the glasses you will use. By all means bring out your best crystal glasses, but for heaven's sake, wash them first in a mild, slight detergent then rinse thoroughly in clear, warm water. Then wipe and polish dry, dry, dry, until the glasses squeak against the cloth. Never store them stem side up because if they aren't perfectly clean when put away, slight bacteria could develop.

I like to get all my glasses out the day before a party. They are washed and rinsed and then dried, but I polish them again about an hour before my guests arrive. I fill a large, wide-topped jug nearly to the top with boiling water from the kettle. Put this on a side table near the laid dining-table and hold each glass top side up over the gentle steam. You will be amazed at the sparkle you can get now with a cloth. Oh yes, when giving a party, I don't think you should attempt to wash the glasses that same evening. You will be tired and perhaps a little the worse for wine. Stack them carefully in one specific place and do them next morning. (When will somebody invent a domestic dish-washer similar to the commercial ones which have special and individual compartments for the glasses. You simply load up, switch on, and let the machine take care of it all. It would revolutionize entertaining! Come on, somebody, there is a fortune to be made.)

I seldom serve liqueurs after dinner, but if I have any duty-free brandy (and we should all *always* bring back our full quota, but do look around as you can be taken to the cleaners on some airlines), I offer that. But I find that everybody likes a glass of port, and I always have in a South African KWV port-style wine. There's some jiggery-pokery whereby they can't call it true port over here, but believe you me, if you can get hold of some your eyes will sparkle when sipping it.

Something I have always done when serving curry is to offer my guests a small glass of gin and ice-cold milk. Eyebrows are often raised, but when I lived in Africa, we always served this at our Sunday curry parties when the actual eating started mid-afternoon. We would start off with light beers or shandies usually.

Buck's Fizz is a wonderful drink with which to start a lazy day, to celebrate a special day, or to start a summer party. I have heard that it was served in California when the prospectors struck gold; it cost a buck a glass. *But*, on more reliable authority, I'm told it was invented by the barman of Buck's Club in the early 1920s. Traditionally made with champagne and fresh orange juice, I make it instead with sparkling white Burgundy or Nederburg Premiere Cuvée Brut, topping half a glass of *fresh* orange juice up with the wine.

Another nice summer aperitif that I discovered in Florence some years ago is Campari based. Put half a measure of Campari into a champagne glass. Liberally dowse a sugar lump with Angostura Bitters, and put into the glass with a twist of orange peel. Top up with a sparkling white wine. It is sharp, sparkling, cool and refreshing.

For a wonderful pick-you-up, the only spirit of which I thoroughly approve, is the vodka served with tomato juice in Bloody Mary (page 170). With all that vitamin C, I feel it does me much more good than harm! The following recipe for lemonade, well-iced and garnished with fresh cherries and lots of fresh mint, is lovely with a generous dash of Pimms No. 1. Over the festive season the home-made Egg Flip on page 18 is delicious, and any cup of hot milk served late at night prior to going to bed is the better for a tot of scotch or brandy

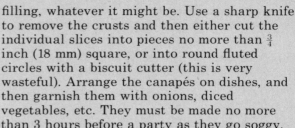

added, as well as a little finely grated fresh nutmeg or chocolate.

Home-made Lemonade

I always have home-made lemonade in the fridge when we have summer weather as it is such a good thirst-quencher and infinitely superior to the fizzy commercial type which is so expensive and 'orrible.

Put the rind and juice of 3 lemons and 1 orange into a large porcelain or earthenware jug. Add 4 oz (100–125 g) castor sugar and pour on $\frac{1}{2}$ pint (300 ml) boiling water. Stir from time to time, and when cool, put in the fridge. Serve with a few slices of fresh lemon and a sprig of fresh mint.

Drinks Party Snacks

The following idea for drinks party snacks are very basic 'finger foods'. The canapés *look* wonderful as well as tasting good; the Portuguese savouries, crispy and sardiney, are good fodder for staving off too much alcohol, and are ideal for this kind of party when you're desperately trying to hold handbags, glasses, food and shake hands all at the same time! Parrots' Eyes are more substantial and very unusual. You could also serve some of the starters throughout the book which are small enough to pick up in your fingers and eat – the avocado balls with smoked salmon (page 47), tiny tomatoes stuffed with avocado (page 48) or the tuna-filled hard-boiled eggs or celery stalks (page 161), for instance.

Canapés

Canapés originally got their name from the French, meaning 'sofa', since these pre-dinner titbits were eaten whilst sitting quite posh in the drawing-rooms and salons! They're a bit of a fiddle to prepare, but with patience and lots of time, you can make a little food go a long way.

I occasionally use a biscuit base but, more often than not, I use thickly buttered wholemeal bread, pumpernickel or, better still, the brown bread recipe on pages 35–6. Use the latter when it is a few days old, and cut each slice about $\frac{1}{4}$ inch (6 mm) thick. Be generous with your best soft butter, and then your

filling, whatever it might be. Use a sharp knife to remove the crusts and then either cut the individual slices into pieces no more than $\frac{3}{4}$ inch (18 mm) square, or into round fluted circles with a biscuit cutter (this is very wasteful). Arrange the canapés on dishes, and then garnish them with onions, diced vegetables, etc. They must be made no more than 3 hours before a party as they go soggy.

Some nice combinations are:

☐ peanut butter spread thickly and topped off with a baby silver onion;

☐ cream cheese coloured with a pea purée, tomato purée, mustard seeds, chopped herbs, apricot purée or turmeric, and then topped off with olive slices, parsley, capers, tomato wedge, lumpfish roe (the red rather than the black), or an avocado wedge;

☐ pieces of tinned sardine topped with finely chopped onion and parsley;

☐ sardines mashed with hard-boiled eggs, topped with an olive;

☐ egg yolk slices covered with 3 drained tinned shrimps, topped with the merest pinch of paprika;

☐ tinned salmon mashed with a little butter and very finely chopped chives;

☐ the thinnest wedge of fresh pear topped with an oily smoked tinned oyster;

☐ finely chopped gherkins mixed with chopped hard-boiled egg, a little salted butter and the merest touch of anchovy essence;

☐ cheese and herb pâté topped with shrimps;

☐ mushroom pâté or chicken liver pâté topped with capers;

☐ well drained and washed tinned red kidney beans;

☐ purée of baked beans with the merest touch of curry powder;

☐ plain, lemon or sweet and sour mayonnaise piped on, garnished with fresh garden peas or washed baby beetroot;

☐ any end bits of cheese 'potted' with a drop of port – use 4 oz (100–125 g) grated cheese to 1 oz (25 g) melted butter and a tablespoon of inexpensive port – and garnished with a walnut half;

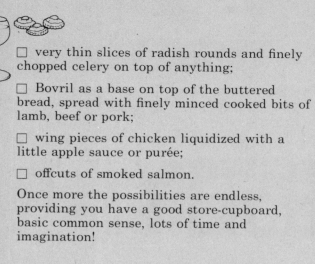
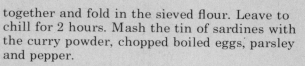

☐ very thin slices of radish rounds and finely chopped celery on top of anything;

☐ Bovril as a base on top of the buttered bread, spread with finely minced cooked bits of lamb, beef or pork;

☐ wing pieces of chicken liquidized with a little apple sauce or purée;

☐ offcuts of smoked salmon.

Once more the possibilities are endless, providing you have a good store-cupboard, basic common sense, lots of time and imagination!

Portuguese Savoury

Whenever I go to a drinks party (and it's not often, I assure you), I nearly always find a quiet corner where I can park my carcase away from the milling crowd, with a convenient table on which I can place both my plate of grub, and more important still, my glass of hooch. Woe betide anybody who tries to make small talk with me during the eating and drinking part of the party!

makes 24 crescents

8 oz (225 g) butter

8 oz (225 g) cream cheese

8 oz (225 g) plain flour, sieved

1 9 oz (250 g) tin sardines, in oil or tomato sauce

½ teaspoon curry powder

2 hard-boiled eggs, roughly chopped

2 tablespoons parsley, finely chopped

freshly ground black pepper

Put the soft butter, cheese and flour into your Kenwood bowl and mix to a dough with the K beater. Otherwise cream the butter and cheese

together and fold in the sieved flour. Leave to chill for 2 hours. Mash the tin of sardines with the curry powder, chopped boiled eggs, parsley and pepper.

On a floured surface roll the dough out very thinly. Cut into 5 inch (12.5 cm) squares and then cut each square in half to form triangles. Place a teaspoon of the sardine filling into the centre of each triangle and then roll from the side edge towards the point to make a shape similar to a croissant, twisting the ends towards each other to make the half-moon shape. Place these crescent-shaped objects on to a baking tray, leave to chill for a couple of hours, and then bake in a pre-heated oven at 425°F (220°C), Gas 7, for 20 minutes.

If serving at a supper or dinner party accompany them with fresh tomato sauce. There's no reason why you shouldn't make them larger, filling them with smoked trout or haddock similarly tarted-up!

Parrot's Eye

This is a dish I always choose when I visit Alan Bobbe's Bistro in Nairobi, and its basic simplicity never fails to satisfy and appeal to me.

From pieces of well-done toast, cut out 3 inch (7.5 cm) round circles. Lightly butter these and then spread them with sour cream or Philadelphia cream cheese whipped up with the rind and juice of a lemon. Smooth dead flat, and coat generously with red Danish lumpfish roe (or better still, with the American red salmon roe which is infinitely better but much more expensive). Plonk the raw yolk of a quail's egg (they can be found now in good poulterers, as more and more quail are being 'farmed' for restaurant tables) in the middle and circle it with a thin onion ring. A few minute sprigs of parsley for garnishing, and you have a 'fishy tartare'!

FIVE
UNIVERSITY

I will never forget when I acquired Miller Howe. I was very low, and virtually out of work, when I read in the *Westmorland Gazette* about the sale of a house with panoramic views. I phoned my long-standing friend and partner, Drew Hendry, in London and when he spoke, I took a deep breath and hurriedly said, 'Have you got £28,000?' to which he immediately replied, 'More than likely.'

Drew came up on the sleeper that night and we drove past Miller Howe around breakfast time. We were excited enough then, but it wasn't until we met the owners Mr and Mrs Boardley at 11 am that we both realized the potential of the house and the site. It was a glorious early summer day and the house seemed to sparkle as much inside as the sun shone outside. We pretended to be cool, but after leaving the house I rushed down to see my bank manager to spell out all my requirements. I wanted to match the sum of money Drew was intending to invest, and although one hears terrible tales about banks and bank managers, the National Westminster Bank in Bowness gave me an encouraging reply in the space of 4 hours (and up to this day have been marvellous in looking after our needs). Later that afternoon, after slight haggling on Drew's part (the Scottish coming out in him) Miller Howe was ours for the princely sum of £26,500.

The next 5 weeks were traumatic as I set the target date of 1 July 1971 for opening – I desperately needed the income. In that short time I acquired carpets, furniture, linen, cutlery, crockery, kitchen equipment, uniforms, sought a licence, applied for change of use, marketed, staffed – and for the 3 days prior to opening, I never went to bed (which those days was in the cellar next to the boiler-house with a wash-basin under the stairs and a Bendix washing-machine as bedside table, a state of affairs lasting until August of 1972)! But despite all that, the eventual launch was a success and even during all the chaos of that first season, we planned the first winter's alterations, and drew up plans for the building of a new wing for the following winter. Although I was so green in those early days, I also seemed to be lucky: everything we planned turned out right, and as the capital outlay grew so did the business.

But it was on the 18th October 1971 that we first started to be noticed nationally, when Derek Cooper kindly wrote in the *Guardian* 'My heart leapt up when I beheld . . .', and from then until the end of the first season it was a matter of full houses. The press, and particularly the specialist food press, is very important to our trade and, having realized how influential *The Good Food Guide* was after a lovely entry in the 1969/70 edition for the 'Tonight at 8.30' Restaurant at the Hydro, Windermere, the new Miller Howe staff and I awaited the publication of the 1972 *Guide* with trepidation. We were tickled pink when not only had Miller Howe got a lovely write-up (with a dreadful caricature of me), but had been given the coveted Pestle and Mortar Award. This was not only good for our morale but excellent for business. Even now as the March publication date approaches everybody gets a bit nervous – it's like waiting for the end-of-term reports from school! We are very proud to have had the top awards now for 10 years, but are certainly not smug or complacent about it.

And it was in May 1974 that we really felt all our efforts had been worthwhile when Margaret Costa wrote a superb article on the Lakes in

Gourmet, with beautiful copy about Miller Howe. From then on we felt we had arrived. Margaret was such an influence in those early days – encouraging me to run my own place, sending media friends up to see what we were doing, bringing order to the kitchens, advising invaluably in every kind of way. I learned so much from her.

Cooking isn't what you know, but what you *still* have to learn, and one of the major joys of the business is that most of the professionals are nice people, and are only too pleased to share their knowledge with you (with one well-known exception, who keeps his recipes locked away in a Fort Knox type safe). And it is when one meets someone like Theodora FitzGibbon who spent 15 years working on her *The Food of the Western World* that one realizes how much there still is to learn (this particular book is our bible at Miller Howe, and it should be on every cookery bookshelf the length and breadth of the country). Each and every time I go off on my travels, I am stimulated by the people I meet, by the food I eat, by the recipes I am given or am inspired to create. Thus my staff and I continually learn, improve, and enlarge our repertoire – so satisfying.

Which brings me back to Miller Howe. Now, of course, 10 years after it was opened, the hotel is established and successful, partly due to the fact that I am blessed with the most loyal, kind, and friendly staff, 8 of whom have been with me for over 9 years. However affected it may sound, we *are* like one big family – mostly happy and always honest with one another – and despite working in such close proximity we all thoroughly enjoy a short holiday together at the end of each busy season. And each winter the cooks and I literally tour the world with British Airways in an attempt to dispel the myths about British Country House Cooking, and to spread the Miller Howe message. In 1980 it was South Africa, Japan, New York, Boston and San Francisco; in 1981 South Africa again, the Middle East and North America; our 1982 plans already include Australia and New Zealand.

Starters

Creamed Apple Soup

serves 10

2 lb (1 kg) Granny Smith apples

4 oz (100 g) butter

8 oz (225 g) onions, finely chopped

1 pint (600 ml) dry cider

1 pint (600 ml) good chicken stock

I made this often at Miller Howe in the autumn of 1980 as our apple trees had a splendid crop, and Mike the gardener seemed to be forever coming in loaded up with cardboard boxes full. Apple sauce with everything became the theme, and this soup featured at least once a week on the menu. There are many different garnishes with which to ring the changes, and the soup can both be served hot, or chilled, when it is ideal for a picnic.

Peel and core the apples, and cut into thin slices. Melt the butter in a large saucepan, and sauté the onions slowly until golden. Add the sliced apples and $\frac{1}{4}$ pint (150 ml) of the cider. Put a double thickness of dampened greaseproof paper over the ingredients, put the lid on, and simmer over a very low heat for about 45 minutes, until the apples have fallen. Add the remaining cider, and the chicken stock, and then liquidize the soup. Pass the liquidized soup through a fine sieve into a clean pan.

If you wish to serve it cold, leave it to cool, and then chill in the fridge. Garnish it, in cold dishes, with a generous sprinkling of finely chopped chives and a thin onion slice. Or you can add a pinch of curry powder or the merest sprinkling of freshly ground cinnamon. Or put it in a vacuum flask to take it on a picnic.

If you want to serve it hot, reheat gently and check the seasoning; both salt and sugar might be needed. Garnish, in hot bowls, with a generous tablespoon of natural yoghurt into which you have stirred a teaspoon of horseradish sauce, and then a liberal sprinkling of grated Lancashire or Cheddar cheese. A tablespoon of chopped chives adds a touch of class (and colour), and if you're feeling in a celebratory and generous mood, a couple of tablespoons of Calvados will really enhance the apple taste.

Sage and Onion Soup

serves 12

2 lb (900 g) onions

2 pints (1·2 litres) milk

12 fresh sage leaves

salt, freshly ground black pepper

12 tablespoons tomato provençale (page 175)

This soup is cooked in the oven and then liquidized, and has such an unusual flavour, particularly if served with tomato provençale.

Peel the onions (remembering to put the skins into a stockpot if you have one on the go), and roughly chop into fairly small chunks and transfer to a casserole. Add the milk and the leaves of fresh sage, cover with a lid, and bake in the oven at 350°F (180°C), Gas 4, for 2 hours. Liquidize and pass through a sieve, and lo and behold, you have your soup.

When re-heating prior to serving add the seasonings, and should the flavour be a trifle bitter (so much depends on the strength of taste in the fresh sage), add a little castor sugar. I usually garnish the soup with a slice of fried apple, floating it on top of each individual dish as an island to carry the tablespoon of tomato provençale. A sprinkling of chopped chives or parsley will finish the dish off.

serves 20

1 lb (450 g) fresh chicken livers

8 oz (225 g) belly pork, off the bone

1½ tablespoons black peppercorns

2 tablespoons walnut oil

2 oz (50 g) butter

1 medium onion, finely chopped

4 cloves garlic, crushed with 2 teaspoons salt

1 tablespoon marjoram

¼ pint (150 ml) orange curaçao

¼ pint (150 ml) double cream

juice and rind of 2 oranges

2 oz (50 g) walnuts, finely chopped

Orange, Walnut and Pepper Chicken Liver Pâté

Check through the livers, remove any stringy pieces, and rinse them in cold water. Put the belly pork in a roasting tray and cook at 425°F (200°C), Gas 7, for 1 hour until well done, and then cut up into 1 inch (2·5 cm) cubes. Do *not* use the crackling.

Fry off the peppercorns in the walnut oil, remove them, then add the butter and fry off the onion, garlic and marjoram until nice and golden. Add the chicken livers and simmer gently for 15 minutes.

When cold, add the pieces of belly pork, the orange curaçao and cream, and blend in a liquidizer. Pass through a metal sieve into a bowl. Check the seasoning, and fold in the juice and rind of the orange together with the finely chopped walnuts.

Leave to chill in the fridge. When serving, scoop out with an icecream scoop and place on watercress lightly coated with walnut oil. Serve with a dessertspoon of natural yoghurt poured over each scoopful, and garnish with chopped walnuts, and red pepper diamonds.

The recipe can, of course, be halved, and it freezes very well.

Sautéed Duck Livers with Watercress Salad

One of my weaknesses is *foie gras*. A tin or jar is always to hand in my refrigerator and, perhaps twice a year on a grey day, when nothing has gone right, I'm tempted to make some wholemeal toast and consume a whole tin by myself. A wicked extravagance, I know, but I always feel better afterwards – and, for the bank manager's peace of mind, I generally confine myself to only 1 or 2 such days out of 365! (See page 162 to appreciate just *how* I spoil myself!)

Good fresh duck livers are a delicious substitute, but *do* try to get fresh ones. They're easily available frozen in supermarkets, in ½ lb (225 g) or 1 lb (450 g) packets, and the flavour is much the same – but it's the texture that's different as the very, very fine skin on the frozen ones is invariably split, making it rather difficult to cook a whole liver without some of it spewing out!

Marinate the fresh cleaned livers in milk for 24 hours. About 2 per person makes a good starter. Place the drained livers on a well-buttered tray and, if available, sprinkle a little fresh marjoram over them. Cook at 350°F (180°C), Gas 4, for 10 minutes only and then serve at once on a watercress salad dressed with a vinaigrette made partially with walnut oil. If fresh cherries are in season they make an ideal accompaniment.

TERRINES

One of the best things about terrines is that they can be made in a quiet time and served when everything is hectic. They store extremely well in the refrigerator. I give here specific recipes for various terrines, but any left-over bits of uncooked meat can be made into a good terrine after marinating in this or that – port, brandy, marsala, yoghurt – and adding bits and bobs – pistachio nuts, stuffed olives, sticks of fresh asparagus. It always reminds me of my childhood when, on Thursdays (the day before pay-day at the shipyard when the purse and belly were both light), my Grandmother used to concoct a mince dish, literally out of nothing, which we always ate with relish. Nowadays these left-overs can easily be made into the more sophisticated terrine.

The best dish to use for terrines is the commercial terrine container, brick-like in shape, measuring 12×3 inches (30.5×7.5 cm), made of steel, and usually a smart terracotta colour, with a close-fitting lid. However, if you haven't got a proper terrine dish, and you intend to make a terrine for the first time, simply use a 1 or 2 lb (450 or 900 g) bread or loaf tin and proceed in the normal way. But when you come to cook the terrine, you must completely cover the filled, finished tin with about 5 layers of foil before you put it in the oven (to substitute for the lid which holds the rising terrine down).

Terrines need always to be lined, to hold the filling together, and to make it more attractive and easier to serve. I usually use good smoked bacon, but some recipes call for pancakes, and others blanched cabbage or lettuce leaves. You can use strips of blanched leeks and there are people who use strips of pork fat. But bacon is the easiest and tastiest, and each dish needs approximately 14 oz (400 g) to line the base, sides and then the top of the filled dish. The better the bacon, inevitably the better the cooked terrine will taste. So many people try to economize by using cheap, tasteless bacon. I always use a smoked rindless middle bacon sold in vacuum packs, which stores well, tastes superb, and has practically no water content so doesn't shrink.

You need to take care when lining the terrine. I usually start by putting the dish in front of me, the short end nearest me, and then run an imaginary line right down the middle of the base. I use this as my starting point for each piece of bacon, putting the fatter end on this and then running the bacon piece to the left-hand side first. After ensuring that it fits tightly into the corner, I run it up the edge of the dish and then leave it flapping out over the side. Do one side and one end and then repeat the process on the opposite side, bearing in mind that you want every single bit of the terrine to be covered so that none of the filling will run out. When the filling/s are in and finished, simply flop the bacon flaps over left/right/left/right ending up with the 2 end bits and, lo and behold, the terrine, looking like a laced-up boot, is ready for cooking.

Cooking is done in a normal roasting tray into which the terrine dishes are placed and into which warm water is poured until it reaches half way up the sides of the dish. If you are going to make 3 or 4 terrines at once, I've found that each individual terrine needs space completely round it to cook evenly, so you may need 2 roasting trays on 2 shelves in the oven.

When the terrines are cooked (to test, remove the lid and gently press the contents, which should feel slightly springy like a perfectly cooked Victorian sponge!), they should be weighted down and left in the warm kitchen to cool. I find an ordinary house brick placed on top of each terrine ideal. They solidify and 'gel' in the coldroom or fridge and then slice perfectly. To get the terrine out of the dish prior to serving, run a palette knife carefully round the 4 sides, easing the bacon (or casing) away from the sides of the terrine (you should feel a slight suction). Then you place the terrine into a basin of boiling water for literally 10 to 20 seconds, have to hand a slicing board, and invert the terrine, giving it a sharp knock and shake, and the terrine block should fall out on the board ready to carve. A sharp serrated knife is the best for carving, and when I do this I place the narrow end of the terrine against the used terrine dish to act as a wedge.

Each terrine should give you from 18 to 24 slices, depending entirely on how much you wish each guest to eat! If you find the carving difficult and the terrine slightly sloppy (fish and vegetable terrines can be so), put the terrine into the freezer for about 10 minutes when out of the mould, but do allow a longer time for serving so that the cut slices come round to room temperature and in no way taste 'fridge-y'. It's also quite a good idea to dip your carving knife into a large jug of boiling water after each slice. When you first slice terrines you could well find it handy to have a fish slice at the end of the terrine so that, when the slice is cut, it topples over onto the fish slice and is then easy to transfer to the serving plate. It becomes automatic after a while, I do assure you!

Salads are very important with terrines, and so with each recipe I also give an idea for a salad to use.

serves 20–24

1 lb (450 g) raw chicken breasts

salt, freshly ground black pepper

3 egg whites

½ pint (300 ml) double cream

2 teaspoons Davis powdered gelatine

1 small green cabbage

8 oz (225 g) frozen peas, defrosted

1 tablespoon cream

4 oz (100 g) mushrooms

1 oz (25 g) butter

4 oz (100 g) baby carrots

2 oz (50 g) small French beans

8 oz (225 g) mushroom pâté (page 173)

Vegetable Terrine

This terrine (which looks stunning) is quite fiddly, but the results are really worth it. Use a terrine measuring 12 by 3 inches (30·5 × 7·5 cm). There are many different ways of doing it, but this is one of my favourites.

The first stage is that of the chicken cream which acts as the base of the terrine and holds the vegetables in place. Cut the chicken into cubes and place in a Magimix or blender. Add the seasonings and the egg whites and whirl until quite smooth. Leave in the container and chill for 2 hours in the fridge, then return to the machine and whisk in the cream and gelatine.

The next stage is to prepare and blanch off the vegetables. Do remember that they will all have a further 45 minutes cooking in the oven so they must be cooked for minutes only, left very, very *al dente*. To add a little more flavour, you could put a sprig of mint with the peas, a little sugar with the carrots, and a touch of coriander with the mushrooms.

Cabbage: Separate into leaves and cut the thick stalks away. Blanch for 1 minute only.
Peas: Defrost thoroughly, and cook lightly for 5 minutes only. Strain. Purée them with the tablespoon of cream.
Mushrooms: Lightly fry them off in the butter and leave to dry on kitchen paper.
Carrots: Cut into thin strips and then cook lightly for about 2 minutes.
French beans: Top and tail and blanch for 2 minutes.

You will need 3 individual piping bags with large nozzles for the third stage. Line the terrine with the blanched green cabbage leaves, making sure they all overlap and are tight enough to prevent any of the filling oozing out. On the base, pipe a thin layer of the chicken cream and then, leaving a small gap from the side edges, place parallel rows of cooked carrot strips lengthwise down the dish. Gently press the carrots down, and then pipe on more chicken cream. Into this, place carefully lengthwise in similar parallel rows, all the small French beans, and gently ease these down into the mixing. Next pipe in the mushroom pâté and scatter the cooked mushrooms on top. Then pipe on the cooked and puréed peas mixed with the balance of the chicken mixture.

To ring the changes you can use asparagus, baby courgettes, artichokes etc, and try always to visualize what the end result is going to be like. (See the photograph for another idea.) Cover the top with the green cabbage leaves, and then cover well with a suitably sized piece of double thickness greaseproof paper, before putting on the terrine lid. Pre-heat the oven to 375°F (190°C), Gas 5, and when you're ready to cook, turn it down to 350°F (180°C), Gas 4. Put the terrine in the bain marie in the oven and cook for 45 minutes.

This terrine can be served warm with a light hollandaise sauce (page 177), but I personally prefer to eat and serve it cold. I let it cool, then I chill it, and eventually serve it with a fresh cold tomato sauce (page 175), lightly flavoured with tarragon vinegar. It needs practically no garnishing as the pattern of the vegetables themselves is a feast for the eye.

Savoury Spinach Terrine

serves 20–24

8 oz (225 g) belly pork

at least 2 lb (or 1 kg) spinach

4 oz (100 g) butter

freshly ground black pepper

14 oz (400 g) smoked bacon

4 oz (100 g) cream cheese

3 eggs

2 fat cloves garlic, crushed

2 tablespoons fresh herbs of choice

Put the belly pork in a roasting tray and cook at 425°F (220°C), Gas 7, for 1 hour, then take off the bone, remove skin, and cut into cubes. Cook the spinach in the butter with the pepper, and drain well. To ensure that no liquid is left after straining in a colander, place the spinach by handfuls on a dinner plate, top it with another plate and press together – you will be amazed at how much additional water comes out. You should end up with approximately 1 lb 12 oz (800 g).

Line the terrine with the smoked bacon and whizz everything else round in the Magimix or blender. When everything has been brought together, pour the mixture into the lined dish. Cook in a bain marie at 350°F (180°C), Gas 4, for 45 minutes.

A generous handful of skinned pistachio nuts make a welcome addition to this and, if you have a few spears of cooked fresh asparagus to hand these can be layered through too – similar to the vegetable terrine.

I like to serve this with a salad of apple, celery and walnuts. Make a French dressing to your personal taste, using a third walnut oil for the oil content. On a mandoline, slice peeled and cored apples (they look much more attractive this way) and leave to marinate for a few hours in the dressing. Then either prepare celery twirls, or finely dice washed dried celery and scatter this with the apples and garnish with shelled halved walnuts.

Marinated Breast of Chicken in Cheese Terrine

serves 20–24

2 chicken breasts

2 tablespoons cooking brandy

rind and juice of 2 fresh limes

8 oz (225 g) belly pork, off the bone

1½ lbs (700 g) cream cheese

2 eggs

3 fat cloves garlic

4 tablespoons fresh herbs

14 oz (400 g) smoked bacon

Skin and bone the breasts (if still on the bone) and marinate in the cooking brandy and rind and juice of the limes. The longer you leave them in the marinade, the more flavoursome your terrine will be. Roast the pork for 1 hour in an oven set at 425°F (220°C), Gas 7, then remove skin and mince finely.

Mix together the good cream cheese, eggs, crushed juicy garlic, and at least 4 tablespoons of finely chopped herbs – chives, parsley, marjoram, what you like or what is available. Beat into this the finely minced belly pork.

Line the terrine with the bacon and then put in half the cheese and pork mixture. Onto this place lengthwise the 2 chicken breasts. Top off with the balance of the cheese and pork mixture. Fold over the hanging smoked bacon and cover with a double thickness of greaseproof paper and the lid, and cook in a bain marie at 350°F (180°C), Gas 4, for 45 minutes.

A pleasant salad to go with this unusual terrine is one of alternate slices of skinned tomato and orange, coated with a French dressing, finely chopped spring onions and fresh seasonal herbs.

serves 20–24

about 6 pancakes (page 86)

1 lb (450 g) good quality frozen prawns

rind and juice of 1 fresh lemon

2 teaspoons horseradish cream

1 tablespoon fresh parsley or chives

5 medium eggs

½ pint (300 ml) double cream

8 oz (225 g) smoked salmon, chopped

4 oz (100 g) cream cheese

2 teaspoons dried dill weed

Prawn and Smoked Salmon Terrine

Line the terrine with the pancakes. Defrost the prawns by leaving them out of the freezer overnight in a cool place then open the bag, and drain the prawns in a colander. Place them in a roasting tray and put them into the warming drawer of an oven – you will be surprised by the amount of liquid that still comes out of them over a drying-out period of about half an hour.

Place the dry prawns into a blender and add the rind and juice of the lemon, the horseradish cream and parsley or chives. Blend to a smooth cream. Add 3 of the 5 eggs one by one, and beat well, and then put the mixture in the container in the fridge for at least 8 hours.

When chilled put back onto the machine and slowly beat in the double cream. Pour half this mixture out into the pancake-lined terrine, and transfer the other half to a bowl. Rinse out the container, add the smoked salmon and cream cheese, and whizz together with the other 2 eggs and the dill weed. Put this rather thicker mixture on top of the prawn cream in the terrine, and top off with the balance of the prawn cream. Flap over the hanging pieces of pancake, and put another pancake or 2 on the top to cover if necessary, and cover with a double thickness of greaseproof paper. Put on the lid and put the terrine into a bain marie and bake for 1 hour at 350°F (180°C), Gas 4. Remove from the oven and leave to cool.

Serve with a cucumber, yoghurt and fresh herb salad. Or a most unusual and pleasant salad to go with this is cucumber, kiwi fruit and yoghurt with a little dill weed on top. both salads are on page 134.

For a more professional-looking terrine, put each of the 2 mixings – the prawn and cream, and the salmon and cream cheese – into separate piping bags. On the base of the lined terrine, pipe one of the mixtures in a strip down the left-hand side, and then another strip down the right-hand side. With the other mixing in the other bag, pipe down the middle. For the second layer the middle mixing is used on the 2 sides and the lower outer mixing in the middle. Rather complicated, but you are trying to achieve a chess-board effect!

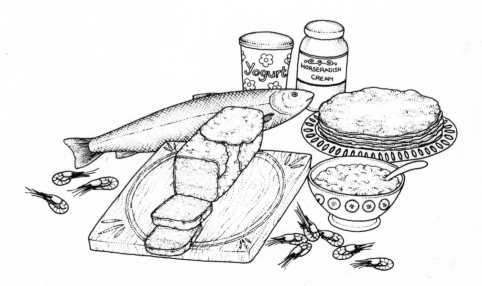

serves 12

1 duck, about 4 lb (1·8 kg)

4 oz (125 g) fillet of pork, in 1 piece

5 oz (150 g) natural yoghurt

10 green peppercorns

4 oz (125 g) kidneys, cleaned and halved

$\frac{1}{4}$ pint (150 ml) madeira

2 oz (50 g) chicken livers

$\frac{1}{4}$ pint (150 ml) milk

$\frac{1}{2}$ lb (225 g) sausagemeat

ground nutmeg and coriander

salt, freshly ground black pepper

Savoury Duck Slice

This is very similar to a terrine but you don't use a terrine mould as the skin of the duck acts as the holder of the ingredients. This is one dish that can use up many left-overs of uncooked meat, but this is how I have done it – and most successfully.

Marinate the fillet of pork in the yoghurt with the green peppercorns for a few days, and the kidneys in the madeira. Soak the chicken livers in the milk for a day at least. Spice the sausagemeat with nutmeg, coriander, salt and pepper.

Bone the duck, and lie it on 4 thicknesses of tinfoil on a board, splayed out rather like a real sheepskin rug. Place half the well-spiced sausagemeat over all the exposed flesh and skin and then place the piece of pork fillet right in the middle. Put the remaining sausagemeat on top and flatten it all round the sides of the fillet. Place the kidneys on next, followed by the chicken livers. Bring the edges of the duck skin together and sew with string to form a plump, full duck, or roll everything up in the foil which acts as a holder. The latter is so much easier, but both methods need support on both sides when cooking, preferably from warm clean house bricks.

Roast for at least $1\frac{1}{2}$ hours in the foil at 425°F (220°C), Gas 7. When cold, slice and serve on a tomato and orange salad, or a tomato herb salad.

POACHED EGGS

After trying all methods imaginable for poaching eggs, I would strongly advise you to invest in a non-stick egg-poaching pan – particularly as there are so many ways to use poached eggs for family meals and entertaining. The pans come in various sizes for 4, 6, 8 and even go up to 16 as used in the hotel. You might think this an extravagance, *but* there is no need at all to limit it entirely to poaching eggs, since the actual saucepan can have many other uses.

Put the saucepan on the stove with all the containers in place except one and fill it with cold water, just up to the base of the containers. Through the peep-hole of the unplaced container, you will see when the water starts to boil, and then you can turn the heat down to a constant simmer. Replace the final container and place a tiny knob of butter in each container. Sprinkle with freshly ground black pepper and a mere touch of salt and break in the fresh eggs. Rather than putting the metal lid back on the eggs I find a large pyrex plate placed over the eggs is best as I can then see all the time how the cooking of the eggs is progressing (continually taking off the lid results in a loss of temperature). Before your very eyes, the insipid albumen soon begins to turn to the set solid white and as you see this encroaching on the yolk, the process can easily be controlled. Have to hand a plastic tray lined with a double thickness of kitchen paper. Taking hold of the handle of each container, gently slide the cooked poached egg out onto the kitchen paper to drain. (Also have at hand a bowl of very cold water into which you dip your hands before taking hold of the little container handles which will be quite hot).

Sautéed Duck Livers (page 122) with a
watercress and orange salad.

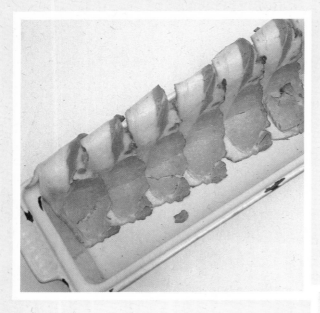

TERRINES (pages 123 to 128).

Lining the terrine with smoked bacon.

Piping the mixing into the fully lined
terrine for a chessboard Prawn and
Smoked Salmon Terrine.

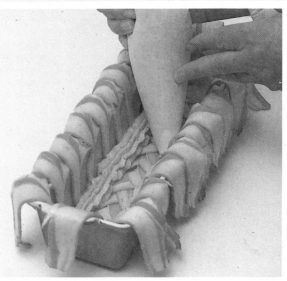

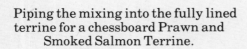

Savoury Duck Slice.

Goujons of Turkey Breast (page 107) with
Sweet and Sour Sauce (page 176),
garnished with parsley and mango slices.

Canapés (see page 116 for many other
suggestions) and Portuguese Savoury
(page 117).

Top. American Wheatmeal Chocolate
Rum Slice (page 141).
Foot. One way of using tinned tuna fish –
in a salad which looks like a flower on the
plate (page 161).

Top. A Pavlova, garnished with kiwi fruit
(page 167).
Foot. Just the job for a Sunday Morning at
home – the papers, baked curried nuts,
some music and a delicious Bloody Mary
(page 170).

Vegetable Terrine.

Prawn and Smoked Salmon Terrine.

Marinated Breast of Chicken in Cheese
Terrine.

LAMB TOURNEDOS WITH BLACKCURRANT CROUTONS (page 132).

Below. The finished tournedos served on blackcurrant croutons garnished with whole cloves of garlic.
Top left. After separating the long thin bones from the flesh, cut out the long thin fillet.
Top right. Two pieces of fillet, one secured with cocktail sticks ready to be fried.
Left. After spreading the crouton with blackcurrant jam, dip the edges into finely chopped parsley.

At breakfast the poached eggs should, of course, be transferred immediately to your pieces of hot, well-buttered toast or placed on a bed of spinach purée (see page 133). But poached eggs can be used in a variety of ways, mainly for starters, and here are a few ideas.

Poached Egg in Vegetable Nest with Hollandaise

This is a dish which needs a relatively large amount of your precious time if it is to be done well, but it's well worth the effort, as it's so pretty to look at (and good to eat). It looks best if you can present it on those china oyster-shaped shells (or the real ones provided by your charming fishmonger). A scorer is also vital (I don't know what I'd do without mine – such a simple gadget creates so many stunning effects), so *do* buy one!

You want to make individual nests of 3 to 4 inch (7–10 cm) strips of vegetables, cut with the scorer. It's difficult to specify the quantities you need of vegetables, but at least 2 oz (50 g) of mixed vegetables per person.

Colour is important too, for the nest, so choose your vegetables with that in mind. Use the purple outside skin of the aubergine, the golden orange of the carrot, the pure white of the turnip, all cut with the scorer. With a very small, sharp-pointed stainless steel knife, make similar lengths of nice thin strips of celery, and white, red and green cabbage. Put a saucepan two-thirds full of water on to boil with a touch of salt and a drop of vinegar, and get a metal sieve that will, when half-filled, submerge the vegetable strips in the boiling water. Blanch them, but *don't* leave them in any length of time or they will be all limp; wanting them nice and crisp, you put them *in*, count 3 slowly, and *out* they come. Leave to one side, well mixed, until the bowl fills up with cooked strips looking rather like a rainbow. I then sometimes leave them all day marinating in a French dressing or, occasionally, in a let-down mixture of coconut milk.

When you want to start putting the dish together for serving, select your serving plate or shell, and place a small handful of the mixed, marinated vegetable strips on to it. Push them out from the centre to make a shape literally like a bird's nest. In the middle of this bare space, pipe or spoon a blob of cheese and herb pâté (page 173), then on this carefully place your cold poached egg.

Make the hollandaise sauce (page 177) to which you have added some chopped, fresh herbs and simply coat the egg with this, remembering that *hollandaise sauce when stone cold is revolting* so this must be done at the last minute. To add a bit of sparkle to the serving, put the dish onto a doyleyed larger plate, and lay on it (if you live in the country) a fresh green fern. You can also garnish it with sprigs of parsley and watercress or, in summer, a sprig of redcurrants which not only look stunning, but add to the flavour.

You might, at this stage, think this is too troublesome a dish for you to do. Well, it isn't, and your trouble will be amply rewarded when you serve the eggs to your guests. You can virtually do it all up to the hollandaise at your leisure and even the ingredients for the hollandaise can be measured out ahead of time into the 2 saucepans and Magimix (but you must coat the egg yolks in the Magimix with some wine so that the egg yolks don't go crinkly and hard).

Poached Egg in Herb Lettuce with Mayonnaise

per person

1 egg

1 large lettuce leaf

1 teaspoon chopped mixed herbs

2 tablespoons home-made mayonnaise (page 177)

Poach eggs as described, and blanch the lettuce leaves in boiling salted water (they will curl up like a cigar but are so easy, when cool, to roll out flat again).

Sprinkle the flattened lettuce leaf with the mixed herbs, and place the poached egg on top *yolk side down*. Bring the 4 edges together forming a small package, and then turn it over. When serving, simply spoon over the mayonnaise.

For a touch of different flavour, a teaspoon of redcurrant or blackcurrant jelly may be whipped in to the mayonnaise, or the merest pinch of curry spices.

Salmon Cream

makes about 14 3 inch (7·5 cm) ramekins or spoon servings

8 oz (225 g) tinned salmon (weighed *after* removing skin and bones)

juices from the tin, made up to 5 tablespoons with cold water

$\frac{1}{2}$ oz (15 g) gelatine

1 pint (600 ml) double cream

1 tablespoon white wine vinegar

1 tablespoon horseradish cream

2 cucumbers, peeled, pipped and finely chopped

salt, freshly ground black pepper

4 egg whites, stiffly beaten

If you are out to really impress your guests, you can line the bases of your ramekins with decorated aspic, and you can also make one whole salmon cream to be spooned out and served on individual beds of shredded lettuce.

Put the gelatine into a small saucepan, cover with the 5 tablespoons of salmon juice and water, and leave to one side. Flake the salmon. Lightly whip the double cream with the vinegar and horseradish cream, and fold in the salmon along with the finely chopped cucumber and seasoning.

Reconstitute the gelatine by heating the saucepan very, very gently, until the gelatine has melted, and then pour it through a warmed sieve into the cream mixture. Fold it in, and then fold in the stiffly beaten egg whites.

Spoon out into the individual ramekin dishes *or* into a plastic bowl. Leave to set in the fridge, remembering to bring the cream or creams out of the fridge at least 30 minutes before serving.

Smoked Trout Cream

serves 6

2 smoked trout, about 6 oz (175 g) each

4 oz (100 g) rich cream cheese

$\frac{1}{4}$ pint (150 ml) double cream

rind and juice of $\frac{1}{2}$ lemon

pinch of nutmeg

$\frac{1}{2}$ tablespoon horseradish cream

2 egg whites

Skin and bone the trout (you should have at least 6 oz or 175 g weight of flesh left), and then flake the meat, being careful to see that you've removed every bone.

With an electric hand whisk, beat the cream cheese until smooth, then incorporate the double cream. Fold in the rind and juice of the lemon, the nutmeg, horseradish cream, and the flaked smoked trout.

In a metal bowl, beat the egg whites until stiff, combine with the trout mixing, and put into 6 individual glasses or 3 inch (7·5 cm) ramekins.

Chill and garnish for serving with a blob of cream decorated with a fanned-out cocktail gherkin, half an olive and a strip of tomato, placing the dishes on to ferned flowered plates. Serve with slices of buttered walnut and date loaf (page 36).

Main Courses

serves 4

2 ducks, about 3½ lb (1·6 kg) each

4 fresh limes

12 juniper berries, lightly crushed

2 tablespoons good oil

2 oz (50 g) butter

salt, freshly ground black pepper

Breast of Duck with Lime and Juniper

I might as well tell you that this is my very favourite new dish of 1981, particularly when served with the gin and lime sauce accompanying the next recipe.

Fresh ducks are the only kind I have used and the plumper the better. If it seems an expensive dish, remember that duck doesn't usually go very far anyway, and you can use the legs for terrines, and all the bones and skin make the most marvellous tasty stock. Remove the breasts from each duck (see page 98 for hints on how to do this) and skin them. Finely grate the rind of the limes and squeeze every drop of liquid out of the fruit into a bowl large enough to hold the duck breasts in one layer. Put in the crushed juniper berries, and soak the skinned breasts in this marinade for at least 4 whole days, turning daily.

I haven't the luxury of a modern barbecue range at Miller Howe but get the desired effect on the breasts by carrying out the following trick. Get an old metal coathanger, bend it in half, and bend more until you get 4 strands of wire, each separated by about ¾ inch (18 mm). Heat these strands over a naked gas light, holding the other end in a gloved or clothed hand, and press it down on each breast of duck, thus making 4 nice burnt brown barbecue marks on the flesh.

Lightly sprinkle the breasts with salt and pepper and fry off in the heated butter and oil for about 2 to 3 minutes on either side, depending on how you like your duck. Serve coated with the gin and lime sauce (following), and accompanied by potatoes with cream and cheese (page 24).

Fried Duck Skin Bits
Never, *never* discard duck skins. If you cut them up into very fine bits, and fry them off over a low heat, they become quite crisp, and when really cooked through are superb scattered over a plain green salad.

serves 4

4 large thin steak-size slices calves' liver

2 oz (50 g) seasoned flour

2 tablespoons good oil

2 oz (50 g) butter

Calves' Liver with Gin and Lime Sauce

The secret of cooking calves' liver is to fry it for as short a time as possible. You will be surprised to find, I am sure, that the cooking time is literally 2 or 3 minutes at the most on each side, resulting in liver that is beautifully soft and delicate, so, so tender, and slightly pink inside.

Pat the liver slices dry with kitchen paper and dip in seasoned flour (plain flour to which you have added salt and freshly ground black pepper). Thinly coat the bottom of your frying pan with the good cooking oil and, when hot, add the butter. With tongs gently lay the liver steak or steaks in to the hot fat and only cook until the blood starts to appear on the top surface and then gently turn over to do the other side. This should always, in my opinion, be done at the last moment and even if you are entertaining it isn't a tricky job to do!

1 oz (25 g) butter

½ medium onion, very finely chopped

juice and rind of 2 limes

1 clove fat juicy garlic, crushed

1 dessertspoon tomato purée

½ teaspoon Dijon mustard

¾ pint (400 ml) good chicken stock

¼ pint (150 ml) gin

salt, freshly ground black pepper

1 tablespoon castor sugar

1 tablespoon arrowroot with 1 tablespoon water

But it is the unusual sauce that for me makes this dish and this can be made in the morning and simply brought back to the temperature at which you wish to serve it. You can use oranges instead of limes, if you prefer that taste (the same *volume* of juice and rind).

Gin and Lime Sauce
Sauté off the onion, rind of the limes and the crushed garlic in the butter, and then add the tomato purée, Dijon mustard, chicken stock, gin, salt, pepper and sugar. Bring to the boil and simmer for at least 30 minutes. Pass through a sieve into a clean saucepan and bring back to the boil.

In a tea-cup mix the arrowroot with the water to a very smooth paste and as the sauce comes back to the boil add the arrowroot mixture. Stir continually over the heat for about 3 to 4 minutes. If leaving until later, cover with a butter paper to prevent a skin forming.

serves 2

2–4 cloves garlic, soaked in ½ pint (300 ml) milk for 30 minutes

2 lamb tournedos, prepared as in method

2 oz (50 g) butter (or dripping) for frying

2 bread croutons, same size as tournedos, fried in 2 oz (50 g) butter until golden

2 teaspoons blackcurrant jam

1 oz (25 g) parsley, finely chopped

¼ pint (150 ml) fresh lamb stock

1 tablespoon red or white wine

¼ oz (7 g) flour

¼ oz (7 g) butter

salt, freshly ground black pepper

Lamb Tournedos with Blackcurrant Croutons

Beef tournedos are expensive, so sometimes I make my own variation from best end of lamb. Neither is this a cheap dish, but it's ideal for special occasions and the meat left over can be used for moussaka or bobotie (see pages 79 and 52).

From 1 unchined and untrimmed best end of neck you should get 2, maybe 3 tournedos. Hold the joint upright, resting on the small flat end of the chops, with the long thin bones in your left hand. Carefully loosen the meat at the base of the bones, working in towards the long thin ones. Pull the skin, fat and meat back towards you, and carefully cut out the long thin fillet (this is like taking out the 'eye' of each chop, but in one long thin piece). Cut this in 2, then cut almost through each one again as if to make 4 pieces. Instead, open out the cut and stand on end. Secure with a cocktail stick.

At the end of the soaking period, bring the garlic and milk to the boil and then remove the garlic cloves (the milk will have taken most of the garlic flavour by this point, and so it is wonderful for using in soups and sauces). Dry the garlic and fry in hot butter until golden. Then fry the meat for 1 minutes on each side, to brown and seal, then 2 or 3 minutes more on each side, according to whether you prefer your lamb to be pink or well-cooked.

Spread the fried croutons with jam and dip the edges of each into the chopped parsley. Arrange on a warmed serving dish, and top each with lamb and garlic. Keep warm in the oven while you prepare the sauce.

Add the stock and wine to the juices in the pan and simmer, stirring in all the residue from the meat, for about 5 minutes. Rub the flour and butter to a paste and then drop tiny pieces of this, one at a time, into the pan, whisking as you do so. Keep adding the paste in this way until the sauce thickens just enough to glaze the meat. Season with salt and black pepper to taste, then pour over the lamb and serve immediately.

Vegetables and Salads

Purée of Spinach

serves 6–8 as one of at least two vegetables

1 lb (450 g) fresh spinach leaves

12 oz (350 g) butter

freshly ground black pepper

This is an extremely rich and delicious dish which is well worth the time and care it needs. It's ideal for a dinner party as it can be prepared the day before then re-heated in a double saucepan. It needs no tarting up at all with herbs or spices, but I must admit the merest hint of freshly grated nutmeg is rather pleasant.

Take the stalks carefully and tenderly off the spinach leaves. Cut 4 oz (115 g) of the butter up into little knobs and melt over a low heat in a thick bottom saucepan. Add the coarsely chopped clean spinach leaves and simmer slowly for 15 minutes. Remove, allow to cool and then liquidize and pass through a fine plastic sieve.

Melt a further 4 oz (115 g) butter and cook the spinach purée again until it has soaked up the second lot of butter. Leave to cool.

Finally repeat the process with the third amount of butter, then serve hot with liberal sprinklings of freshly ground black pepper.

Cabbage Baked with Lemon and Mint

1 lb (450 g) firm green cabbage

rind and juice of 2 lemons

½ teaspoon sea salt

freshly ground black pepper

2 tablespoons olive oil

2–4 sprigs fresh mint, chopped

One of the most popular vegetable dishes that we serve at Miller Howe is Baked Cabbage with Garlic and Juniper. This recipe is prepared in much the same way, but with the marvellously different tastes of lemon and mint. These quantities will serve 4 to 6, as one of 2 vegetables in a meal.

Remove the outer leaves and cut the cabbage into 4 sections. Cut out the firm, hard stalk from each quarter and then slice the cabbage very finely with a sharp stainless steel knife. Transfer to a bowl and mix with the finely grated rind of the lemons, the juice, salt, lots of pepper, and the chopped mint.

Slowly heat the olive oil in a 9 pint (5 litre) saucepan and, when beginning to smoke, throw in the cabbage and stir vigorously with a wooden spoon until each little bit of the cabbage is coated with the oil. Bake in a pre-heated oven for 15 minutes at 425°F (220°C), Gas 7, *or* if you're the proud owner of a Hostess trolley, transfer when well coated with oil to the appropriate dish, *without* baking in the oven, and it will come to no harm for up to 45 minutes.

Cucumber, Yoghurt and Fresh Herb Salad

serves 4

4 lettuce leaves

¼ cucumber (16 thin slices)

5 oz (150 g) natural yoghurt

2 tablespoons fresh herbs, chopped

This is a pleasant simple salad that can be served as a side dish with roast lamb, with prawn and smoked salmon terrine (page 127), or, on a sunny day, as a first course.

Finely shred your lettuce leaves at the last moment and arrange them in the middle of the serving plates in the shape of a small pyramid. Score and thinly slice the cucumber and then fan out 4 slices around the edge of the plate, but sloping towards the centre of the pyramid. Trail the natural yoghurt over the centre of the fanned-out cucumber circle, and then sprinkle on whatever fresh chopped herbs you have to hand.

If you are serving this salad as an actual course, it can be enhanced with sprigs of fresh mint cut up finely with the lettuce, and garnished at suitable intervals around the edge of the plate with black or green olives. If you have a sweeter tooth, black and green grapes and perhaps a couple of thin wedges of sweet greenhouse tomatoes. I have also, on occasions, left the thin scored cucumber slices for a couple of hours to marinate in a French dressing of my choice.

Cucumber, Kiwi Fruit, Yoghurt Herb Salad
This is just a little bit more special than the above but made in exactly the same way, alternating slices of kiwi fruit with the cucumber slices.

Caesar Salad

serves 8

about 4 slices good bread, crusts off

2 large cloves juicy garlic

¼ pint (150 ml) best olive oil (I personally use half walnut, half corn oil)

¼ teaspoon sea salt

2 large crisp heads of lettuce

rind and juice of 1 lemon

2 oz (50 g) Parmesan cheese, grated

freshly ground black pepper

a few drops of Worcestershire sauce

Practically every single American restaurant claims to make the finest Caesar Salad, and they are invariably served with much aplomb and showmanship, but varying in quality from simply superb to downright disgusting. I am a sucker for them and when travelling in the States I am drawn to a Caesar Salad like a bee to honeysuckle. I understand they originated at Caesar Cardini's restaurant in Tijuana in North Mexico, practically on the Californian/Mexican border, where Californians went to drink in their hordes, as if there were a second gold rush, during prohibition. The salad achieved its fame principally through the fact that lettuce – which we today take for granted – could only be consumed where it was grown, as refrigerated transportation was unknown, and salads were thought therefore to be rather grand.

I am sure I will offend someone by giving my version of this dish, and to him/her/them I apologize immediately if I haven't dug out the original recipe. There is so much to learn in cooking, but do try this version, and I think you/they will like it!

In the olden days, only cos lettuce was used, being taken up in the fingers and dangled into the mouth, as it was thought criminal to cut or tear the leaves. Much drama was attached to the actual making of the salad in the restaurant at the side of the diner's table. I must admit cos lettuce is delightful, but I use Iceland or Butterhead lettuce and often include some spinach leaves (at this stage puritans will put the book down and throw up their hands in horror).

The salad is enhanced and brought to life (as far as I am concerned) by the addition of lovely garlic croutons, and here absolutely no short cuts should be taken (not like some American restaurants, who use pre-packed croutons, tasting of oily polystyrene). The croutons (cut into small squares of about 1 inch or 2·5 cm) should be left, spread over the base of a baking tray, in the warming drawer of your oven, in the airing cupboard or on top of the kitchen boiler (to start the drying-out process). Remove the skin from the cloves of garlic and press the flesh to a smooth paste with the sea salt. Transfer this lovely mushy mess to a tea-cup and dribble in about 3 tablespoons of the olive oil to make a garlic sauce which you put in a medium sized frying pan and heat until it begins to smoke. Turn down the heat and cook off the dry bread croutons until they are brown and crisp, but do watch them and keep stirring them gently with a palette knife to make sure they don't burn.

The salad should be brought together as late as possible, so the only thing you can do earlier is to remove the stem from the lettuce, wipe the leaves clean with a dampened cloth, and store in the salad drawer of the fridge. I don't like to dump lettuce into a sink of water, and then whirl it around as the tender leaves become bruised. When you wish to serve the salad, simply toss the prepared lettuce in the rest of the olive oil which has been mixed with the juice of the lemon. Don't go about this operation as if you were bashing dough, but do it gently and lightly as you, again, don't want to harm the tissue of the leaves. I think it's done best in a large 14 inch (33·5 cm) plastic bowl which I find invaluable in my kitchen. Then fold in the grated Parmesan cheese (do try to use fresh, but the little sealed sachets are an acceptable substitute), and the rind of the lemon. Dole out into individual wooden bowls or china soup bowls, divide the croutons between them, and finish off with a generous sprinkling of pepper and a few drops of Worcestershire sauce.

Sometimes, if I use half lettuce and half fresh spinach, I give everybody a tablespoon of really well-cooked, very finely diced smoked bacon and half a finely chopped hard-boiled egg. Other pleasant additions I have had are chopped chives, the actual bacon fat used as part of the oil content, and a few leaves of basil to garnish the salad. But don't, whatever you do, be tempted to add some anchovies!

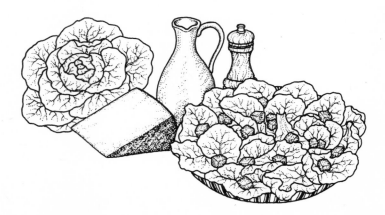

serves 8

1 large clove garlic

1 large lettuce

at least 8 oz (225 g) potato salad (page 174)

4 large or (better still) 8 small young tomatoes

16 anchovy fillets, halved lengthwise (about 2 tins)

32 small Kenya French beans

8 oz (225 g) tin tuna, in oil

32 black olives

6 teaspoons very small capers

1 tablespoon finely chopped chives (not essential)

8 large sprigs fresh parsley

2 tablespoons parsley, finely chopped

4 eggs, boiled for 8 minutes (see page 16)

about ¼ pint (150 ml) French dressing

Salade Niçoise

This is another one of those salads seen often on restaurant menus, and which can vary so much from place to place. A good salade niçoise is a joy to look at and an enormous pleasure to eat, while a bad one – with stale, over-cooked potatoes, commercial creams full of preservatives, limp soggy lettuce, vinegary dressings – is unspeakably horrid. Whatever you do, *don't* bring this salad together until the very last minute. But by all means, prepare the potato salad in its dressing in the morning, have the tomatoes wiped or skinned, the anchovies soaking in milk (if you prefer them less salty), and the lettuce wiped and stored in the salad drawer of the fridge.

Make the potato salad (page 174), and prepare the French beans. Top and tail them and pop into boiling water. When the water has come back to the boil, cook for 2 minutes at the most, then strain, put under a cold running tap, dry, and leave to get cold.

I'm the sort of person who likes, whenever possible, to serve individual dishes of salad for guests (then each guest has an eye-appealing treat placed in front of them, and also doesn't have to help himself!). I rub a peeled clove of garlic round the base and sides of the dishes and then repeat with a teaspoon of the French dressing. Arrange the torn-up lettuce leaves on the base of each dish, and in the middle place the potato salad. Arrange your segmented tomatoes around the perimeter of the bowl, with the flaked tuna fish and segmented hard-boiled eggs, so that they all resemble the outside petals of a daisy (the potato salad being the centre of the flower). Then arrange the French beans and anchovies in a lattice pattern on top of the potato salad. Sprinkle on the small capers and 4 black olives per plate, along with the chopped chives and parsley, and just as you're about to serve, spoon over the French dressing of your choice (see page 176) and garnish with the sprig of parsley.

Desserts, Cakes and Biscuits

COLD SOUFFLÉS

Whenever I announce that I'm going to demonstrate how to make a cold soufflé at one of the residential cookery courses, a 'holy' hush seems to descend on everybody in and around the kitchen. Eyes glaze, mouths open, and there is a look of horror on everyone's face! I must be honest and say that when I first tackled the following recipe, I had sleepless nights before I took the plunge. I now realize how stupid I was, and how easy it is to make a good cold soufflé.

The following recipe might at first sound rather off-putting, but I have attempted to make the whole process as clear as possible and then, at the end, I summarise the various points you should watch out for. Believe me, your soufflé will be very good indeed at your *first* attempt, but a damned sight better at about your sixth. But that is what cooking is all about: we continually learn and improve!

Lemon Soufflé

for 12–14 individual 3 inch (7·5 cm) ramekins

½ oz (15 g) gelatine

5 tablespoons dry white wine

6 eggs

10 oz (275 g) castor sugar

4 large lemons

1 pint (600 ml) double cream

4 oz (100–125 g) toasted nibbed almonds

First of all, prepare your ramekin dishes. You need 6 inch (15 cm) deep strips of good greaseproof paper of sufficient length to go one and a half times round each ramekin. Fold the greaseproof paper in half and wind this strip round the outside of the ramekin so that it stands proud of the top, and hold in place with a thick rubber band. When you pour the prepared soufflé into these dishes the mixture comes well over the top of the china/porcelain ramekin, with the greaseproof paper acting as the holder.

Place the powdered gelatine into a small saucepan and quickly add the dry white wine all at once. Shake until all the powder has dissolved and leave to one side.

Warm your mixing bowl by half filling it with hot water from the tap. Leave it for several minutes before emptying and then drying with a clean tea towel. Break the egg yolks into the clean warm bowl, putting the egg whites into a separate, perfectly clean metal bowl. Weigh out the sugar and have to hand. Grate the rind finely off the lemons onto a small plate. Cut the lemons in half, extract all the juice and put it in a small saucepan.

With the beater, start to whisk up the egg yolks, and when they have begun to look much lighter in colour, add a little of the castor sugar and continue to beat. Add a little more, and beat well after each addition. It will take about 15 minutes altogether to add the entire weight of sugar if you are to do it correctly, and this is why you have to have such patience at this stage. A soufflé is only as light as you make it, and the time spent at this stage, adding the sugar little by little, is vital. The more fluffy you can make the egg yolks, the more air is in the mixture; if you were to plonk all the sugar in at once, the poor yolks wouldn't have a chance of becoming feathery and white. So make sure you don't add another bit of sugar to the mixture (your beater working away at top speed) until you see that the texture is super light and white. When you do add sugar, the mixture will momentarily go down a fraction, but will very soon come back up again.

Meanwhile, start the fresh lemon juice warming through, and very lightly beat ½ pint (300 ml) of the double cream with the rind of the lemons. Don't beat the cream until it is as stiff as a poker, as you want to be able to combine it as lightly and as speedily as possible with the mousse-like egg yolk and sugar mixing. When the cream has just started to show outlines as your hand beater goes through it, *stop*! Rather it too sloppy than too stiff and do, *do* remember that should you take your cream out of a cold fridge it could well look thick. Don't be taken in by this as cold stiff is totally different in texture to beaten stiff. If your cream is fairly stiff when removed from the fridge, you will be surprised to see that, almost as soon as you start to beat, it goes quite limp and then takes time to come back to the streaky stage. (This may all sound terribly complex, but I think it important to explain things as fully as possible – and do double check with the summary at the end.)

When you are quite satisfied that the egg yolk and sugar mixture is ready (and it will have multiplied at least 4 times in volume) start to add the hot lemon juice tablespoon by tablespoon. Once again, remember to add it a little at a time, returning the saucepan to the heat to keep the juice warm until the mousse mixture has had time to absorb what you've just put in. This step will take quite a few minutes but there is no point in rushing things – if there were an easier way of doing a soufflé, believe you me, I would have found it. I *have* tried, but got nothing like the super results from this old-time correct way!

Pour the juice/egg yolk/sugar mixture out into the lightly beaten cream and with a long-handled spoon combine the 2 mixtures. This is where my large 14 inch (35·5 cm) rounded bottom plastic bowls come into their own – they're *super* for this type of job, and make light work of this stage of the recipe.

Put the gelatine in the saucepan over a low light, and when all soft and runny (remember to keep the temperature as low as possible so that you can put the saucepan base on the palm of your hand without discomfort), pour the melted gelatine through a warmed fine metal sieve onto the soufflé mixture. Once again use the long-handled spoon to make sure that the gelatine is evenly distributed.

Nowadays, at this stage, I tend to act the clever clogs by leaving the process of folding in the beaten egg whites as long as possible, but, for goodness sake, don't you be so 'grand' the first time you do a soufflé. As soon as the gelatine is folded in, beat the egg whites until they are quite stiff, but again, don't *over*-beat them. They should be billowy and wispy like clean white clouds for, remember, they have to be gently folded into the super light mixture you have already taken such pains to achieve.

When the whites are fluffy, put one-third of them on top of the soufflé and with that invaluable metal spoon, fold them in. Sometimes they are a bit prima-donna-ish, separating into small snowballs, and not blending in. If this is the case, don't panic, but swiftly zig-zag your spoon from side to side, breaking up the balls, and lo and behold, they will soon vanish. Don't forget to beat the remaining egg whites up again (even after a minute, beaten egg whites seem to drop), and fold them in gently.

Pour the soufflé mixture gently into the prepared greaseproof-collared ramekins, then put the ramekins into the fridge to chill. Just prior to serving, remove the rubber band and gently ease off the greaseproof paper. Use a palette knife to lightly coat the sides showing above the top of the dish with the remaining $\frac{1}{2}$ pint (300 ml) of cream which you have lightly whipped. Then, turning the ramekin on its side, roll this creamed bit in the toasted nibbed almonds. This is incredibly simple and it makes your sweet look very professional. Top off with a blob of cream and a quarter of a thin slice of lemon.

Summary of Important Points
1. Use *good* greaseproof paper for lining side of ramekins.
2. Add white wine to powdered gelatine in one fell swoop.
3. Have mixing bowl very warm for initial beating of egg yolks.
4. Add sugar little by little.
5. Add heated lemon juice little by little and keep it warm.

6. *Don't* beat the cream until it is thick and stodgy.
7. Only fold in one-third of the beaten egg white at first.

Orange Soufflé

Use the juice and rind of 2 to 3 oranges instead of the 4 large lemons. You want a similar volume of juice as that from the lemons.

Lime Soufflé

Use 6 limes, and add 3 finely chopped large sprigs of fresh mint.

Strawberry Soufflé

Use $\frac{1}{4}$ pint (150 ml) of the strawberry purée on page 140.

STRAWBERRIES

I always used to think that the name 'strawberry' had something to do with the fact that a lot of gardeners, then and now, spread straw underneath the growing fruits to keep them clean, keep pests away, and help build up the heat to let them ripen. But this is not so. The name is derived from the Anglo-Saxon *streowberige*, and means the berry that creeps, that 'strews' itself all over the place – which of course, both wild and cultivated strawberries do.

Although strawberries are available practically the whole year round nowadays, I personally still prefer to use them in their original season and, without wishing to cause any controversy, there is no doubt in my mind that English ones are the best. Israeli, Californian and New Zealand strawberries found in high-class greengrocers around Christmas hold no fascination for me as they are usually tasteless and tough and not worth the money. And *frozen* or *tinned* strawberries – words fail me.

1 lb (450 g) strawberries, hulled

2 oz (50 g) icing sugar

2 tablespoons cooking brandy (optional)

Strawberry Purée

Freshly picked in season, English strawberries need nothing else but a little castor sugar and fresh farm cream. But as the weeks pass by, you will be only too aware of when the strawberries begin to go off. When purchased they aren't as firm, you tend to damage them slightly as you remove the stalk, and that first fruity flavour has gone. This is the time to begin playing around, and make some of the following dishes, particularly the purée. Better still, keep your beady eyes well and truly open at the greengrocer's and pounce when they have any strawberries on offer that are definitely past their prime. With these make the purée which will be a boon for months afterwards if you store it in the freezer. It can be used for icecreams, sorbets, mousses, soufflés, milk shakes and many other recipes.

Simply liquidize all the ingredients together, pass through a nylon sieve, and then freeze in individual containers.

You can also make the purée with raspberries when past their best.

serves 4

1 lb (450 g) strawberries, hulled

½ pint (300 ml) stock syrup (page 178)

1 tablespoon green peppercorns

2 tablespoons mint, chopped

Strawberries Poached with Mint and Green Peppercorns

This might sound a very odd recipe at first, one to be dismissed with disdain. Please don't. Try it, and I'm sure you will be surprised by the successful combination of flavours – and also find the dish relatively inexpensive. Anyway, for years people have been sprinkling freshly ground black pepper on both under-ripe and over-ripe berries, so now that green peppercorns have made such a mark on the culinary scene, why not use *them*.

When you want to serve your strawberries (and don't do anything except hull them until the very last minute), put the stock syrup and peppercorns into a saucepan and simmer gently for 10 minutes. Put in the strawberries and poach them for literally 1 minute only, drain through a plastic sieve and serve at once with a generous dollop of double cream, whipped up with the faintest touch of ground nutmeg.

serves 8

1 lb (450 g) strawberries

2 tablespoons dark rum

8 tablespoons double cream, lightly whipped

4 teaspoons demerara sugar

2 digestive biscuits, liquidized

Hot Strawberries and Cream

Once again, make this dish when strawberries are neither firm nor young. Hull the fruit and put into the individual ramekin dishes. Sprinkle with the rum. Spoon over the double cream and scatter the demerara sugar and liquidized digestive biscuits on the top. Brown under a hot grill and eat at once.

*   *   *

Fruit Sorbets

serves 10–12 generous portions

1½ pints (900 ml) water

12 oz (350 g) cube sugar

rind and juice of 3 fresh lemons

fruit purée (as on chart below)

1 egg white

¼ pint (150 ml) double cream

It is most important that you always use a spotlessly clean saucepan when making the basic syrup. Place the cube sugar into the pan and add the water with the juice and rind of the lemons. Bring to the boil and simmer for 12 minutes.

When cool fold in any of the following fruit purées:

MANGO   3 lb (1·4 kg) mango flesh, puréed in a liquidizer
MELON   3 lbs (1·4 kg) melon flesh, puréed in a liquidizer
RASPBERRY or STRAWBERRY   2½ lb (1·1 kg) fruit purée (page 140) with 3 tablespoons redcurrant jelly
APPLE   2½ lb (1·1 kg) apple purée (page 168) with 6 tablespoons Calvados
PEAR 2½ lb (1·1 kg) pear purée (page 168) with 6 tablespoons brandy

Put the mixture into plastic containers and leave in the freezer overnight. I can finalize this dish in minutes in a Magimix, but if you haven't got one, sorbets still aren't all that difficult to make. But in either case you need to remove the frozen purée/syrup mixture and allow it to soften before you beat it again. In the Magimix or by hand, beat the mixture back to a sloppy smooth texture and add the egg white and the double cream. Freeze again and use preferably within 48 hours.

If you have some left over, and wish to use it a week later, simply remove from the freezer, allow to become soft, and re-beat again in the Magimix or by hand (an electric hand beater is the best), and freeze once more. This way you always get a pleasant texture. Serve in chilled glasses with individual sponge cakes (page 37), sesame biscuits (page 65) or cigarette russe biscuits (pages 144–5).

American Wheatmeal Chocolate Rum Slice

fills an 11 inch (28 cm) square cake tin

8 oz (225 g) butter

4 large fresh eggs

8 oz (225 g) soft brown sugar

5 level teaspoons baking powder

4 level tablespoons good old-fashioned cocoa

2 tablespoons rum

8 oz (225 g) wheatmeal flour

for the filling

1 pint (550–600 ml) double cream

3 tablespoons castor sugar

2 tablespoons dark rum

This is undoubtedly the easiest (and most delicious) cake I make these days. It's literally all done in a mixer, requiring no skill whatsoever, so I urge you to try it.

Put all the ingredients into your mixer, and slowly whizz it round until you have a soft, drippy batter. Line the tin with greased greaseproof paper. Gently spread the batter over the base of the lined tin and cook in a pre-heated oven at 350°F (180°C), Gas 4, for approximately 30 minutes. The cake is cooked when it has come slightly away from the sides of the tin and is springy to the gentlest of touches.

When absolutely cold, turn out of the tin and simply cut in two down the middle. Each one of these halves will serve, when finished, about 6 to 7 slices, so if you don't want to use it now, keep one of the halves for another time. Whether you're feeding 6 or 12, each cake half or just the one should now be cut in half once more, and then sliced *through* the middle – so you end up with 4 5½ inch (13–14 cm) squares from *each* original half cake!). You could well find the cake slightly crumbly, so do be careful when cutting and slicing.

To make the filling, whip the cream lightly, add the sugar and rum little by little, and whip lightly after each addition. Be generous with the filling and build your cake up with the cream until you have 4 layers of cake and 3 of the flavoured cream.

The cake will cut into about 6 or 7 slices (or 12 to 14 if you're using both original halves, naturally), which you flop down onto your serving plates – no way will these crumbly slices stand up. If you have any of the cream left, pipe attractive rosettes on the middle of the slice or round the edge.

Banana Yoghurt Rum Slice

3 ripe bananas

6 tablespoons natural yoghurt

3 eggs

2 tablespoons dark rum

5 oz (150 g) butter

10 oz (275 g) castor sugar

12 oz (350 g) self-raising flour

1 teaspoon bicarbonate of soda

for the filling

$\frac{1}{2}$ pint (300 ml) double cream

2 tablespoons castor sugar

3 bananas, well crushed

$\frac{1}{2}$ pint (300 ml) natural yoghurt

about 2 tablespoons rum

These ingredients will make 4 8 inch (20 cm) sponge flans. It's rather a filling, heavy pudding, but one that I like to have occasionally. If you're not going to use all 4 at once (4 flans will serve 16 generously), use 2 for your party, and freeze the other 2. Halve the filling ingredients.

Set the oven to 350°F (180°C), Gas 4. If you have a Magimix, put in the peeled and broken-up bananas, the yoghurt, eggs and rum, and whizz round to make a purée. If you haven't a blender of any sort, break up the bananas in a bowl, mash with a fork and then, using a hand beater, combine with the yoghurt, eggs and rum.

In a separate bowl, cream the butter and the sugar, and do make a good job of this. Beat away until the mixture is quite white and crystally, and then beat in the sloppy banana/yoghurt mixture. Fold in the flour with the bicarbonate of soda.

Divide into 4 floured and sugared sponge flan tins and bake for 25 to 30 minutes. Turn out onto a wire tray and, when cold, you can use them straightaway, but they're the better for storing (in a polythene bag inside a tin, or, as I said, they freeze beautifully).

To make the filling, beat up the double cream with the sugar and rum until fairly thick and then beat in, a little at a time, the crushed banana and yoghurt.

Cut the sponges into 2 through the middle, and build up into tiers, sandwiching them together with the cream mixture. Serve in wedge slices and, if there is any of the filling left, pour it over the top and decorate with halved walnuts or pecan nuts. This is an ideal pud for a picnic.

Walnut Lemon Meringue Gâteau

10 egg whites

18 oz (500 g) castor sugar

rind of 1 lemon

1 tablespoon fresh lemon juice

9 oz (250 g) walnuts, chopped

for the filling

2 eggs

4 oz (100 g) castor sugar

juice and rind of 2 lemons

$\frac{1}{2}$ pint (300 ml) double cream

some extra walnuts (or hazel or pecan nuts)

This recipe will make 4 8 inch (20 cm) round circles of meringue but the recipe can easily be halved. If you do make the full recipe, 2 of the meringue circles can either be stored in an airtight tin, or frozen. You could use hazelnuts or pecan nuts instead of walnuts, but remember to change the title of your gâteau!

Use a spotless mixing bowl and also ensure that your whisk is equally clean. Line the base and sides of the tins with good greaseproof paper.

Beat the egg whites until stiff and dry and then beat in about 14 oz (400 g) of the castor sugar, *a little at a time*. Using a long-handled metal spoon, gently fold in the remaining castor sugar along with the rind of the lemon, the lemon juice, and the chopped nuts. Dollop out into the 4 prepared sandwich tins and, using a palette knife, spread gently and carefully over the base. Put into a pre-heated oven at 275°F (140°C), Gas 1, for 2 hours. Turn the oven off then and slightly open the door (using a wooden spoon as a doorstop) and leave as long as you like. When absolutely cold, store, or make 2 gâteaux with the 4 circles of meringue, or 1 gâteau with 2 circles. Sandwich them together with the filling.

You need a Christmas pudding type bowl which will fit into a small saucepan without touching the bottom of the saucepan. In the bowl, beat together the eggs and sugar, then beat in the juice and rind of the lemons. Put the bowl into the pan of simmering hot water and, from time to time, stir the contents. It will take 10 to 15 minutes for the contents to begin to thicken. When the sauce will coat the back of your wooden spoon, remove from the heat and leave to cool. When stone cold, pass this thick 'essence' through a fine plastic sieve into the double cream, and beat to a piping consistency.

Fill the gâteau or gâteaux with this cream. You can leave some over to pipe little rosettes on the top, and garnish these rosettes with whichever nuts you used for the gâteau. It will cut very easily (crumbling a bit, I must admit), if you use a serrated bread knife, and 1 gâteau will generously serve 8 to 12 guests.

Apple and Hazelnut Galette

Beat the sugar and butter for the galette together to a creamy consistency, and then fold in the flour and ground hazelnuts. Divide the mixture into 4 and chill for 30 minutes. Lightly grease and flour 4 9 inch (23 cm) cake tins, and spread each ball of the dough lightly over the base of these tins. Chill again for 15 minutes and then bake at 350°F (180°C), Gas 4, for 10 minutes. Leave to cool.

For the filling, peel, core and slice the apples, and put into a saucepan with all the other ingredients. Cook off until you have a nice thick gooey mess. This, when cooled, is what you layer between the 4 rounds of cooked galette, and to cut it you'll need a very sharp serrated knife.

If you prefer to do individual portions to save portioning out at the actual party, simply roll the galette mixing out and use a fluted biscuit cutter of the size you wish. Chill the rounds on greaseproof paper, cook on a baking tray for a slightly shorter time, and when cooked, make up individual dishes as above.

Creme Brulée

Mix the egg yolks in a bowl with the castor sugar and beat until white. Bring the runny double cream to the boil with the split vanilla pod in it. Pass the cream through a fine nylon sieve – to remove any loose seeds from the vanilla pod (which you simply wash for use again) – onto the egg yolk and sugar mixture, and beat this together. Put the 8 ramekins into a roasting tray partly filled with warm water and pre-heat the oven to 275°F (140°C), Gas 1.

Wash out the saucepan and return the mixture to this. Over a medium heat, continually stirring with a wooden spoon, cook until the cream and eggs thicken like an egg custard and really coat the back of the wooden

---

serves 8

6 oz (175 g) soft butter

4 tablespoons castor sugar

10 oz (275 g) plain flour, sieved

6 oz (175 g) hazelnuts, ground

for the filling

1 lb (450 g) Granny Smith apples

grated rind and juice of 2 lemons and 2 oranges

6 tablespoons sultanas

1 oz (25 g) butter

½ teaspoon mixed spice

1 tablespoon icing sugar

fills 8 3 inch (7·5 cm) ramekins

4 egg yolks

2 level tablespoons castor sugar

1 pint (550–600 ml) runny double cream

1 vanilla pod, split

8 tablespoons demerara sugar

spoon. *Do not under any circumstances allow this mixture to boil.* Strain into a large jug that has a good pouring lip and then fill the ramekins in the roasting tray with the custard mixture. Place the filled ramekins into the warm oven and leave for 15 minutes as you are wanting a thin layer of skin to form on the surface of each custard. Remove from the oven and allow to cool.

For an absolutely foolproof caramelizing, light your grill at least 45 minutes ahead, and I recommend you use a metal tray about 1 inch (2·5 cm) deep which you fill with crushed ice. Onto this bed of ice, place the individual ramekins. Spread a tablespoon of demerara sugar evenly on top of the skin of the custard (very, very carefully as you do not want to split the skin: if you do, the sugar sinks, the custard is exposed, and curdles under the intense heat of the grill). When the grill is at its hottest, simply push the sugared ramekins underneath. Leave them there (watching like an eager beaver), and if the middle ones are obviously cooking quicker than those at the edges, turn the tray round with a gloved hand, and manipulate the dishes around.

The top, when allowed to cool, is crunchy like toffee, and the custard below quite rich and delicious. To enhance this recipe even more, fresh strawberries or raspberries can be sunk into the dishes of custard before cooking them in the oven.

Another way of cooking Creme Brulée is to follow all the instructions up to the cooking stage, but then you cook the ramekins in a bain marie at 375°F (190°C), Gas 5, for 30 to 35 minutes and then allow to cool before starting the caramel topping. This is obviously a less runny and creamy pudding, a texture which many prefer.

Cigarette Russe Biscuits

2 egg whites

4 oz (100 g) castor sugar

2 oz (50 g) butter, melted

2 oz (50 g) plain flour, sieved

I have always drooled over these delicacies served up in the finer French restaurants, and made in abundance at enormous expense to the consumer by a commercial firm just south of the coastline of Brittany. It was only when I started to do them myself I realized that the only thing really required was time and a little patience. The first time you attempt them, set aside about three-quarters of an hour to make 20 or so. Provided you store them in an airtight container, when absolutely cold, they will last for several days.

Set the oven at 375°F (190°C), Gas 5, and line a 10 × 14 inch (25·5 × 35·5 cm) metal tray with good thick greaseproof paper. (The Bakewell silicone treated paper is the best, bought in rolls at stationers, and whatever you do, don't skimp on this as you will have one hell of a job trying to get the cooked biscuits off the paper while they are still quite warm in order to roll them.)

In a small metal bowl, beat up the egg whites until dry and stiff, then beat in the sugar a little at a time. Gently fold in the sieved flour, and then scoop the mixture to the top half of the bowl and add the cooled, melted butter to the bottom and gently stir the 2 together.

Your tray will only take 3 biscuits and I would respectfully suggest that, on your first attempt to make these biscuits, you lightly pencil in 3 equal sized circles – one at the top left-hand corner, one on the right-hand side in the middle and then the third in the bottom left-hand corner, and use this as a guide. Each biscuit requires barely one dessertspoon of the batter mixture, and this is liberally spread over the circle area by using a flexible palette knife. You might think it impossible to spread a dessertspoonful over such an area, and quite right you are. It doesn't matter a hoot if each circle has occasional bare areas as long as you spread out the batter like a flat thin pancake.

Put the tray into the oven and, if you are fortunate enough to have a glass-fronted oven with inside lights, you have no problem as you will be able to see the rich yellow mixture start to turn fawn, light brown, and cooked right through to the colour of a good ginger biscuit. If you see that one is cooking more quickly than another, simply turn the tray round. If you haven't a glass-fronted oven you will just have to look in after about 5 minutes to see how things are doing, and keep on doing so (turning the tray as often as you require) until all 3 are evenly cooked.

Remove the tray from the oven and have to hand a palette knife, a long-handled wooden spoon, and a cooling tray. A mistake that many people make is to be in too much of a rush to get the cooked biscuits off the paper, onto the table, and wound round the handle of the wooden spoon. If you start this process too soon, the biscuit will still be quite limp and it wrinkles up. Leave to cool for a few moments and then you can slide your palette knife underneath, and flick the circle over top side down. Place the handle of your wooden spoon at the edge nearest you and roll the biscuit up around it. Give a very gentle squeeze to the whole cigar shape, quickly slide it off the handle on to the cooling tray, and go on to the second biscuit. You will soon develop the knack and become quite expert.

Miller Howe Savoury Dinner Rolls

makes 16–18 rolls

1 oz (25 g) fresh yeast

½ teaspoon castor sugar

2 oz (50 g) butter, melted

1 lb (450 g) plain strong flour

2 oz (50 g) Cheddar cheese, finely grated

1 teaspoon salt

¼ teaspoon freshly ground black pepper

1 bunch watercress, finely chopped

1 teaspoon dry English mustard

½ pint (300 ml) tepid milk

Cream the yeast with the castor sugar in a small basin using a wooden spoon and then combine with the cooled melted butter. Place the flour, cheese, salt, pepper, watercress and mustard in the Kenwood bowl and fit the dough hook. Add the tepid milk slowly to the yeast mixture in the bowl (the temperature should be like that of the water for a baby's bath: never, never have it too hot or you will kill the yeast). With the Kenwood on slow speed, start to add the milk mixture. Carry on 'kneading' on the machine slowly until the mixture is quite smooth and springy. Take out of the bowl and knead into a ball shape. Lightly flour the Kenwood bowl and return the ball of dough to it.

Cover with a warm tea towel, and leave to prove in a warm draught-free corner of the kitchen (at Miller Howe we use the old airing cupboard in the office next to the kitchen). After about 1 hour carefully look at the mixing and when it is literally doubled in size, remove from the warm place and knock the dough back down with your fist, to more or less its original size. Turn out onto a floured board.

Cut into 16 to 18 pieces to make individual rolls. To do this if right-handed, place your right hand palm down on the board and then slowly bring your finger ends up underneath your palm. Put each individual piece of cob dough beneath this cup-shaped 'mitt', and roll your hand round in a circle, applying very little pressure, to make your cob. Should your hands be hot and sweaty (and often the first time you make the bread you are hot from nervous tension), lightly flour them.

Transfer the cobs to baking trays lined with greaseproof paper, allowing space round each one for them to rise. At this stage you could sprinkle some finely chopped nuts and cracked wheat on the top of each cob, which is unusual and looks lovely when cooked.

When the individual cobs are all rolled out and placed on the baking trays, put the trays back into your warm spot and leave them to double in size again – normally about 30 minutes – and then bake in a pre-heated oven at 450°F (230°C), Gas 8, for 15 to 20 minutes. Remove from the oven, paint liberally with melted butter, and serve as soon as possible.

ENTERTAINING OCCASION
Dinner Parties

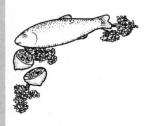

Menu
1

Savoury Duck Slice (page 128)
on Tomato and Herb Salad (page 165)

Baked Trout with Hazelnuts and Orange
(page 50)
Fried Mixed Vegetables (page 60)

Pear Frangipane (page 110)
with Whipped Cream

Rich, Easy Brown Bread (page 35)

Serve a glass of chilled dry Madeira (Sercial) with the
duck slice, a Chablis or South African dry Steen Chenin
blanc with the trout, and a small glass of chilled
Sauternes or pear brandy with the frangipane.

Although the duck slice is quite complicated, *all* the work is done beforehand, and there is very little on which you have to concentrate the day of your party. Just make everything look good, and have a good time!

FOUR DAYS BEFORE
Marinate the fillet of pork and the kidneys for the duck slice.

THREE DAYS BEFORE
Marinate the chicken livers for the duck slice.

TWO DAYS BEFORE
Make the savoury duck slice.

THE DAY BEFORE
Make the pear frangipane and leave covered in a cool safe place. Make the bread.

MORNING
Double-check your shopping and the table setting. Put dishes in the warming drawer and prepare the coffee tray.
Check:
the lamps
the heating
the room for coats and the cloakroom
the records and tapes
the flowers

Fillet the trout, coat each half (2 per person) with the butter and ground hazelnuts, and leave on a well-buttered baking tray covered with clingfilm.

Prepare and portion the tomato herb salad and leave in the fridge covered with clingfilm.

Prepare the vegetables, cutting them up into small pieces ready for frying (leaving anything that might discolour in a bowl of water).

Segment or slice the oranges for the fish and leave covered with clingfilm. Leave the cream for the frangipane in a bowl ready to be whipped up at the last minute.

EVENING
Take the tomato herb salads out of the fridge in time for them to come round. Take off the film and place on the table.

Slice the savoury duck, and put one slice on each plate of salad.

Just as you're about to sit down, take the clingfilm off the trout and put the trays into the pre-heated oven for 20 to 30 minutes.

About 5 to 10 minutes before the trout is ready, heat the oil and butter for the vegetables, and start stir-frying them.

Have ready the warmed plates for the fish, and when the cooking time is up, turn the oven off, garnish each portion of fish with the orange slices or segments and flash them under a hot grill.

Put the pear frangipane into the still hot, turned-off oven to warm through. Whip the cream and garnish the frangipane when you're about to serve it.

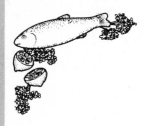

Menu
2

Vegetable Terrine (page 125)
with Fresh Home-made Tomato Sauce (page 175)

Breast of Duck with Lime and Juniper
(page 131)
with Gin and Lime Sauce (page 132)

Potatoes with Cream and Cheese (page 24)
Peas with Mint

Lemon Soufflé (page 137)
with Cigarette Russe Biscuits (page 144)

Rich Easy Brown Bread (page 35)

Serve a Pouilly Fumé with the terrine (preferably
Ladoucette), and a good robust inexpensive claret with
the duck. The soufflé doesn't need anything at all.

Once again, the starter is quite complicated, but it's all done beforehand, and you can just concentrate on the main course basically, the day of the party.

FOUR DAYS BEFORE

Marinate the breasts of duck in the lime juice and crushed juniper berries, and turn daily.

TWO DAYS BEFORE

Prepare and cook the vegetable terrine, leave in the dish, and chill. Make and sieve the fresh tomato sauce and chill.

THE DAY BEFORE

Make the bread, and the cigarette russe biscuits (which you should store well in an airtight container).

MORNING

Double-check your shopping, and set the table. Put the serving dishes and plates into the warming drawer, and prepare the coffee tray, hiding it discreetly away.
Check that:
all lamps are working, and have bulbs
the heating is OK
the spare bedroom for coats and the cloakroom are organized
tapes or records are selected for the background music
the flowers are watered

Make the lemon soufflés, and leave to chill in the fridge.

Make the Gin and Lime sauce and leave to one side covered with butter paper to prevent a skin forming.

Cook the potatoes almost to the final stage.

EVENING

Portion out your vegetable terrine. If you have plain white china, dollop 2 tablespoons of the tomato sauce into the middle, and then tilt the plate so that a larger circle is formed. Gently place your slice on top of this. It looks fantastic.

Have ready your saucepan with the gin and lime sauce, and a frying pan with oil and butter for the duck.

Gently heat the potatoes through in a warm oven and then, when you're frying off the duck for the 2 or 3 minutes each side, sprinkle the cheese over the top of the potatoes and brown under a hot grill.

Warm the sauce and simmer the peas – and I just use frozen – with a sprig of mint.

Whip the remaining cream from the soufflé recipe and use this to cream the sides of the souffles. Roll them thereafter in the nibbed almonds.

Menu
3

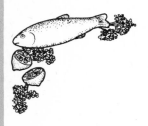

Avocado Pear stuffed with Tuna, Smoked
Salmon and Water Chestnuts (page 48)
with Lemon Mayonnaise (page 177)

Baked Suprême of Chicken (pages 97 to 100)

Aubergines with Cheese (page 61)

Walnut Lemon Meringue Gâteau (page 142)

Rich, Easy Brown Bread (page 35)

Serve a South African Riesling with the pear, a Côtes
du Rhône with the chicken, and a glass of Boschendal
Bouquet de Fleurs with the gâteau.

With this menu, there is quite a lot to do just before the party, but I think you will agree the tastes and textures are worth it.

TWO DAYS BEFORE

Marinate the chicken suprêmes in the marinade of your choice.

THE DAY BEFORE

Make the lemon mayonnaise and store in a screw-top jar in a cool place.

Make the aubergine 'stew'. Make the bread.

Stuff the chicken suprêmes with the stuffing of your choice, and store in their foil parcels in the fridge.

Make the meringues for the gâteaux and store when cold.

MORNING

Check your shopping and set the table. Prepare the coffee tray and put the plates and dishes in the warming drawer.
Check:
the heating
the lamps
the room for the coats and the cloakroom
the tapes or records
the flowers

Divide the aubergine stew between individual ramekins and top with the breadcrumbs. Grate the cheese.

AFTERNOON

Make the lemony filling for the gâteau. Fill the gâteau, and store in the fridge.

EVENING

Prepare the avocado pears and their stuffing. Brush the cut tops of the avocadoes with lemon juice. Lay them on the table shortly before you sit down.

Have ready the roasting and cooling trays and the water boiling before you start cooking the chicken. Pre-set the oven, and 35 to 40 minutes before you want to eat the chicken (allowing time for pre-dinner drinks and the avocado) put the chicken suprêmes in.

About half-way through the chicken cooking time, put in the aubergine ramekins.

As you unwrap the foil parcels, and put the chicken suprêmes and juices onto the warmed plates, top the aubergine ramekins with cheese, and brown quickly under a hot grill.

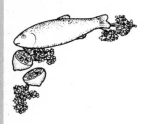

Menu
4

Cold Cucumber Soup (page 45)

Sorrento-Style Cod (page 77)

Goujons of Turkey Breast (page 107)
with Sweet and Sour Mayonnaise (page 176)

Triple Purée Vegetable Pots (page 165)

American Wheatmeal Chocolate Rum Slice
(page 141)
with Butterscotch Sauce (page 33)

Rich, Easy Brown Bread (page 35)

As the soup is so delicate and the fish so robust, I
suggest a white Châteauneuf du Pape to accompany the
first two courses, followed by a South African Cabernet
Sauvignon with the turkey goujons. With the pudding,
serve an inexpensive non-vintage champagne.

This 4-course dinner is no less easy a menu for entertaining as almost everything can be done in advance, and the only major thing you have to do at the last minute is to fry off the goujons (preferably in a deep fryer).

TWO DAYS BEFORE

Make the butterscotch sauce and store in the fridge.

Make the wheatmeal cake and store in an air-tight tin.

THE DAY BEFORE

Soak the raisins for the soup in the brandy for 12 hours or so. Make the soup, stir in the plumped-up raisins, and leave to chill.

Make the mayonnaise and leave in a screw-top jar in a cool place. Make the bread.

MORNING

Check the shopping and the table setting. Put the dishes in the warming drawer and prepare the coffee tray.
Check:
the lamps
the heating
the room for coats and the cloakroom
the records and tapes
the flowers

Prepare the triple purée vegetable pots up to the custard stage and leave the ramekins, covered, sitting in the bain marie ready for cooking off in the evening.

Prepare and fry the floured cod cubes and the sauce, and portion the cod out onto the dishes in which they'll be baked.

Chop the parsley for the cod, and have ready your sprigs of dill or fennel for the soup.

Cut and slice the wheatmeal cake, make the cream filling, and layer the cake up with the cream. Cover with clingfilm. Put any cream left over into a piping bag.

Cut the turkey breasts into fingers, flour and egg them, then coat with desiccated coconut. Leave uncovered on greaseproof paper in the fridge or larder.

EVENING

Portion the soup out and put on the table, garnishing just before your guests sit down.

Coat the dishes of cod cubes with their sauce, and put them in the pre-heated oven just as you sit down to your soup.

When you serve the cod, turn the oven up and put in the vegetable pots in their bain marie, covered with the custard.

Fry the goujons off in your deep-fryer (keep hot while you finish), and serve with the triple purée vegetable pots and the mayonnaise.

Unwrap the wheatmeal slice, divide into portions, and pipe rosettes onto each. Warm the butterscotch sauce gently.

SIX

NIGHT SCHOOL

Even though I supervise all the running of Miller Howe, I still have to look after the running of my own home in Bowness. I value my time at Brantlea very much, and I delight in entertaining close friends there, although I rarely have time. Spending so much time at the hotel, and eating there most evenings, I don't like having too much food around at home, but like most people I am often caught 'on the hop' with friends turning up suddenly around lunch, tea or supper time. A bottle of wine is opened and I desperately ask myself, 'How long are they going to stay?' and, 'What the devil can I conjure up?', and when the second bottle is broached, I plunder the store-cupboard – which is the answer to all unexpected entertaining occasions.

My Nan always had a well-stocked store-cupboard even in the leanest of times – both when money was short, and during the war. Each week some item of what we considered luxury was bought for the top shelf: tinned John West salmon for dainty, thin, brown bread sandwiches; condensed milk for a quick butterscotch sauce; tinned Fray Bentos corned beef for making bread, butter and egg fritters; Carnation milk for topping off a fruit salad or – horror of horrors, thinking about it now – for adding to the cloggy chicory-full Camp Coffee (made with panache and served with a sense of one-upmanship on Sunday mornings); Heinz tinned vegetable salad to enhance a winter salad tea; calves foot jelly for when we were ill; tinned Heinz tomato soup and, of course, tinned Heinz baked beans!

I tend to keep even the store-cupboard fairly bare purely and simply because if I have food in the house *I eat it*! I would win any award going for middle-of-the-night bean-feasting: if I know there is some left-over joint in the fridge, you can bet your bottom dollar I will wake up at 3 a.m. simply dying for a bit of this and a spoonful of that! Likewise if there are cakes left over from tea, or soup from a snack lunch, they won't last long in my house.

WHAT'S IN STORE

But, basically, I always keep the following in fridge, freezer and store-cupboard, and although they don't at first sight look promising, it's amazing what you can do, with a little imagination.

Store-Cupboard

Tinned
corned beef
red kidney beans
Italian whole tomatoes (usually 2 tins)
baby purées
sardines, in olive oil and tomato sauce
tuna fish, with and without oil
lumpfish roe
spam
smoked oysters
soups made by Baxters, various, but always Heinz tomato soup

Heinz baked beans
red salmon
baby carrots

Packets, jars etc
flour for making sauces
oatmeal
desiccated coconut
lots of different teas
lots of spices
Davis gelatine
plenty of nuts
marmalade (pages 65–6)
jam
masses of home-made chutneys (page 60)
pickled onions
2 packets of Hovis crackers
anchovy essence
tomato and brown sauces, and Lea & Perrins Worcestershire sauce
dry English mustard, Dijon mustard and Moutarde de Meaux
white and red wine vinegar
olive oil
walnut oil
sugar, castor and soft brown
sea salt
black pepper
dried herbs
small packets of Kellogg's cornflakes for those unexpected overnight guests (you should be so lucky)
sealed packet of ground coffee and Nescafé Blend 37
fresh fruit

Fridge

tinned *foie gras* (that's a personal indulgence of *mine*!)
American red caviare salmon roe
plenty of eggs
Philadelphia cream cheese
small cartons cream, single and double
butter, unsalted and salted
block of Cheddar cheese
packet of Emmenthal cheese
tomato juice
jar of butterscotch sauce (page 33)
jar of onion marmalade (page 83)
jar(s) of French dressing(s)
jar of savoury breadcrumbs (page 173)
milk, of course

In the salad drawer
lettuce
carrots
tomatoes

lemons
oranges
grapefruit

Freezer

Petit pois
sweetcorn kernels
prawns
Wiltshire smoked middle bacon
concentrated orange juice
concentrated grapefruit juice
spinach purée (page 133)
loaf of wholemeal bread
half a dozen pavlovas (page 167)
small container of vegetable soup
dozen uncooked sweet scones (page 179)
block home-made (page 166) or bought icecream
sponge cakes for quick trifle (page 37)
tomato provençale (page 175)
apple purée (page 168)
individually wrapped marinated steaks or lamb chops (pages 69–70)
individual portions of curries (pages 55–9)

Store-Cupboard Favourites

Baked beans are definitely always to be found in my store-cupboard, and although I'm loath to become associated with any particular product, I must honestly say there are no baked beans in my opinion quite to match those of Heinz. I have tried most makes in most parts of the world but I still come back to these. It is all the *different* things that can be done to and with them that appeal to me: they can be curried, puréed, fried, served cold, grilled – a wonderful standby. I always buy the large 15 oz (425 g) tins.

Curried Beans

serves 2

1 tin Heinz baked beans

1 medium onion, about 6 oz (175 g)

1 oz (25 g) butter

1 teaspoon curry powder

½ Granny Smith apple, finely diced

1 oz (25 g) sultanas

If I have time to spare, curried beans are delicious. Simply fry off the chopped onion in the butter, and add curry powder to taste (I sometimes add a pinch of turmeric and a little allspice too). At the end I put in the finely diced raw apple, a few sultanas, and then I add the baked beans to cook through. They are nice served on toast, in a nest of mashed potato or with rice.

Puréed Baked Beans

Butter slices of hot toast, and spread them lightly with a little prepared English mustard. Liquidize the beans, and coat the toast liberally with the purée. Pop under the grill and top off with lots of onion rings and chopped parsley.

Fried Baked Beans with Bacon

Cut up your fatty bacon – about 4 oz (100 g) good streaky – into very small pieces and cook in the frying pan until the bacon is lovely and crisp and there is a lot of fat out of the bacon in the pan. Add the tinned beans, heat through and serve with rice or inside a half baked potato.

Cold Baked Beans

On spinach or lettuce leaves arrange wedges of apples or pears (or any seasonal fruit you may have to hand) and simply spoon the cold baked beans into the centre. Scatter liberally with chopped fresh herbs. Grated raw carrots set around the perimeter of the plate in small blobs blend well with this, and you could add quarters of hard-boiled eggs.

Grilled Baked Beans

serves 6

1 oz (25 g) butter

salt, freshly ground black pepper

2 oz (50 g) lettuce, spinach or chicory, chopped

2 oz (50 g) Cheddar cheese, grated

1 tin Heinz baked beans

1 oz (25 g) breadcrumbs

6 teaspoons chutney of choice (optional)

A real 'cowboy' dish this, but one that I like! Butter and season individual ramekin dishes and place on the base of each some chopped spinach, lettuce or chicory. Fill the ramekins by layering the finely grated cheese with the beans alternately. Warm through in a bain marie in the oven at 350°F (180°C), Gas 4, for about 20 minutes, and then top with grated cheese and breadcrumbs and finish off under the grill.

I'm also very greedy about chutneys, and occasionally I put a teaspoon of chutney on the leaves in the ramekin dish before I start layering the cheese and beans. It's a nice thing for the person eating it to find!

Baked Custard Baked Beans

serves 6

1 tin Heinz baked beans

2 oz (50 g) left-over fruit or veg, finely chopped

½ pint (300 ml) double cream

2 eggs

1 egg yolk

Mix with the baked beans some finely chopped banana, apple, red or green peppers, celery, fennel – in fact anything you have left over in the fridge – and divide between individual buttered seasoned ramekins. Make the egg custard and pour over the contents of the ramekins and bake at 375°F (190°C), Gas 5, for about 25 minutes.

Left-over finely chopped cooked meat can be added to make this even more substantial, and a little grated cheese too, if you like.

Hovis Crackers. Although reading the packet alone is enough to put off any true gourmet (the ingredients are flour, fat, wheatgerm, sugar, salt, *whey powder*, baking powder, *autolysed yeast*, malt flour, *emulsifiers*, soya flour and *antioxidant*), the actual biscuits are a godsend in any store-cupboard. They can form such an excellent base to a snack, and they never, like bread, go stale. Topped with any of the pâtés, cold meats, chutneys, salads etc they are delicious, and can also be filled, with a top and bottom biscuit, to make appetizing, filling sandwiches. They can be a base for mashed sardines, mixed with a little cream cheese and herbs; left-over scrambled eggs, mixed with chopped chives and a little curry; minced cold meats, mixed with tomato sauce and chutney; cold fish blended with mayonnaise, purée of vegetables, thickened with bread-crumbs and possibly desiccated coconut; sour cream mixed with grated carrot, turnip, parsnip and fresh herbs. Imagination can run riot, so long as you do the toppings more or less at the last moment. *Don't* use these biscuits as a buffet piece: if you do, they go soggy far more quickly than the wheatmeal bread given on pages 35–6.

Tuna fish. My store-cupboard always has tins of tuna fish in oil as they are such a good standby for a salad should somebody pop by and, of course, are needed for Salade Niçoise (page 136). But tuna fish simply made into sandwiches, grilled and served on hot toast or – better still – with little triangles of buttered toast, is good. I also like to serve raw onion rings when eating tuna fish and a few very thin rings of red peppers add a sense of colour and excitement to any dish.

There is a classic Italian dish of cold escalopes of veal coated with tuna fish purée and I have, on occasions, put a small tin of tuna fish into the liquidizer with a drop of white wine and used this thick sauce as a coating for thick slices of cold pork or cold chicken.

I also like to use hard-boiled eggs with tuna fish. After shelling the eggs, cut them lengthwise, take out the yolk and add that to the liquidizer along with the tuna, a little cream cheese, curry powder, a few pine kernels if you're feeling extravagant, or a tiny drop of walnut oil (all to add further flavour). Simply pop this resultant purée (after testing for seasoning) into a piping bag and pipe back into the scooped-out centres of the eggs. Quite filling, and attractive too if garnished with sprigs of fresh parsley.

A base of cream cheese with chopped dill is good, too, with tuna fish – especially if you pipe a nest of the cheese out on to the plate and put the tuna fish in the middle. Surrounded by alternate wedges of tomato and hard-boiled egg, it looks like a flower on the plate.

When puréeing tuna fish you can also throw into the liquidizer watercress, parsley, fresh herbs, skinned and pipped tomatoes. Serve on individual salads, as a sauce, as a filling for eggs, tomatoes or avocadoes, and garnish with pipped grapes to make the dish look more attractive.

Another idea is to cut 3 inch (7·5 cm) sticks of celery and pipe the purée of flavoured tuna fish along the sticks. Ideal for a finger-snack supper or for a buffet party.

Foie Gras. My ultimate self-indulgence, at least once a year, is to greedily gobble an enormous portion of tinned *foie gras* with lots of hot buttered toast, swilled down with a really good bottle of Alsace wine. I'm apparently a very difficult person for whom to buy presents, so to some selected friends I say, 'I'll settle for a tin of *foie gras*'. And seek it out they kindly do on various holidays on the Continent. I unwrap it with joy, immediately put it into the fridge, and every single time I open the fridge door I think affectionately of the donors! Although at the same time, I hate to think of the *original* donors – the poor geese or ducks which have been fattened by force-feeding in Strasbourg, Toulouse, Perigueux or Nancy – when I open my tin or jar and see the lovely, light, creamy brown colour, just slightly tinged with pink, I know I am in for a right royal feast.

When I actually get round to serving this luxury, I do it with enormous ceremony: place mats are put on the glass dining-table, candles are lit, the best glasses highly polished, individual butter dishes, silver decanter and tray, best china plates, all set out. The whole effect is ruined, of course, by the fact that I bring the electric toaster to the table, purely and simply because I like my toast for the delicacy to be really *hot*. I use very little butter on my pieces of thick hot toast, but I must admit I am very, very liberal with the scoops of *foie gras*. I am usually a very quick eater of food (I know no caterer who is slow, as we're more often than not called away from food to see to a guest or take a telephone call), but when I eat this dish I slowly and religiously chew my way meltingly through every highly appreciated mouthful. The wine is good too!

Brantlea Favourites

Although the store-cupboard is raided often, there are many other recipes which are firm favourites of mine at home – good, basic cooking, simple and tasty.

Scrambled Eggs

per person

3 eggs

1 tablespoon double cream

salt, freshly ground black pepper

1 teaspoon oil

1 oz (25 g) butter

Since I work 6 days a week, never getting home until the early hours of the morning, I feel that 11 or 11.30 is a sensible time to start my Sunday, my only day off. I almost always have scrambled eggs – a bit of a ritual really – and I find that many people have *very* fixed ideas on how they like this done (or is it that so many people aren't at their absolute best first thing in the morning?).

Beat the eggs and cream well together with a liberal dash of freshly ground black pepper and a touch of salt (I always keep more cream at hand in case I cook the eggs too much). For *each* portion of 3 eggs, heat 1 teaspoon oil and 1 oz (25 g) butter, and allow them to melt slowly in the saucepan. When combined and sizzling a little, pour in all the mixed eggs and, *using an electric hand beater*, whisk away in the saucepan (or use a wire whisk and keep on working it continually). The important thing to remember is that when the contents of the saucepan are obviously beginning to cook – turning firm rather than liquid – *remove from the heat at once* and continue to beat. You want to end up with a fluffy, runny mixture. The mistake so many people make is waiting for the eggs to reach their desired consistency whilst on the heat, forgetting that they continue to cook for a few minutes *afterwards*, in the heat of the pan itself.

See that you have a warmed plate to hand as well as triangles of toast, and for goodness sake, make sure your guests are in position waiting to dive into the dish. I can throw a tantrum if I find, when I get to the table with the lovely, soft, shimmering, delicious scrambled eggs, that my guests have gone to the loo or off to get something or other! Mind you, this is only at home. If that happens at Miller Howe, the staff bring the plate back to the kitchen and, when the guest is re-seated, we start again from scratch.

Hot, well-buttered toast is a vital accompaniment to scrambled eggs, but I almost always enhance it with tiny cubes of smoked salmon mixed in. (If doing this, omit the salt from the eggs as you will find most smoked salmon has more than its fair share of salt.) Freshly chopped herbs and chives added are tasty, butter-fried mushroom caps make the dish more filling, and bacon rolls stuffed with prunes baked in the oven make a nice cartwheel effect on the plate. I often fry triangles of bread in bacon fat too.

Scrambled eggs with some tiny cubes of cooked ham added and spooned out onto a couple of thin slices of Emmenthal cheese make a tasty starter. I have also surrounded the mountain of scrambled eggs with some Granny Smith apple wedges and put at the north, south, east and west of the hill a teaspoon of grated carrot and generous sprigs of watercress or parsley. Tomato provençale (page 175) or mushroom pâté (page 173) can also ring the changes with this platter.

Toasted Sandwiches

I'm a toasted sandwich addict, and I never tire of these effortless, quickly-made, belly fillers. Even at this moment in your cupboard, fridge or freezer you will have *something* with which to make a toasted sandwich. I must admit I do possess a special machine, which is almost vital for a proper sandwich, but do be careful if you invest in one as some are a load of rubbish and no more cook the insides of the sandwiches than fly to the moon.

A toasted sandwich should be served piping hot, with the toast *and* the filling hot too! So many commercial establishments have the audacity to serve cold food between cold slices of dried-up toast and pass them off as the real thing. If this should happen to you, send the ruddy thing back! Being a bit of a fanatic, though, I like the actual *inside* of my sandwich to be toasted too. First of all heat your machine, then put together 2 slices of bread to fit, lightly butter the top and bottom, and toast them. If your machine is the moulded type (and they are really better) the toast will

come out slightly warped but that doesn't matter. 'Top and tail' these slices, and put the filling on the toasted sides.
Here are some pleasant combinations you could use:
cheese, tomato and chutney;
cheese, fried onion and chutney;
diced left-over meat with a touch of curry and lots of cheese;
apple slices or pear wedges are nice added to anything;
practically any kind of tinned fish combined with lightly chopped onions;
left-over cooked bacon and tomato;
avocado and smoked salmon bits (a little more exotic);
tongue with asparagus;
any left-over vegetable mashed with some bottled sauce and fresh chopped herbs;
cold chicken, turkey or game lightly painted with redcurrant jelly and a smattering of chopped nuts;
peanut butter with raw onion slices;
Bovril with cheese and chutney;
offcuts of steak bashed out very, very thin;
cold left-over scrambled egg mixed with horseradish and tomato or anchovy paste;
any left-over mushroom, cheese and herb or liver pâtés;
and so you can go on and on . . .

When you have put your filling in, don't allow any overhang but leave about $\frac{1}{4}$ inch (6 mm) space round the edges, and make sure your guests are ready to eat the moment the sandwiches are cooked. Toast for the time stated on your machine. Garnish with a whole tomato, a few shreds of lettuce, some apple wedges, or strips of raw vegetables and, of course, a fresh sprig of parsley or watercress.

Pan-Fried Sirloin Steak

For me the sheer simplicity of this dish is stunning and it's delicious. I usually buy a 10 oz (275 g) sirloin steak with lots of buttery-looking fat which I snip with scissors at $\frac{1}{4}$ inch (6 mm) intervals. I then put the steak into a deep soup plate and pour 2 tablespoons of good olive oil over it. I leave it overnight and turn it the next morning. When I want to cook the steak, I melt 2 oz (50 g) unsalted butter in pieces over a low heat, then turn up the heat until the butter sizzles, and throw in the steak. Using a wooden spoon I keep on pressing all corners of the steak down on to the hot base of the frying pan and, depending on the thickness of the steak, I turn it as the first sign of blood shows. At this stage I pepper generously and when it is cooked to my liking (medium rare) I immediately transfer it to a very hot plate. I wield the sea salt mill equally generously and tackle the steak *at once*. No hanging about or messing about.

A generous helping of onion marmalade goes well with this, or simply fried onion rings . . . and, oh yes, don't forget to pour over the steak the delicious juices from the pan, and what can't pour, mop up with a thick slice of bread!

2 lb (900 g) shoulder of
lamb, boned

1 small ham hock, about 10
oz (275 g)

8 oz (225 g) each of carrot,
onion, turnip, celery, diced

2 tablespoons parsley,
chopped

2 lb (900 g) potatoes, peeled
and evenly sliced

1 tablespoon tomato purée

salt, freshly ground black
pepper

Bobby's Irish Stew

Robert Lyons (Bobby to us all) has worked with me and Tom in the kitchen for over 9 years now, and when we are all fed up with the exotic things of life (oh, doesn't that sound grand, my Nan will turn in her grave), a dish of Bobby's Irish Stew brings us all well and truly down to earth. When the staff hear that a stew is on the way, everybody stays behind for dinner and even those on days off come in especially to enjoy it. I often take left-overs home and freeze them.

Cut the boned shoulder of lamb into strips, leaving the fat and skin on. Blanch the strips in boiling water for 10 minutes to remove the excess fat. Remove, drain, and simmer gently in fresh water with the ham hock for a further hour. Add the carrot, onion, turnip and celery, and cook for a further hour, simmering gently, and stirring occasionally with a wooden spoon. Add the parsley, potatoes, tomato purée, salt and pepper and cook slowly for a further 45 minutes. During this final cooking period you may have to keep gently topping up with a little water as the stew starts to thicken. Remove the ham hock before serving and if you can leave the stew for a further 24 hours and re-heat, it's even better. Served with pickled red cabbage and, in the winter, pickled onions, it's a feast fit for a king (and caterers)!

serves 8

2 oz (50 g) butter

salt, freshly ground black
pepper

8 oz (225 g) parsnips

8 oz (225 g) peas

8 oz (225 g) carrots

10 fl. oz (300 ml) double
cream

2 eggs

nutmeg

Triple Purée Vegetable Pots

This is an ideal way of serving 3 different vegetables in individual 3 inch (7·5 cm) ramekins to your guests, provided they don't mind eating something akin to nursery food! It's simple, good for you, and good to look at, and practically all the work can be done either early in the morning or even the day before.

Butter and season the 8 ramekins. Cook the vegetables in separate saucepans in salted water until well done. Strain and return to the saucepans to dry out a little, and then liquidize each separate vegetable with a quarter of the cream. Pass through a sieve, and then put layer by layer into the buttered and seasoned ramekins, leaving about $\frac{1}{4}$ inch (6 mm) space for the custard.

When you wish to serve the pots, whisk up the remaining double cream and eggs with a little nutmeg, salt and pepper. Pour this on the top of the vegetable purée in each pot, and bake at 350°F (180°C), Gas 4, in a bain marie for 25 minutes.

Tomato Herb Salad

When you can get hold of those lovely small, fresh, seasonal tomatoes that have such a sensuous smell around the stalk, this is the best way to prepare and serve them. Allow 4 small tomatoes for each individual portion. Wipe them with a damp cloth, remove the stalk and then slice them very thinly (cross-wise with the core running parallel to the cutting surface). Discard the base and top slice of each tomato (these can be used for tomato purée or popped into the stock pot if you have one on the go), and place one slice in the middle of each of your small plates. Fan out the slices from this middle slice in an ever-enlarging circle. Sprinkle with very finely chopped onion and then scatter over finely chopped mixed fresh herbs – parsley, basil, tarragon, dill, marjoram, mint – in fact anything you have to hand. Put a mere sprinkling of your favourite French dressing over the salad and the meanest pinch of castor sugar as well. Cover with clingfilm or saranwrap and leave as long as you wish in the fridge. Don't forget to remove from the fridge in time for the salad to come back to life.

Served with slices of thickly buttered wholemeal bread it is a feast, but with the following spinach salad, it's sheer bliss.

Spinach, Bacon and Apple Salad

serves 4

1 lb (450 g) fresh spinach

6 oz (175 g) de-rinded smoked bacon, finely diced

2 Granny Smith apples, cored and finely diced

Fresh spinach is a *must* for this recipe. Simply tear the green away from the fairly strong stems, and then cut it up with a sharp stainless steel knife into fine shreds (rolling the leaves up into a cigar shape makes it easier to cut). Scatter over 4 small plates.

Meanwhile fry off the smoked bacon in a frying pan without any additional fat or oil until the bacon bits are quite brown and firm, and there is a fair amount of bacon fat in the pan.

Add the finely chopped apples, stir-fry for a further minute, and then sprinkle bacon bits, apple dice and every little drop of bacon fat over the spinach. Wonderful.

Home-made Vanilla Icecream

makes 2 pints (1·1 litre)

4 eggs, separated

4 oz (100–125 g) icing sugar

1 teaspoon vanilla essence

½ pint (300 ml) double cream

This is an easy-to-make, simple-to-serve icecream that Jean Butterworth often makes and serves for me when I go on a Sunday night off to have dinner at White Moss House. Jean is a super cook and in many ways I envy her as I would so like to change the style of dinner at Miller Howe and make it less theatrical and more basic, and each time I dine with her and Arthur, I come back *so* aware of every single morsel being good basic home-cooking, with every taste coming through clean and clear.

In a clean metal bowl beat up the 4 egg whites until gently stiff, and then slowly beat in the icing sugar, a tablespoon at a time. *Do* take time and care with this initial stage. When once again the mixture is nice and fluffy, beat in the egg yolks, one at a time, and also the vanilla essence.

In a separate large bowl, lightly beat up the double cream and then fold the cream and egg white mixtures together. The 2 mixtures should be of the same consistency, as this helps them to combine more evenly.

Freeze in a large container, or 6 to 8 3 inch (7·5 cm) ramekins. It's always soft to serve and keeps for up to a month. Serve it in portions of about tablespoons per person, or in the ramekins, and you can dress it up with any of the suggested toppings on pages 85–6.

6 egg whites

12 oz (350 g) castor sugar, sieved

2 small teaspoons white wine vinegar

Pavlovas

In *Entertaining with Tovey* I gave a recipe for pavlovas which I had used for years. It was a good recipe, and family and friends never complained. But on a recent cookery course at Miller Howe, a small contingent of intense, super ladies from Belfast remarked kindly on the pavlovas served for dinner one evening and politely asked for the recipe. When I told them, one of the ladies quietly said, 'How nice. Have you ever tried making them without cornflour? I do, and I'd like to hear what you think.' Being one for constant experimentation and possible improvement I did just that, and I discovered how mediocre my previous pavlovas had been!

This updated version of pavlova stores quite well in airtight polythene bags and freezes extremely well. The mixing will make at least 15 individual pavlovas, and is very economical.

Make sure your Kenwood or mixing bowl is completely clean, then put your cold whites in and start to whisk them up. Whites can reach a stage when they begin to fall back a little, so watch the mixing very carefully, and when firm, dry, fluffy and well-risen, beat in 1 tablespoon of the sieved castor sugar. The egg mixture will fall a little but soon comes back to its former peak, and you repeat this with 1 further tablespoon of sugar. Stop beating after this and transfer the contents to a clean enamel or pot bowl. Using a large spoon, gently fold in the balance of the castor sugar, a third at a time. You will definitely think you are doing wrong, for after each addition your egg mixing will become more limp and slightly soggy (contrary to everything you've ever been told about beating egg whites). But have faith.

Fold in the wine vinegar, and have to hand 2 upturned baking trays lined with good greaseproof paper. Using 2 rounded silver serving spoons, scoop out individual portions of the egg white and plonk onto the greaseproof paper, taking care to leave plenty of room around each one. Sprinkle generously with vanilla sugar (page 178), and put into a pre-heated oven set at 325°F (170°C), Gas 3, for 45 minutes. Turn off the oven and leave as long as you like.

The meringues are a light brown on the outside, as crisp as a toffee apple, and lovely and marshmallowy inside. Serve them with whipped cream, summer fruits, sandwiched together with fruit purée, however you like.

When cold, you can freeze them on a baking tray until stiff and solid, then put into polythene bags. When you wish to use them, take out of the freezer, and they only need minutes at room temperature.

serves 4–6

½ pint (300 ml) double cream

2 tablespoons castor sugar

1 tablespoon Camp Coffee

2 tablespoons dark rum

2 ripe bananas

Brazilian Coffee Rum Banana Cream

For a bit of 'dash' to end an easy supper evening, this beats the lot, and I blush when I tell you it is one of the favourite puds served at Miller Howe (only done these days when a regular requests it).

Whip the cream with the castor sugar and Camp Coffee essence, and fold in the good dark rum. Simply roughly chop up the peeled bananas (you can use bananas past their best) and fold them into the whipped cream and spoon out into tall knickerbocker-glory type glasses.

You can, if you like, top each one off with finely grated chocolate and a pinch of ground nutmeg. Enhance each portion with some chopped or crumbled stale meringue and, better still, a few lovely chocolate coffee beans.

serves 8

1 pint (600 ml) double cream

4 tablespoons icing sugar

rind and juice of 2 lemons

¼ pint (150 ml) gin

2 egg whites

Lemon Posset

Beat the cream with the icing sugar until quite thick, and then beat in the rind and juice of the lemons, and the gin. Make sure you beat in these liquids slowly, a little at a time, otherwise it will be difficult to whip your cream back to a thick consistency.

Beat up the egg whites in a separate metal bowl until dry, and fold them into the cream. Spoon out into glasses and leave to chill. Serve with small individual sponge cakes freshly baked that day (page 37).

This sweet can quite easily be changed simply by substituting for the lemons and gin. You could use orange rind and juice and Drambuie; lime rind and juice and vodka; pineapple juice and Kirsch.

2 oz (50 g) butter

at least 2 lbs (900 g) Granny Smith apples, peeled, cored and sliced

4 oz (100 g) demerara sugar

1 tablespoon fresh lemon juice

Apple Purée

When apples are cheap or readily available, make a supply of apple purée which you will bless each time you remove some from your freezer. It has endless uses: as apple sauce; as a quick hasty dessert, sweetened with a touch of Calvados; served with icecream; warmed through as a dessert with a generous spoonful of butterscotch sauce (page 33); as a fool with either crème de menthe or Calvados.

Butter the base and sides of a 10 pint (5½ litre) saucepan or casserole well and then just pile in the peeled, cored and sliced apples. Add the demerara sugar and fresh lemon juice. Cook either on top of the stove or in the oven until they have fallen (you will just have to keep on looking at them, but as a guide this amount of apples cooked on a medium heat on top of the stove take about 15 minutes, and in an oven at 350°F (180°C), Gas 4, take 40 minutes).

Liquidize, pass through a nylon sieve, and freeze when cold. At home I use old clean cream and yoghurt cartons for storing, with the original top or cling film to close.

This recipe will give you ¾ pint (400 ml) or 1 lb 2 oz (500 g). Make a pear purée in exactly the same way, adding a spot of brandy.

ENTERTAINING OCCASION

Holidays at Home

Holidays at home, whether Bank Holiday weekends, ordinary weekends, or simply a day off, can, if planned carefully, turn into a happy holiday for one and all. When holidaying at home, it is of the utmost importance that you break away from traditional eating habits: if breakfast at half-past seven, lunch prompt at one, then tea followed by supper is your usual style of living, change it. In the morning, let the family all have a long lie-in and take their own trays up to their rooms. If you haven't enough posh trays, improvise with empty peach or similar fruit boxes, lined with foil or greaseproof paper. With an added fancy doyley, it looks quite good enough to eat from!

Organize everything the night before, laying out plates, cups, individual pats of butter, marmalade, little jugs for milk etc. Then everyone gets up in their own sweet time to make toast, tea or coffee, or help themselves to cereal, and then can potter back to bed. Toast crumbs in the bed are a small discomfort to be suffered for the sheer luxury of knowing there is nothing pressing to make you get up from between the bedcovers.

Or, if you are the head cook and bottle-washer, tell everybody *you* are going to have a lie-in, and say that, at 11 am, you plan to serve a hearty breakfast with fruit juice, porridge and then a good old fry-up of bacon, egg, sausage, black pudding, tomato, fried bread and fried apple followed by lots of toast and coffee. That will save you then having to cook a meal at midday.

Squeeze the oranges the night before and store in the fridge. Soak any commercial oats in milk overnight, and lay out on separate baking trays or dishes the ingredients for the fry-up (bake-up would be more appropriate). Per person, you need a rasher of bacon, a sausage, a slice of apple, and a half tomato on the greased trays. Cut out triangles of bread, and place them, mushrooms and slices of par-boiled potatoes in the frying pan. When you're ready to cook the next morning, after a wonderful lie-in, pre-heat the oven to 350°F (180°C), Gas 4, and cook in the order:
Sausages for 30 minutes
Bacon and black pudding for 15 minutes
Apple for 10 minutes
Tomato for 5 minutes
As you put in the apple slices, start frying off the potatoes and mushrooms in the butter in the frying pan.

Eggs are different, and can be fried, too, but

often scrambling is the easiest for 6 or more people (see page 162).

Instead of another cooked meal that day, why not have a slap-up North Country high tea. Cold meats and salads with chutney, pickled onions, cucumber in vinegar and lots of well-buttered brown and white bread, followed by trifle and jellies with a real feast of baking – scones (pages 36 and 179), rock cakes (page 37), sponges (page 37), cakes and gâteaux (see pages 64, 87 and 141–3). After all that everyone should have had enough for the day!

Or you could have a substantial meal around noon and a kitchen supper in the evening of baked potatoes with buttered or fried eggs. Or what can beat simple fried egg and chips with a generous dollop of HP or Heinz tomato sauce. Makes a change from the 'oat' cuisine!

But *I* personally organize my holidays at home entirely around my store-cupboard (see pages 157–62). Accustomed as I am to working most of the time with rich exotic food it is a welcome relief to find that on the occasional Sunday there is absolutely nobody staying or coming round. Then the store-cupboard comes into its own, and is raided (to be replenished on the Monday).

I start off a store-cupboard eating day with lightly scrambled eggs done with double cream (see page 162), an ideal way to start any lazy day (and the later the better). A pinch of curry powder adds a little spice to the dish, and if you decide to open the tin of smoked oysters, they can be gently folded in at the end, substituting for the smoked salmon which you would probably normally use if you'd planned the meal. Chopped chives or parsley straight from the garden enhance this dish, and if you haven't any wholemeal bread, use those delicious Hovis crackers, buttered. (You could also cream the butter and add a few drops of anchovy essence which adds a bit of life to the bread or crackers.)

Into the dishwasher go the dishes, and then the Sunday papers are read in a leisurely fashion from cover to cover. It never ceases to amaze me how 2 different papers report the same event, function or performance so differently. Quite often I get so confused I have to resort to an early Bloody Mary! Out comes the vodka from the freezer (yes, I do mean freezer. Vodka doesn't freeze hard, and you should *always* serve it freezer cold), the tomato juice from the fridge, the Worcestershire sauce, the lemon (or better still, lime), the sea salt, egg white, stick of celery if there is any, and the grand performance begins!

Into the posh cocktail shaker or liquidizer goes the measure of vodka topped up with the tomato juice (1 part vodka to 4 parts juice), Worcestershire sauce (Tabasco?) freshly ground black pepper, lemon or lime juice (occasionally I add a pinch of curry spices, and less occasionally, a half clove of fresh juicy garlic), and then I whizz it all round or shake it up.

Meanwhile the rims of the glasses are dipped in egg white and then immediately into a saucer of lovely chunky sea salt. Pour the Bloody Mary into these frost-rimmed glasses and serve at once – a wonderful pick-you-up and cure-all. Accompanied by some nuts from the store-cupboard, this amply passes the time between late breakfast and afternoon tea. Lunch really is *too* bothersome, so to keep the pangs of hunger at bay, I might delve into those pickled onions, accompanied by chunks of Cheddar cheese and the odd spoonful of this or that chutney.

Even on the laziest of Sundays I can rustle up enough energy to make a few scones for tea (page 179), and I devour them more or less straight from the oven, with far too much butter soaking into them. Drinking pot after pot of rather weak mint tea, I feel truly cosseted on a cold afternoon, listening to tapes, records or the radio, in front of the fire.

Supper can be simply thick slices of tinned spam fried and served with tarted-up baked beans (pages 159–60), a few spoonfuls of frozen petit pois, a fried apple slice, a fried banana with a dollop of grated Emmenthal cheese. If I feel soupy, this emergency home-made vegetable soup is a godsend. Simply mix a can of Italian tomatoes with a can of baby carrots and a tablespoon of concentrated frozen orange juice, then liquidize and pass through a sieve. If you do this use the grated Emmenthal cheese for garnishing this rather than the spam fry-up.

I am quite content to end this down-to-earth basic supper with a slice of icecream with some butterscotch sauce (page 33) poured over it.

Other ideas which can quickly and easily form

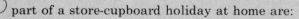

part of a store-cupboard holiday at home are:

Sardines on toast accompanied or topped with either a poached or softly boiled egg.

Grated carrots and apple dolloped out onto slices of skimmed tomato and then topped with poached or softly boiled eggs. The lovely runny yolk serves as a sauce to the grated veg. and the combination is very nice – particularly if you add a teaspoon or two of French dressing and finish off with finely chopped nuts.

Poacher's Salad (pages 107–8) with different dressings.

Tinned red salmon mashed up with all the juice and then mixed with Philadelphia cream cheese (you can also quickly beat up an egg white and fold this in). If you intend to leave the store-cupboard bare, garnish with a teaspoon or two of the red lumpfish roe.

Tinned soups tarted up with a generous pouring of brandy, sherry or any booze you might have in your cupboard which you think will give the dish a lift. Grated cheese and finely chopped herbs add texture, yoghurt or cream add richness. Cheese croutons or even solider pieces of cheese on toast are good to serve with a tarted-up soup. A pinch of curry mixed in, and a liberal topping of toasted coconut enhances any meat soup.

Tinned red kidney beans freed of their 'orrible brine, marinated in or dressed at the last minute with a French dressing. They can even be delicious combined with a strong cheese sauce, ladled out into individual dishes, topped with further grated cheese and breadcrumbs, and finished off under the grill.

SEVEN

ENTERTAINING WITH TOVEY FAVOURITES

In *Entertaining with Tovey*, published in 1979, I told you how to star in your own kitchens, and the majority of our Miller Howe basic recipes were reproduced there. But it is impossible to avoid repeating some of the favourites here, as so many of our new, newly evolved, and improved recipes involve those *Entertaining* basics. If you can't find the recipe you want here, I can only urge you to rush out and buy *Entertaining with Tovey*, which is now in its second impression!

Miller Howe Cheese and Herb Pâté

5 oz (150 g) butter
1 lb (450 g) cream cheese
3 cloves garlic, freshly crushed with a little salt
1 tablespoon chervil, chopped
1 tablespoon parsley, finely chopped
1 tablespoon chives, finely chopped

Melt the butter slowly in a saucepan. Mix the other ingredients together in a mixer bowl (or by hand), making sure that the herbs are evenly distributed.

When the melted butter has cooled, pour it gently into the cream cheese mixture. Fold it into the cheese gently (*do* take care, as the mixture could curdle), and transfer the pâté to a loaf tin, or leave it in the bowl, to cool and set.

Miller Howe Mushroom Pâté

4 oz (125 g) butter
8 oz (225 g) minced onions
2 lb (1 kg) mushrooms, minced
generous pinch of sea salt
freshly ground black pepper
1 pint (600 ml) red wine

Melt the butter in a large saucepan over a gentle heat, then add the minced onions. Simmer for approximately 10 minutes, then add the mushrooms, salt and pepper and stir well. Add the red wine and leave to simmer over a low heat for 2 to 3 hours, stirring occasionally. The idea is to let the liquid evaporate until the mixture is fairly dry. When cold, it can easily be stored in a suitable plastic container in the fridge or freezer.

Savoury Breadcrumbs

2 oz (50 g) onion, finely chopped
2 tablespoons parsley, finely chopped
1 clove garlic, crushed with salt
8 oz (225 g) fine breadcrumbs
1 oz (25 g) strong Cheddar cheese, finely grated

Breadcrumbs, whether savoury or not, are much easier to make if you have a food processor, Magimix or sophisticated mincer/blender, but obviously they *can* be done by hand. The first requisite is *stale* bread – left-over dinner rolls, crusts from toast, any bread left over at the end of a loaf or from making round croutons etc – and the crisper the better. Leave any bits of bread that you want to use for breadcrumbs in a tray in the oven, where the heat from the pilot light will turn it harder.

If you have an electric 'kitchen helper', simply put in the ingredients in the following order – garlic, onion, bread, parsley, cheese – and everything will be done for you. If you're doing it by hand, make sure the onions and parsley are chopped *very* finely. Crush the garlic to a smooth paste with the salt, and grate the cheese very finely. Make the breadcrumbs on a grater (their crispness makes this much easier), and combine everything together in a mixing bowl.

Store any left-over crumbs in a screw-top jar in the fridge.

2–3 slices bread

1 tablespoon good oil

1 oz (25 g) butter

1 egg

2 teaspoons cooking brandy

salt, freshly ground black pepper

1 teaspoon Moutarde de Meaux

about 4 oz (100–125 g) strong Cheddar cheese

Croutons with Brandied Cheese Topping

Cut the slices of bread into croutons about 1 inch (2·5 cm) square (minus the crusts, which you can use for breadcrumbs), and leave them on a baking tray in a warm spot in the kitchen or in your gas oven where the pilot light will generate enough heat to harden the croutons. The staler the crouton, the less fat it will absorb in the cooking. Do this in the morning.

Smear the base of the frying pan lightly with the good oil and then, when really hot, add the butter. Toss in the croutons and cook off as quickly as possible. Always drain 2 or 3 times on kitchen paper.

Break the egg into a small bowl, add the brandy, salt, pepper and mustard, and beat together. Grate the cheese into the mixture until the texture of the paste is fairly firm. Using a small palette knife, spread this paste onto each cooked and drained crouton and heat under the grill at the last minute.

New Potato Salad

To me the first of the new season's new potatoes heralds the arrival of summer. I always pick out the smallest potatoes possible, and as soon as I get home I wipe them with a damp cloth and simmer in salted water, to which I have added a little French dressing (a few parsley or mint stalks in the water improve the flavour, but good potatoes will stand on their own). They are ready when the tip of a sharp knife will pierce them effortlessly, and I drain and serve them as quickly as possible with lashings of butter.

When the potatoes are getting longer in the tooth I tend to heat some French dressing through slightly and have it ready when the potatoes are cooked. Drain the potatoes well, slice fairly thickly, and return to the empty pan. Put on low heat to dry out and then toss the potato slices in the warm French dressing. Serve garnished with chopped chives.

1¾ oz (45–50 g) butter

¾ pint (400 ml) milk

pinch of salt

1½ oz (40 g) plain flour, sieved

White Sauce

I always make a fairly thick basic pint (600 ml) of white sauce as it is easier to thin a sauce down than thicken it up.

Melt the butter in a saucepan (the deeper, narrower kind is better), and put the milk on to warm through with the pinch of salt in another pan. When the butter has melted, and is bubbling away, add the sieved flour all in one go and, using a curved backed wooden spoon, stir vigorously until the mixture is smooth.

Do not over-cook or burn at this stage, and make certain that your milk is quite warm. Add a little of the milk at a time to the flour and butter roux, and never, never add any more until the milk has been absorbed and the mixture is smoothly creamy. This first addition of milk produces quite a fierce heat so start beating with your spoon immediately. I tilt the saucepan so that I can *really* beat the mixture together before starting to add any further milk.

When all the milk has been absorbed, and the sauce is shiny smooth, I pass it through a fine sieve just to make sure there are no lurking lumps. The sauce might be too thick for your requirements, so simply add more milk, or better still, some cream.

Cheese Sauce

To the basic white sauce mix, add about 4 oz (100–125 g) grated cheese. Cook until the cheese has melted into the sauce, and I often flavour naughtily at the end with $\frac{1}{4}$ gill (35 ml) Kirsch or cooking brandy.

Fresh Home-made Tomato Sauce

$\frac{1}{4}$ **pint (150 ml) olive oil**

2 medium onions, about 12 oz (350 g), finely chopped

6 plump fresh cloves garlic

fresh basil, tarragon, and marjoram to taste

5 lb (2$\frac{1}{2}$ kg) fresh ripe tomatoes

This sauce should always be made when there is a glut of cheap tomatoes. It can be kept in the fridge for up to a week, but can be frozen and used, most successfully, for months.

Heat the oil in a large saucepan, add the onions and fry until golden brown. Add the chopped garlic along with the chopped herbs. Add the quartered tomatoes and bring to the boil. Cover the saucepan and leave to simmer for about an hour. Look at it occasionally and stir gently with a wooden spoon. After an hour the juice from the tomatoes should have evaporated, leaving a thickish mixture which you liquidize then pass through a sieve. Season to taste prior to cooling and storing.

Tomato Provençale

2 oz (50 g) butter

4 fat cloves juicy garlic, crushed with 2 teaspoons salt

4 oz (125 g) onion, finely chopped

1$\frac{1}{2}$ lb (700 g) tomatoes, peeled, seeded and roughly chopped

Melt the butter in a saucepan and fry off the garlic paste and onions until nice and golden and then add the chopped tomatoes. Simmer slowly until you have a lovely thick purée mixture (at least 1 hour).

In the winter when tomatoes often lack that deep red colour, a teaspoon of tomato purée helps, and a mere touch of wine vinegar adds a bit of bite.

Store in the fridge for up to a week, or freeze.

enough for about 16 portions

1 pint (600 ml) good chicken stock

2 oz (50 g) butter

2 medium green peppers, diced very small

$\frac{1}{2}$ fresh pineapple, peeled, cored and finely chopped

6 level dessertspoons cornflour

4 tablespoons cold water

$\frac{1}{2}$ pint (300 ml) white wine vinegar

juice and rind of 2 oranges

$\frac{1}{2}$ lb (225 g) castor sugar

1 level teaspoon ground ginger

1 level teaspoon salt

4 tablespoons soya sauce

Sweet and Sour Sauce

Put the chicken stock in a large saucepan with the butter, peppers and pineapple and cover. Simmer for about 20 minutes until the liquid has reduced by about a quarter.

Make the cornflour and cold water into a smooth paste, and when the chicken stock mixture has reduced, add along with all the other ingredients, except the soya sauce. Stir continuously until the sugar dissolves and the sauce thickens. If you are going to use it immediately, stir in the soya sauce, otherwise leave to one side and re-heat when needed, adding the soya sauce at the last moment.

Without the soya, this sauce stores extremely well.

---

1 pint (600 ml) oil (see method)

$\frac{1}{4}$ pint (150 ml) wine vinegar

2 generous teaspoons soft brown sugar

pinch of salt

2 level teaspoons dry English mustard

juice of $\frac{1}{2}$ lemon

French Dressing

French dressing must be made with the very finest of ingredients, wine vinegar (*never* malt), walnut oil and olive oil. As you may have noticed, I love walnut oil (although it's so expensive), and I think its inclusion in a dressing makes it taste marvellous. You can just use olive oil, of course, but try making your dressing with one-third walnut oil to two-thirds olive, and taste the difference.

I just plonk all the ingredients into the liquidizer goblet and blend for a few seconds. The dressing is slightly heavier as a result, but the taste is the same. I make this large quantity at one time as, in the summer especially, so many salads are eaten, and it stores perfectly well in the fridge for up to a week. If you want to make it in smaller quantities, do remember the equation of 4 measures of oil to 1 of vinegar.

To ring the changes, you can add flavourings such as: chopped chives, parsley, basil, mint or crushed garlic; diced hard-boiled egg, onions or apples; a teaspoon of tomato purée, Tabasco, Worcestershire sauce; finely chopped walnuts or pine kernels at the end; different vinegars – red or white wine, cider or herb.

Home-made Mayonnaise

makes ½ pint (300 ml)

2 egg yolks

few drops fresh lemon juice

½ teaspoon dry English mustard

½ teaspoon castor sugar

½ teaspoon salt

½ pint (300 ml) best olive oil

2 tablespoons white wine vinegar

I find it easier to use an electric hand whisk, but a blender can be used. First of all, combine the yolks thoroughly in a warm bowl with the lemon juice and seasonings. Having measured out the good olive oil, gently dip your fingers into it and then trail the oil off your fingers into the egg mixture, beating vigorously and continuously. At this stage you must literally *dribble* in the oil and take your time: if you put too much in at once or hurry the making, your mayonnaise could curdle. If this happens (and it *shouldn't* if you follow my instructions to the letter), just add a tablespoon of hot water to bring it round or, in a fresh bowl, beat the curdled mixture teaspoon by teapoon into a further egg yolk.

When you have incorporated about one-third of the oil, add the vinegar, tablespoon by tablespoon (if you throw the 3 tablespoons in all at once the mixture becomes too thin), and then add the balance of the olive oil, a bit more quickly than before.

This mayonnaise might be too thick for you, but can be thinned down with a little warm water or single cream. If too sharp, cut down on the vinegar content; if too sweet leave out the sugar. And you can ring the changes in the flavour of the mayonnaise by using different vinegars – mint, garlic and tarragon.

Sweet and Sour Mayonnaise

Add to the basic ½ pint (300 ml) mixing, 1 tablespoon of black treacle, 1 tablespoon of Moutarde de Meaux, and 1 dessertspoon of soft brown sugar. This is lovely coated over a cold breast of chicken and goes particularly well with any grilled fish.

Lemon Mayonnaise

To the basic mayonnaise you add the finely grated rind of lemon with the fresh juice, using 1 or 2 lemons, depending on the strength of flavour you require.

You could also make orange mayonnaise in the same manner.

Blender Hollandaise

4 tablespoons fresh lemon juice

2 tablespoons white wine vinegar

12 oz (350 g) butter

6 egg yolks

2 teaspoons castor sugar

pinch of salt

You can halve this recipe, but you can't *double* it in the normal home blender.

Place the lemon juice and vinegar in one small saucepan and the butter in another. Put both on the stove – to heat the lemon juice and vinegar to bubbling point and to completely melt the butter, without burning.

In the blender goblet, blend the egg yolks, castor sugar and salt for literally 2 seconds, just to break up the yolks and incorporate the other 2 ingredients.

When the vinegar and lemon juice mixture is boiling, gently trickle into the blender while it whizzes at high speed (a jug with a good pouring lip is better than a saucepan). When all that is absorbed, do the same with the melted butter and, lo and behold, you have a smooth, rich, tangy hollandaise.

Basic Stock Syrup

2 lb (900 g) preserving or cube sugar

1 pint (600 ml) water

Simply dissolve the sugar in the water over a low heat in a very clean saucepan and infuse at first over this same low heat. Then turn up the heat and allow the liquid to simmer for about 15 minutes. Now you can poach your fruit in it. If you wish to have a tangy flavour, you can add 3 tablespoons of wine vinegar whilst simmering.

Vanilla Sugar

Every kitchen should have a tin of this, as it has so many uses, and adds such a nice look and taste to so many biscuits, cakes, meringues, puddings etc. Simply place 2 or 3 vanilla pods inside a tin with a tight-fitting lid, and fill it up with castor sugar. Shake it occasionally and leave for at least 5 days before using, by which time the sugar will have acquired a good flavour. Every time you use some sugar, fill the tin up again with castor sugar. At Miller Howe we change the pods about twice a year.

To sprinkle the sugar on, I use a large salt shaker like those in fish and chip shops, as the top comes off freely when you want to fill it up, and the sugar comes easily out of the large holes in the top.

Savoury Pastry

1 lb (450 g) plain flour

pinch of salt

2 tablespoons icing sugar

10 oz (275 g) softened butter

2 eggs (at room temperature)

These ingredients make enough pastry to line 3 10 inch (25·5 cm) quiches, or 16 individual 3 inch (7·5 cm) quiches.

Sieve the flour with the salt and icing sugar onto a clean mixing board or working surface, and make a well in the centre leaving the surface exposed. Into this well put the butter – which must be soft enough to hold your thumb imprint. It is hopeless to try to make any pastry with butter straight from the fridge; not only would it take an age to soften, but you would have such a job getting the egg worked into the butter that the sheer exhaustion would put you off making pastry for ever!

Break the eggs onto the butter and then, using the tips of your fingers at a 90° angle to the butter, pat the egg into the butter. Don't *press* the eggs into the butter. You want a mixture resembling the fluffiest and lightest scrambled egg, and it doesn't matter if you accidentally incorporate the odd bit of flour. Tap, tap, tap away for about 8 minutes.

When you are satisfied that you have obtained the correct result, hold a large palette knife at right angles to the board and scoop the flour up from left to right, right to left, top to bottom, bottom to top, literally parcelling it over the butter mixture. Then swiftly cut through the mixture, always hitting the board with your palette knife at an angle of 90°. Remember that in the middle of your board you still have the wet, gooey egg and butter mixture, so, from time to time, scrape your knife along the board and turn the mixture over so that it all blends in. (It's tiring!)

The mixture slowly begins to form larger and larger crumbs. If your kitchen is warm, this won't take too long, but if it's cold, you could be at it for 20 minutes or more. When you begin to get a texture resembling a shortbread mixture, stop, and divide the mixture into 3 equal parts. Bring each section together with the palms of your hands to resemble a ball, but don't squeeze too hard (after all that trouble you've taken to get air into it!). Put the balls into a polythene bag, tie up and leave to chill overnight or it can be frozen, as long as you remember how it felt and looked *before* you put it in the fridge or freezer; you *must* let it come back to the same look, feel and texture.

When you're ready to make the case, with your pastry back to its original state before chilling or freezing, place the base of a loose-bottomed flan tin onto the board and flour lightly round the outside edge of the base. Place the ball of pastry in the centre of the base then, very gently, press it down to start the flattening-out process. Lightly work with your rolling pin from the centre of the dough, easing the pastry towards the edge and then out over the base onto the floured board. The pastry outside the base will be the walls of your quiche so don't stretch it too far. With a palette knife, carefully fold the outside rim back over the pastry, put the base into its ring and, using your thumbs, ease the turned-over pastry up the walls of the flan tin to form the sides of the flan. Lop off the excess and patch any defects. I roll out little snakes from the surplus pastry and run these round inside the edge of the base in order to strengthen it there, at its most vulnerable point. Leave the case to chill – or even freeze – at this stage.

Bake as outlined in the Frangipane recipe on page 110.

Scones

2 lb (scant 1 kg) self-raising flour

12 oz (350 g) very soft butter

generous pinch salt

6 tablespoons castor sugar, sieved

sultanas to taste

4 eggs, lightly beaten

milk or sour cream to mix

These scones are very easy to make, and I usually make this 2 lb (1 kg) mixing which gives approximately 40 scones. If you aren't going to use them all at once, they are best frozen uncooked. Or you can, of course, just halve the quantities.

Pre-heat the oven to 425°F (220°C), Gas 7. Sieve the self-raising flour into a large plastic bowl and divide the soft butter up into 1 oz (25 g) pieces. Bring the flour and butter together very gently and carefully, allowing lots of air into the mixing. It soon starts to come together and resemble fine crumbs, but do not overwork.

Add the salt, castor sugar, sultanas and the lightly beaten eggs and start to bring together. Do not squeeze and do not knock out any of the air.

It is virtually impossible to define how much milk or sour cream you need to get the mixture to the right consistency as so much depends on how soft the butter is, how warm the room is, etc, but the mixture should not be too soft (or your scones will spread during baking) or too dry (when they won't be so light). When you are satisfied with the mix, turn it out onto a lightly floured board, pat it down with your hands and, using a palette knife, cut it into diamond shapes. *Do not* roll the mixture out and then cut into delightful scalloped circles and then economically re-roll – if you do this, your scones are bound to be heavier. Put the scones onto trays and bake for approximately 10 minutes.

To ring the changes, savoury scones can be made by substituting grated cheese and crushed coriander or curry powder for the sugar and sultanas.

Even chopped prunes may be used instead of sultanas, or try diced dried apricots. And occasionally I have included a smattering of desiccated coconut or a few ground almonds.

Home-made Lemon Curd

makes about 1 lb (450 g)

4 oz (100–125 g) butter

8 oz (225 g) castor sugar

grated rind and juice of 2 lemons

4 egg yolks

Melt the butter, sugar, lemon rind and juice together in a bowl set over a saucepan of simmering water and beat until quite smooth. Then beat in the egg yolks and continue cooking until the mixture will coat the back of your wooden spoon (i.e. when you take the spoon out of the mixture, run your index finger along the middle of the back, and the indentation remains there quite clearly). Do not over-cook, as the mixture sets and thickens further when cooling.

Do take your time with this, and don't allow the water to boil fiercely, otherwise you will have speckled bits of cooked egg yolk which would spoil an otherwise smooth lemon curd.

Pour into pots, cool and store in the fridge. Serve with bread and scones at tea, and in many other ways outlined throughout the book.

INDEX

A

The **bold** figures denote actual recipes

B